ILLEGALLY STAYING IN THE EU

Principally, this book comprises a conceptual analysis of the illegality of a third-country national's stay by examining the boundaries of the overarching concept of illegality at the EU level. Having found that the holistic conceptualisation of illegality, constructed through a combination of sources (both EU and national law) falls short of adequacy, the book moves on to consider situations that fall outside the traditional binary of legal and illegal under EU law. The cases of unlawfully staying EU citizens and of non-removable illegally staying third-country nationals are examples of groups of migrants who are categorised as atypical. By looking at these two examples the book reveals not only the fragmentation of legal statuses in EU migration law but also the more general ill-fitting and unsatisfactory categorisation of migrants.

The potential conflation of illegality with criminality as a result of the way EU databases regulate the legal regime of illegality of a migrant's stay is the first trend identified by the book. Subsequently, the book considers the functions of accessing legality (both instrumental and corrective). In doing so it draws out another trend evident in the EU illegality regime: a two-tier regime which discriminates on the basis of wealth and the instrumentalisation of access to legality by Member States for mostly their own purposes.

Finally, the book proposes a corrective rationale for the regulation of illegality through access to legality and provides a number of normative suggestions as a way of remedying current deficiencies that arise out of the present supranational framing of illegality.

Volume 85 in the Series Modern Studies in European Law

Modern Studies in European Law

Recent titles in this series:

Republican Europe
Anna Kocharov

Family Reunification in the EU
Chiara Berneri

EU Liability and International Economic Law
Armin Steinbach

The EU and Nanotechnologies: A Critical Analysis
Tanja Ehnert

Human Rights Between Law and Politics:
The Margin of Appreciation in Post-National Contexts
Edited by Petr Agha

The European Union and Social Security Law
Jaan Paju

The Rule of Law in the European Union: The Internal Dimension
Theodore Konstadinides

The Division of Competences between the EU and the Member States:
Reflections on the Past, the Present and the Future
Edited by Sacha Garben and Inge Govaere

Unity in Adversity: EU Citizenship, Social Justice and the Cautionary Tale of the UK
Charlotte O'Brien

The Use of Force and Article 2 of the ECHR in Light of European Conflicts
Hannah Russell

Environmental Crime in Europe
Edited by Andrew Farmer, Michael Faure and Grazia Maria Vagliasindi

Questioning EU Citizenship: Judges and the Limits of Free
Movement and Solidarity in the EU
Edited by Daniel Thym

The European Union under Transnational Law: A Pluralist Appraisal
Matej Avbelj

For the complete list of titles in this series, see
'Modern Studies in European Law' link at
www.bloomsburyprofessional.com/uk/series/modern-studies-in-european-law

Illegally Staying in the EU

An Analysis of Illegality in EU Migration Law

Benedita Menezes Queiroz

• HART •
PUBLISHING
OXFORD AND PORTLAND, OREGON
2018

Hart Publishing
An imprint of Bloomsbury Publishing Plc

Hart Publishing Ltd
Kemp House
Chawley Park
Cumnor Hill
Oxford OX2 9PH
UK

Bloomsbury Publishing Plc
50 Bedford Square
London
WC1B 3DP
UK

www.hartpub.co.uk
www.bloomsbury.com

Published in North America (US and Canada) by
Hart Publishing
c/o International Specialized Book Services
920 NE 58th Avenue, Suite 300
Portland, OR 97213-3786
USA

www.isbs.com

HART PUBLISHING, the Hart/Stag logo, BLOOMSBURY and the Diana logo are trademarks of Bloomsbury Publishing Plc

First published 2018

British Library Cataloguing-in-Publication Data
A catalogue record for this book is available from the British Library.

ISBN: HB: 978-1-50991-287-2
ePDF: 978-1-50991-285-8
ePub: 978-1-50991-286-5

Library of Congress Cataloging-in-Publication Data

A catalogue record for this book is available from the Library of Congress

Typeset by Compuscript Ltd, Shannon

To find out more about our authors and books visit www.hartpublishing.co.uk. Here you will find extracts, author information, details of forthcoming events and the option to sign up for our newsletters.

For Quiquinha

Acknowledgements

I would like to start by thanking the European University Institute, the institution that hosted me for the first few years that I was writing this book, for the incredible opportunity it offered me to grow, both personally and academically. I am also grateful to Hart Publishing, and in particular to the team that helped me through the period of revision and publication.

I will always be indebted to Professor Loïc Azoulai. His kindness during my time at the EUI will not be forgotten, as well as all the conversations we had about my project, which were always challenging but relaxed, and from which I learned so much. I want to thank Professor Miguel Poiares Maduro for having inspired my interest in EU law. Thank you Dr Cunha Rodrigues for everything you taught me, which will stay with me forever. To Professor Ruth Rubio-Marín I thank the precious advice and friendship.

During the third year of my PhD I was lucky to spend a term writing this book in the beautiful rooms of the Bodleian Library in Oxford. I would like to thank COMPAS for that opportunity and, in particular, Professor Bridget Anderson who was my mentor at the centre. I also want to thank Professor Cathryn Costello not only for having met me in Oxford but, most of all, for giving me the incredibly helpful comments she did for the revision of this book. Professor Philippe De Bruycker, I am very grateful for the interesting conversations we had about my project in which I learnt a lot about migration. I would like also to thank Nicki for her support and for making the writers group such an important and lovely experience.

Fiesole and Rustici will always be my home every time I go back to Florence. There I met a group of people who became friends and to whom I owe many of the wonderful moments I lived in Italy. To Emily, Emma Linklater, Emma Nyhan, Agustin, Jon, Philipp, Michèle, Robin, Dónal, Octavio, Alexandra, Jan, Vera and Frank: thank you! To my dearest Filipa de Sousa I say thank you for all the help and unconditional friendship throughout the years. I was welcomed to Florence by a group of people who soon became my family there, thank you Guilherme Sampaio and Guilherme Almeida! Gaminha, to you I am truly indebted, thank you for always being there and for taking me to La Loggia when I most needed. Tiago, thank you for everything from Florence to Lisbon (you know what). Most of all, thank you for being the friend who I feel like I have known all my life. Carleto, thank you for our strong friendship, without a doubt, it is one of the best gifts I brought from Italy. It's a privilege to have friends like you!

To Micas, Zézinha, Maria Montenegro, Kikas, Inês, Rosinha, Teresinha, Chica, Ana, Helena, Lu and Inês Aguiar, thank you for every celebration and every tight hug, you are a huge part of my heart.

At age 26 I gained a sister, my Lu. You shared with me the happiest and the saddest moments, every achievement, a home, a dining and a working table. Thank you for having been my companion and the best friend I could have during these years. I believe that it wasn't just luck that put us on the same plane in April 2011, and I know that even though we might need planes to see each other now, we will never grow apart.

To my Vóvó Laura, Tia Jójó, Tátá, Ana, Tio Tozé, Catarina, Bia, Mati, Ricardo e João, my dearest family, I am grateful for all your support. Tio Ricardo, my adopted godfather, I have to thank you for all our lively debates around the table in Cabanelas, which tested every inch of my arguments. Thank you Pecanha, for all your love all my life.

To my parents I owe everything. I have come this far because, since I was a little girl, they taught me to follow the path I felt was mine. Even though the geographical distance always hurts, it was always with love that you pushed to go further. Our road trip together to Florence will always be a happy memory of our family and one of the happiest I have. You gave me unconditional freedom and support to dream and grow and certainty of our home and your love in Portugal and I am the luckiest for that. Mãe, Pai: thank you, you are the best part of me.

Jimmy, thank you is not enough to say what I feel, including every time you told me I would make it in the end, or those times you helped me re-writing, editing or rationalising my most emotional arguments. I will keep in my heart forever the perfect six months we lived in Portugal by the sea, as well as the three years in Florence that came before that. I could write another book, even longer and with different volumes, about everything you made forever better, more special and happier in my life. Those memories (and certainties) that we built together are what make me hope for 'the rest of [my] life to start as soon as possible'.[1]

[1] 'When Harry Met Sally' (1989), 1h 29 min 29 sec.

Contents

Table of Cases

European Court of Human Rights

Court of Justice of the European Union Cases and Opinions AG

Judgments

Opinions AG

National Case Law

Table of Legislation

International and European Legislation

Primary Sources

Secondary Legislation

National Legislation

Introduction

IRREGULAR MIGRATION IS an extremely relevant and controversial topic in contemporary European migration law. Not only has it been a high priority issue for the EU in the last decade, it has also been a crucial topic in every national and international political debate. In this area of law national sovereignty is strongly challenged by the implementation of EU legislation. However, this book illustrates that a wide margin of manoeuvre is left for Member States in implementing immigration-related legislation. The concrete focus of the book is the sensitive phenomenon of the illegality of a migrant's stay within the EU. The book engages in that task due to the fact that there is a lacuna in legal research on this particular topic.[1] It does so by attempting to answer the questions of what is covered by the overreaching EU law conceptualisation of 'illegality' in relation to a migrant's legal status, which statuses are left out of this conceptualisation and which are covered but not acknowledged, for instance.

There are a number of different ways to construct an individual's illegal stay or to look at illegality as a phenomenon including social, anthropological, cultural, political, legal or a combination of these means. These constructions have different premises and content depending on factors such as the geographical focus (for example, a focus on the EU or in the US), the category of migrant that the illegality is attached to (such as mobile EU citizens, third-country nationals, third-country nationals accompanying a spouse who is a citizen of the Union, for instance), or whether they are being examined through a national or a supranational lens. This book looks at the concept of illegality of an individual's stay from a legal perspective with a particular focus on EU law. The main goal is to analyse the ways in which the EU deals with different types of illegal stays and to provide a clear study of illegality within the EU.

Before examining how EU law affects the shape of illegality, there is a clear need for a justification of the perspective chosen. There are two primary reasons. First of all, EU law (like national law) is a source of illegality. Whether voluntarily or otherwise, EU law can be the origin of an illegal migration status. For instance, the violation of supranationally imposed requirements to enter, stay, move and work in the EU can result in an illegal status. This is so in relation to third-country nationals who, for instance, overstay their visa and consequently violate the Visa Code, for example.[2] Similarly, the same can be said in relation to mobile EU

[1] G Sciortino and M Bommes, *Foggy Social Structures: Irregular Migration, European Labour Markets and the Welfare State* (Amsterdam, Amsterdam University Press, 2012) 13.

[2] European Parliament and Council Regulation (EC) No 810/2009 of the of 13 July 2009 establishing a Community Code on Visas (Visa Code), [2009], OJ 2009, L 243/1 (hereafter Visa Code).

citizens within the context of intra-EU migration who no longer fulfil the compulsory conditions imposed by Directive 2004/38/EC.[3] Consequently, if the origin of illegality situations is multi-layered, its regulation, enforcement and remedies have the same nature. The underlying aim of this research is to understand the role that the supranational level of regulation plays and to examine what potential that may have with regard to illegality.

Clarity with regard to the perspective chosen to look at illegality is needed since, as mentioned above, there is a combination of different layers of jurisdiction dealing with the phenomenon. As such, there are three relevant jurisdictions which regulate different issues in the area of irregular migration and therefore touch upon the issue of illegality, namely international law, EU law and the national laws of the Member States. This is important since the different sources of law look at different dimensions of illegality. For example, international law (and in particular human rights law)[4] generally takes a more rights-based approach.

There is no comprehensive international law framework that tackles the issue of what illegality means, and there is no 'conceptual clarity' with regard to a definition of irregular migration for that matter.[5] A selection of international documents highlight the fact that the main shared purpose is that of providing general protection to irregular migrants, crucially through affording them rights (although unfortunately this has often been met with a lack of support from States.) For instance, beyond refugee protection, international law establishes general binding obligations on States party to such instruments in relation to the rights of migrants irrespective of their migration status (unless they are expressly excluded from its scope).[6] For example, Articles 1 and 2 (1) of the Universal Declaration of Human Rights contains a notion of human dignity applicable to all regardless of whether they are in possession of a regular migration status or not.

Further, even though the International Convention on the Elimination of All Forms of Racial Discrimination allows for a distinction to be drawn between citizens and non-citizens,[7] it simultaneously guarantees protection against discrimination of citizens and non-citizens alike.[8] A further example is the 2003

[3] Arts 6, 7 and 8 of the European Parliament and the Council Directive 2004/38 on the right of citizens of the Union and their family members to move and reside freely within the territory, [2004] OJ L 158/77 (hereafter Citizens Directive 2004/38).

[4] See for an example Arts 1 and 2 (1) of the UN General Assembly, Universal Declaration of Human Rights, 10 December 1948,217 A (III) (hereafter Universal Declaration of Human Rights).

[5] J Handmaker and C Mora, '"Experts": The Mantra of Irregular Migration and the Reproduction of Hierarchies' in M Ambrus and others (eds), *The Role of 'Experts' in International and European Decision-Making Processes* (Cambridge, Cambridge University Press, 2014) 267.

[6] For example, Arts 1 and 2 (1) of the Universal Declaration of Human Rights. See also for a more comprehensive analysis of the development 'soft law' on the field of vulnerable irregular migrants A Betts, 'Towards a "Soft Law" Framework for the Protection of Vulnerable Irregular Migrants' (2010) 22 *International Journal of Refugee Law* 236.

[7] Art 1 (2) of the UN General Assembly, International Convention on the Elimination of All Forms of Racial Discrimination, 21 December 1965.

[8] Committee on the Elimination of Racial Discrimination, General Recommendation 30, Discrimination against non-citizens, 64th session, 2004.

International Convention on the Protection of the Rights of All Migrant Workers and Members of their Families. This document represents an effort to establish a minimum standard of social rights available for all migrants irrespective the regularity of their status,[9] which shows that even from a rights-based approach considerable efforts have been made to expand the bundle of rights that irregular migrants can enjoy (ultimately, however, without the support of EU Member States, none of whom opted to ratify the Convention). Additionally, Article 9 (1) of the International Labour Organization (ILO) Convention No 143 on migrant workers posits the right to equal treatment for migrants who enter a state irregularly and cannot be regularised. This article is related to the rights that arise from past employment with regards remuneration, social security and other benefits. However, although some EU Member States have ratified this Convention it was not subscribed to in a widespread manner.[10] Consequently, we can see that there is no conceptual clarity in international law and that it establishes general binding obligations on States party to such instruments in relation to the rights of migrants irrespective of their migration status, unless they are expressly excluded from its scope.

Rather than focussing on such international instruments this book examines the existence of a concept of illegality in EU law. This is a conceptual question that attempts to challenge simplistic assumptions about such a complex phenomenon (that of illegality), rather than arguing for a (still very important) expansion of these rights. As such, the first reason why an EU law take on illegality was the most appropriate relates to the nature of the research question.

The second reason for the choice of EU law over other possible sources of law that deal with the issue of the illegality of a migrant's stay relates to the need to clarify and clearly distinguish different concepts and phenomena such as illegality and criminality which are commonly conflated in the EU migration discourse.[11] It is crucial to distinguish between the two in order to understand the scope of the former. Chapter four addresses the issue of the criminalisation of migrants and discusses whether the way EU immigration databases are designed contributes to the conflation of migrants and criminals. One particularly important finding is that border controls may have a significant impact on the way migrants are categorised. In Bigo's words:

> The uncertainty about the borders of the EU plays a major role about feelings of fear among the population but it creates also the capacity for governments to manufacturing

[9] This Convention focuses particularly on providing irregular migrants equal treatment with national workers in matters of: conditions of work, remuneration, terms of payment and the right to join and participate in trade unions (see Arts 25 and 26).

[10] EU Member States that ratified the International Labour Organization (ILO), Migrant Workers (Supplementary Provisions) Convention, C143, 24 June 1975,C143: Cyprus, Italy, Portugal, Slovenia and Sweden.

[11] V Mitsilegas, 'The Changing Landscape of the Criminalisation of Migration in Europe: The Protective Function of European Union Law' in MJ Guia, M van der Woude and J van der Leun (eds), *Social Control and Justice—Crimmigration in the Age of Fear* (The Hague, Eleven International Publishing, 2013) 87.

unease and to use it as a technology of domination where the control of some people is more important than the control of the territory at the borders.[12]

The book analyses how this control over mobile people within the EU, in particular illegally staying third-country nationals, affects not only their legal categorisation but also their marginalisation, for example through conflation of the concepts of illegality of stay and criminality (as we will see in chapter four).

I. EU LAW'S IMPACT ON THE DEFINITION OF ILLEGALITY

EU law sources that touch upon the regulation of illegality are 'scattered', similar to the rest of EU migration law.[13] At the level of primary sources, the Union recently saw its competence increased in the area of immigration.[14] That having been said, EU law's regulation of irregular migration is constrained to the development of a common immigration policy that takes 'enhanced measures to combat, illegal immigration and trafficking in human beings'.[15] The book identifies three main trends that are illustrative of the impact that EU legislation has in the creation of a concept of illegality at a supranational level. First, EU legislation has contributed to the erosion of the traditional distinction between legal and illegal migrants and has failed to solve the situation of those whose status is somewhere between these two categories. Second, EU law only partially regulates the regime of illegality. For example the definition of 'illegal stay' is revealed to be broad enough to allow Member States to create their own categorisation of the same phenomenon, as will be shown below. Third, there has been a shift in what it means to 'have papers' or to be registered in the host Member State since EU law has been implemented in this area. Each of these three impacts deserves to be examined in greater detail.

To elaborate, the first impact is the way in which the EU contributes to a blurring of the distinction between legal and illegal migration. An example of this lack of clarity is the fact that the migration status of certain categories of individuals not clearly covered by illegality under EU law is left to the discretion of Member States (such as the categorisation of non-removable migrants, or migrants who are illegally staying but cannot be removed from the host Member State).[16] These migrants may be kept in limbo for a certain amount of time and, although some safeguards are provided by EU law, there is not (yet) a straightforward answer to this issue that, in practice, 'disturbs the coherence of the legal-illegal dichotomy'.[17]

[12] D Bigo, 'Criminalisation of "Migrants": The Side Effect of the Will to Control the Frontiers and the Sovereign Illusion' in B Bogus and others (eds), *Irregular Migration and Human Rights: Theoretical, European and International Perspectives* (Leiden, Martinus Nijhoff Publishers 2004) 72.

[13] P Boeles and others, *European Migration Law* 2nd edn (Cambridge, Intersentia, 2014) 37.

[14] Art 79 TFEU and ibid, 37.

[15] Art 79 TFEU.

[16] The status of non-removable migrants is the object of chapter three of the present book.

[17] Handmaker and Mora (n 5) 28.

The existence of non-removability situations, created or at least tolerated by EU law, shows that although illegality is meant to be a temporary phenomenon by definition, the lack of effective supranational regulation prevents this from being the case.[18] Even if it is agreed that this group of migrants are illegally staying within the territory of the host Member State (if they are not granted authorisation to stay), this is an atypical situation.[19] The presence of such individuals is acknowledged but there is no duty imposed by EU law to recognise them at the national level, apart from a written confirmation that 'shall' be issued stating that the return decision 'will temporarily not be enforced'.[20] This is not the place to analyse in detail the case of non-removable migrants in the EU, as that is the focus of chapter three, but it is important to show that EU law partially regulates this phenomenon which may have a negative impact on both the scope of the safeguards granted to migrants in this situation and the lack of clarity as to what it means to be illegally staying in Europe.

Second, the complex regulation of illegality from a supranational view is not only scattered and partially developed, it provides half-baked definitions of components of the phenomenon of illegality and allows Member States at the national level to complete them. The examples of these incomplete definitions vary. For instance most national immigration laws do not provide a satisfactory definition of who is an illegal migrant.[21] Furthermore, the definition of 'illegal stay' is a striking example of the incoherence (between domestic and supranational legislation) that may be generated at the domestic level. It must be stressed that the creation of these scenarios does not contravene EU law as the Court of Justice of the European Union (CJEU) clarified in the *Achughbabian* case, stating that the Return Directive, which provides a definition of 'illegal stay', is not 'designed to harmonise in their entirety the national rules on the stay of foreign nationals'.[22]

For instance, the Belgian Immigration Act does not include a definition of illegally staying migrants.[23] This national legislation distinguishes between third-country nationals who have fulfilled the formal requirements imposed by law (being registered by the commune or more generally by the competent national authorities) and those who have not.[24] However, Belgian law adds a further

[18] Especially visible in the non-mandatory character of the regularising power of Art 6 (4) of the Return Directive.

[19] The reasons as to why this is so will be explored in much greater detail in chapter three.

[20] Art 14 (2) of the European Parliament and of the Council Directive 2008/115/EC on common standards and procedures Member States for returning illegally staying third-country nationals, [2008] OJ L 348 (hereafter Return Directive).

[21] E Guild, 'Who is an Irregular Migrant' in C Cholewinski B Bogusz, A Szyszcak (ed), *Irregular Migration and Human Rights: Theorectical, European and International Perspectives, Immigration and Asylum and Policy in Europe* (Leiden, Martinus Nijhoff Publishers, 2004) 15–16.

[22] Case C-329/11, *Achughbabian*, [2011], EU:C:2011:807, para 28.

[23] Art (1) of the Loi 15 décember 1980 sur l'accès au territoire, le séjour, l'établissement et l'éloignement des étrangers.

[24] Guild (n 21) 21: 'This case is covered by article 79: "Est possible d'une peine d'amende l'étranger qui contrevient aux articles 5, 12, 17 ou 41bis ou qui circule sur la voie publique sans etre porteur d'un des documents prévus à ces articles ou à l'article 2".'

distinction (that of irregular stay and illegal stay) that is not made by (but crucially is also not prohibited by) EU law. Falling into an illegal stay in EU law depends on not fulfilling the 'conditions of entry as set out in Article 5 of the Schengen Borders Code or other conditions for entry, stay or residence'[25] in the host Member State. As such, there are no obstacles to national immigration legislation that creates another regime for a type of stay (irregular) that simply does not accomplish the formalities (such as registering in the commune) and for that reason is sanctioned differently from an illegal stay.[26] The Belgian legislation is cited as an example in order to demonstrate that the role played by EU law in defining certain parts of the phenomenon of illegality leaves gaps in this definition which can be filled, often in a problematic manner, at the national level by Member States.

II. THE LANGUAGE OF ILLEGALITY: TERMINOLOGICAL CHOICES

Despite the fact numerous studies have been published concerning the terminological choices inherent in addressing not only the phenomenon of illegality but also the immigration status of the migrants living within it,[27] it is nonetheless necessary to briefly address the reasons behind the terminological choices made in this book. Illegality and irregularity are used interchangeably when referring to an immigration condition that structurally is a product of policy choices, subsequently translated into immigration legislation.[28]

Second, (with regard to the personal element of illegality) the terminology used for the individual who is not granted a legal immigration status by the host country's immigration authorities is illegally or irregularly staying migrant, or simply an irregular migrant. The expression 'illegal migrant' is not used throughout this book due to the fact that it is not considered to be legally precise and at the same time harmful to the conception of illegality by conflating it with criminality. Scholars, NGOs and most actors working in this area do not encourage the use of the term 'illegal migrant'[29] due to the fact that illegality arises as a result of the migrant's act of breaching immigration law rather than from the individual

[25] Art 3 (2) of the Return Directive.

[26] In the Belgian example irregular stay is sanctioned with a fine and not imprisonment as an illegal stay may be, see Guild (n 21) 21.

[27] K Groenendijk, 'Introduction: Migration and Law in Europe' in E Guild and P Minderhoud (eds), *The First Decade of EU Migration and Asylum Law* (Leiden, Martinus Nijhoff Publishers, 2012) 5; M Jandl, D Vogel and K Iglicka, 'Report on methodological issues' Research Paper, Clandestino, Undocumented Migration: Counting the Uncountable, 2008; A Triandafyllidou, *Irregular Migration in Europe: Myths and Realities* (Farnham, Ashgate Publishing Company, 2010) 2.

[28] See chapter one of this book for a comprehensive version of the concept of illegality.

[29] For an example, the Platform for International Cooperation on Undocumented—PICUM—an NGO actively campaigning for a change in terminology (see: http://picum.org/en/news/picum-news/45168/, or http://picum.org/en/news/picum-news/42546), or RI Cholewinski, *Study on obstacles to effective access of irregular migrants to minimum social rights* (Council of Europe, 2005) 8.

themselves.[30] Some believe that categorising people as illegal clashes with the recognition of their humanity[31] and as such there is a clear preference for referring to these migrants as irregular migrants, rather than illegal, in order to avoid the pejorative connotations that associate migrants who are illegally staying in a country with 'criminals' and criminality.[32]

Much ink has been spilled in an attempt to find the perfect terminology with which to categorise migrants who have an irregular immigration status. The terms which are typically used include: 'illegal', 'clandestine', 'unauthorised', 'unlawful', 'non-compliant', 'sans papiers', 'irregular', 'aliens without residence status', 'undocumented' and 'precarious'.[33] These are only a few of the examples of the creative semantic exercises that dominate the debate in this area.[34] A definition must in its essence look at the phenomenon as it is and avoid becoming a normative argument in relation to what the author believes the phenomenon may be. One such example is Bauder's 'illegalized refugee and immigrant' proposal.[35] This author argues for the adoption of a term that focuses on the 'systematic process that renders people "illegal"', instead of making these migrants responsible for the situation where they find themselves.[36] On the face of it, Bauder's idea that illegality is a product of the governments and institutions in charge of enforcing migration and refugee laws seems correct. However, it also seems biased for not taking into account the agency of migrants who do not possess a residence permit, or have not renewed their visa, or even refused to leave after being issued an expulsion order. As such, Bauder's definition does not recognise the possibility that migrants can themselves be responsible for their irregular immigration status.

The challenge of finding the essence of what the concept of illegality means in EU law starts by understanding and demystifying the wording used at this level of governance. To avoid adding fuel to the fire of the debate about the terminological options in the area of irregular migration, and at the risk of not doing justice to the already extensive sociological literature on the topic, the term 'illegally staying

[30] R Andersson, 'Illegal, Clandestine, Irregular: On Ways of Labelling People,' Border Criminologies (http://bordercriminologieslawoxacuk/illegal-clandestine-irregular/), 2014, and H Bauder, 'Why We Should Use the Term 'Illegalized'Refugee or Immigrant: A Commentary' (2014) 26 *International Journal of Refugee Law* 2.

[31] P Nyers, 'No one is Illegal between City and Nation' (2010) 4 *Studies in Social Justice* 127.

[32] The relationship between illegality and criminality is analysed in further detail in chapter four.

[33] See, for example: Andersson (n 30) and B Vollmer, *Policy Discourses on Irregular Migration in Germany and the United Kingdom* (Basingstoke, Palgrave Macmillan, 2014) 9.

[34] For examples of scholars using the different terms see: J McDonald, 'Migrant Illegality, Nation Building, and the Politics of Regularization in Canada' (2009) 26 *Refuge: Canada's Journal on Refugees*; M C LeMay, *Illegal Immigration: A Reference Handbook* (Santa Barbara, Abc-clio, 2007); Bauder (n 30); M Jandl, 'The Estimation of Illegal Migration in Europe' (2004) *Studi Emigrazione* 141, L Chavez, *Shadowed Lives: Undocumented Immigrants in American Society* (Andover, Cengage Learning, 2012); A Błuś, 'Beyond the Walls of Paper. Undocumented Migrants, the Border and Human Rights' (2013) 15 *European Journal of Migration and Law*; and A McNevin, 'Political Belonging in a Neoliberal Era: The Struggle of the Sans-Papiers' 10 *Citizenship Studies* 135.

[35] Bauder (n 30) 1.

[36] ibid, 5.

third-country national' and 'unlawfully staying EU citizen' is preferred as this is the terminology used by the source of law that is at the heart of the present study: EU law.[37]

Third, leaving aside the terminological choices that focus on the role of the migrant, or those that focus on the role of the host countries and institutions, this book opts to look at illegality from the perspective of what it is legally linked to: the right to stay or to reside. Thus, the terms adopted in the present study when referring to the individuals that are part of illegality is illegally staying third-country national or irregular migrant. This choice is also motivated by the fact that this is the terminology used in official EU documents and CJEU jurisprudence dealing with illegality and irregular migration in EU law. Hence, in order to avoid unnecessary misconceptions with regard to, first, the perspective taken in the book (EU law) and second, the phenomenon under analysis (illegality in relation to migration statuses), the decision was taken to opt for a more legal and perhaps literal approach to the terminology.

It is important to clarify that the position taken does not simply dismiss the importance of the problem discussed by the various scholars referred to previously. It is rather a conscious choice that considers this book not the best and most useful forum for a detailed discussion of this issue once more. Rather, the book attempts to challenge the 'unspoken assumption'[38] that the definition of who falls into illegality and what illegality is exactly is unproblematic.[39] This is the issue that lies at the heart of the book, an issue of substance, and which will be explored in the following chapters.

III. OVERVIEW OF THE BOOK

The book is divided into two blocks of analysis. The first includes the first three chapters and has the main objective of addressing a holistic conceptualisation of illegality in the EU. As such, chapter one starts with a conceptual analytical part which deals with the legal sources of illegality and EU institutional framework that regulates this phenomenon. It then moves on to demonstrate why the traditional binaries of legal and illegal or alien and citizen are inadequate in terms of migrant statuses of the regulation of illegality within the EU in chapters two and three. The cases of unlawfully staying EU citizens and non-removable third-country nationals serve to illustrate the premise that the concept of illegality as it stands at present

[37] Used interchangeably with irregular migrant throughout the book. For example see: Art 2 (b) of the European Parliament and the Council Directive 2009/52/EC providing for minimum standards on sanctions and measures against employers of illegally staying third-country nationals, [2009] OJ L 168, (hereafter Employers Sanctions Directive).

[38] On 'unspoken assumptions': R Andersson, *Illegality, Inc: Clandestine Migration and the Business of Bordering Europe*, vol 28 (Oakland, University of California Press, 2014) 8.

[39] Guild (n 21) 3.

falls short of adequacy in relation to the group of migrants it affects. Simultaneously, these cases highlight the legal gaps left by EU law in the regulation of illegality and that Member States are forced to step in to fill in what is left unregulated. Illegality then becomes a phenomenon within a fragmented, multi-level regime which produces multiple migrant statuses with a heterogeneous interpretation at the domestic level. An example of this heterogeneous interpretation and application of the law is the scope of protection of non-removable migrants, or even the enforceability of the expulsion of an EU citizen from the host Member State.

The second stage addresses the side effects and problematic implications of the EU's approach to the illegality of a migrant's stay at national and supranational levels, as presented in earlier stages of the book. Chapters four and five look at ways in which the regime of illegality may produce perverse consequences (criminalisation at the level of border control (EU level) and the instrumentalisation of the access to legality (national level)). In relation to the issues covered by chapter four, it is shown that the EU databases, biometrics and information exchange used as tools to track illegality have somewhat deviated from their initial purpose, while the generalised surveillance of movement erodes the distinction between alien and citizen as well as criminal and illegally staying third-country nationals. It is shown that the combination of these two factors allied to greater access by national police authorities to the personal data stored in those systems risks violating the principles of proportionality, necessity and discrimination. In particular, chapter four considers the interconnection between the repositories of information as the Schengen Information System, the Visa Information System, the EURODAC, the EUROSUR, the Entry Exit System proposed by the Commission. It is shown that the unclear boundaries of irregularity and criminality have striking consequences not only for the individual per se but also for Member States' sovereignty and Europe as a whole. EU databases are a clear example of the potential conflation of illegality and criminality; access to their wide range of information along with the growing interoperability of agencies and bodies consequently associates millions of mobile third-country nationals with criminality in the EU.

Finally, the book has the broader goal of offering a comprehensive view of how the two levels of governance—EU and national—overlap in the implementation of illegal stay rules in relation to the access to legality as a way to bring to a close the cycle of illegality. Chapter five focuses on the idea of accessing legality and first looks into how Member States may instrumentalise the rules that grant a legal migration status to third-country nationals. The analysis moves on to a more normative take on this mechanism and suggests that by using it in a corrective way, from a supranational level, potential remedies to the consequences derived from the regime of illegality previously addressed could be extrapolated.

All things considered, the corrective rationale for the access to legality has a broader purpose of limiting the domestic instrumentalisation of who the EU citizenry should be, as well as implicitly delimitating the group of people for whom leaving illegality is revealed to be a harder task. Instead of suggesting a new categorisation of people, given that by the 'way we label, define, and categorize people who move, we obscure and make invisible their actual lived experience',[40] the book takes a closer look within the competences as objectives of EU law and draws its normative claim from the need for a 'reset' in the context of regulation of illegality at the EU level. This is an important task to complete, as strides have been made in recent years in the area of migration, but there remains something to be said in a systematic matter about illegality in the EU and how the rules that regulate a exclusionary phenomenon such as this, impact more broadly on the definition of the people of Europe.

[40] A Crosby, 'The Boundaries of Belonging: Reflections on Migration Policies in the Twenty-First Century' in S Pratim Basu (ed), *The Fleeing People of South Asia: Selections from Refugee Watch* (London, Anthem Press, 2009) 52.

1

'What Part of Illegality Don't You Understand?'[1]: Illegality in EU Migration Law

I. INTRODUCTION

WHAT IS ILLEGALITY? In order to answer this question it is necessary to examine two different cycles of illegality and their various stages in order to provide a holistic view of the phenomenon of illegality. Illegality is a condition linked to a migrant's status and may be shared by both citizens of the Union and third-country nationals (even if different labels are used and different consequences arise from this status depending on whether the individual is a Union citizen or a third-country national). The idea of creating two cycles of illegality aims to illustrate two different dimensions of the creation of illegality (one migrant-centred and the other State-centred) as a way of providing a comprehensive analysis of the possible causes of illegality. The first cycle, the migrant's cycle of illegality, is divided into four stages: entry, stay or residence, employment, or return (voluntary) in case they do not acquire a legal migration status. The second cycle, the State's cycle of illegality is also divided into four fundamental stages: the moment of the decision to grant or not grant a residence permit, the registration and documentation stage, the border control stage and lastly the removal stage or granting a legal status. This cycle is only complete when combined with the stage of access to legality. This stage is further developed in the final chapter as a way of remedying the problematic consequences that arise from the EU regulation of illegality.

Most scholars focus on the discussion of the moral legitimacy of the right to stay in the EU.[2] Others focus on the social, anthropological and political construction of illegality.[3] In contrast, this book does not intend to adopt any of these

[1] L Downes and G Steinbrenner, 'What Part of "Illegal" Don't You Understand?' *The New York Times*, 28 October 2007 (www.nytimescom/2007/10/28/opinion/28sun4html?_r=0).

[2] J Carens, *The Ethics of Immigration* (Oxford, Oxford University Press, 2013).

[3] E Balibar, *We, the People of Europe?: Reflections on Transnational Citizenship* (Princeton, Princeton University Press, 2003); Bas Schotel, *On the Right of Exclusion: Law, Ethics and Immigration Policy* (New York, NY/Oxford, Routledge, 2011) 218; A McNevin, *Contesting Citizenship: Irregular Migrants and New Frontiers of the Political* (New York, Columbia University Press, 2011); L Bosniak, *The Citizen*

approaches; instead it clarifies the ways in which illegality is constructed from a legal perspective, mainly (although not exclusively) through the lens of EU law. However, it should be noted that national immigration legislation of Member States is not dismissed as it plays a crucial role in regulating illegality, and as such specific examples of the interaction between domestic law and EU law (often producing unsatisfactory and incoherent scenarios in the area of illegality) are given.

II. CONCEPTUAL ANALYSIS

A. The Concept of Illegality

'I am a human pileup of illegality' was how Downes described himself in 2007 in an editorial that attempted to address the question of what having an illegal immigration status means in the US.[4] Edwin Ackerman similarly concluded that it is the notion of illegality that is at the origin of the current debate on irregular immigration.[5] As such it is necessary to first of all analyse the concept of illegality and the perspective adopted in an attempt to understand it in order to subsequently test the current conceptualisation of illegality in EU migration law.

Scholars from different areas of law agree that conceptualising illegality is complex: some by pointing out that illegal immigration is fundamentally a political question;[6] others by stating that attitudes towards this concept are generally careless and uncritical, lacking more detained analysis.[7] And indeed it is difficult to find a sufficiently comprehensive analysis in legal scholarship that addresses EU law and illegality.

It will be shown that, first, the dynamic character of illegality as a phenomenon is susceptible to shifts and is inherently temporary.[8] Second, there are different categories of migrants that arguably do not fit within illegality.[9] Last, the fact that

and the Alien: Dilemmas of Contemporary Membership (Princeton, Princeton University Press, 2008); P Nicholas and D Genova, 'Migrant "Illegality" and Deportability in Everyday Life' (2002) 31 *Annual Review of Anthropology* 419; LR Chavez, 'The Condition of Illegality' (2007) 45 *International Migration*.

[4] Downes and Steinbrenner (n 1).

[5] E Ackerman, '"What Part of Illegal don't you Understand?": Bureaucracy and Civil Society in the Shaping of Illegality' (2014) 37 *Ethnic and Racial Studies* 181, 199.

[6] B Anderson and M Ruhs, 'Researching Illegality and Labour Migration' 16 *Population, Space and Place* 175, 178; E Longo, 'Seeking a Better Life: Human Welfare of Migrants in Irregular Situations in the United States and Europe',Working Paper Series #5, (2013) The Program on Law & Human Development, University of Notre Dame, 3.

[7] C Menjívar and D Kanstroom (eds), *Constructing Immigrant "Illegality"—Critiques, Experiences and Responses* (Cambridge, Cambridge University Press, 2014) 4.

[8] K Koser, 'Why Migration Matters' (2009) 108 *Current History* 147, 149–50: 'What is more, an individual migrant's status can change—often rapidly. A migrant can enter a country in an irregular fashion but then regularize her status, for example by applying for asylum or entering a regularization program. Conversely, a migrant can enter regularly then become irregular by working without a permit or overstaying a visa'.

[9] A Kubal, 'Conceptualizing Semi-Legality in Migration Research' (2013) 47 *Law & Society Review* 555, 556.

illegality results from a combination of laws is the cause of the difficulty in finding a sole satisfactory definition of illegality.

For some, illegality is a condition that results from governmental and institutional enforcement of migration legislation[10] whereas for others it is a phenomenon that affects people who are in a vulnerable situation and whose identity is precarious.[11] However, for most, the idea of illegality in migration is 'used too often, without proper questioning'.[12] Illegality, as Kubal argues, is a socio-legal phenomenon usually tautologically defined.[13] In order to avoid the circular discourse of what illegality is about, this chapter rejects the traditional approach of definition by exclusion (in other words that those who do not have a legal immigration status are illegal) and proposes a comprehensive definition of the concept.

i. A Holistic Version of the Concept of Illegality

As De Genova has stated, the very origin of illegality is law:

> 'Illegality' is the product of immigration laws—not merely in the abstract sense that without the law, nothing could be construed to be outside of the law; nor simply in the generic sense that immigration law constructs, differentiates, and ranks various categories of 'aliens'—but in the more profound sense that the history of deliberate interventions that have revised and reformulated the law has entailed an active process of inclusion through 'illegalization'.[14]

Although De Genova refers specifically to immigration laws that may create illegality, other branches of law also increasingly deal with situations of illegality of a migrant's status. Administrative and criminal law are two such examples, especially with regard to the domestic regulation of illegality. At this stage it is crucial *a priori* to set aside the conceptualisation of illegality as a 'problem', a perspective that was argued by Portes in the 1970s.[15] Illegality is a phenomenon that has a legal source such as legislation, either national or supranational (or a combination of both), establishing the conditions to legally stay in a host country. It is the violation of this legislation that consequently results in an immigration status which is against the law.[16] Consequently, illegality is an immigration condition

[10] H Bauder, 'Why We Should Use the Term 'Illegalized'Refugee or Immigrant: A Commentary' (2014) 26 *International Journal of Refugee Law* 2, 5.

[11] MJ Guia, 'Crimmigration, Securitisation and the Criminal Law of the Crimmigrant' in Maria João Guia, Maartje van der Woude and Joanne van der Leun (eds), *Social Control and Justice: Crimmigration in the Age of Fear* (The Hague, Eleven International Publishing, 2013) 23.

[12] Kubal (n 9) 561.

[13] ibid, 560.

[14] Nicholas and Genova (n 3) 439.

[15] A Portes, 'Introduction: Toward a Structural Analysis of Illegal (Undocumented) Immigration' (1978) *International Migration Review* 469, 470, and M Ruhs and B Anderson, 'Semi-compliance and Illegality in Migrant Labour Markets: an Analysis of Migrants, Employers and the State in the UK' (2010) 16 *Population, Space and Place* 195, 196.

[16] G Sciortino and M Bommes, *Foggy Social Structures: Irregular Migration, European Labour Markets and the Welfare State* (Amsterdam, Amsterdam University Press, 2012) 217.

that, structurally, is a product of policy choices that define which types of migration are legal,[17] subsequently translated into immigration legislation dependent on the violation of these laws to create an illegally-staying status.

Dauvergne has pointed out that classifying migrants as illegally staying is in itself a type of exclusion.[18] Following this line of thought, as Scortino and Bolmes have stated, it is argued that illegality is first of all a type of exclusion:[19] the first that illegally-staying migrants face. As such, it is important to attempt to move away from the conventional conception of illegality by exclusion, which reinforces the idea that of illegality as a generator of outlaws. Traditionally, establishing the boundaries of regular migration has been used as a tool to determine what, by default, is covered by illegality. By defining who has a legal migration status and leaving others outside that scope, the contours of the personal component of illegality are commonly defined.

In contrast, it is necessary to first set out the stages of two types of relationships that define the dynamics between the migrant, the State and the creation of illegality. First, different stages of illegality are distinguished in order to reproduce the cycle of an illegal stay in an attempt to draw special attention to cases or situations where migrants may bear some responsibility for producing a situation of illegality.[20] Second, from the perspective of the State, a similar exercise is carried out with the sole nuance that, instead of looking at stages of illegality, the focus is more on the role of documentation and registration (factors within the realm of the State) and their impact on the way illegality is created. From these exercises, two conflicting perspectives of who is responsible for the creation of illegality can be distinguished:[21]

(a) The view of the individuals who have migrated to another State and who are in breach of the host country's immigration laws; and,
(b) The view of States that believe it is an exercise of their sovereignty to decide who to exclude from having a legal immigration status, which consequently generates illegality.

The aim of this holistic analysis is to demonstrate that, as a result of the complexity of the factors involved and the ways in which illegality may be caused,

[17] F Duvell, 'Framing and Reframing Irregular Migration' in Bridget Anderson and Michael Keith (eds), *Migration: The COMPAS Anthology* (Oxford, COMPAS, 2014) 20.

[18] C Dauvergne, *Making People Illegal: What Globalization Means for Migration and Law* (Cambridge, Cambridge University Press, 2008) 17.

[19] Sciortino and Bommes (n 16) 220.

[20] The situation of children who are born already with an irregular migration status is that they are not considered to be part of this cycle as this young group is not exercising their agency when their parents enter irregularly or overstayed. No Member States grant automatically citizenship to children who are born in their territory (*jus soli*) in the EU.

[21] F Duvell, 'Paths into Irregularity: The Legal and Political Construction of Irregular Migration' (2011) 13 *European Journal of Migration and Law* 275, 276.

the conventional binary of legal or illegal is increasingly becoming obsolete.[22] This is so as a result of the multiplication of migrant categories (regular and irregular),[23] the limbo situation that arises from non-removability[24] and the type of illegality that unlawful EU citizens may fall into[25] (which relates more with the limits to access social benefits in a host Member State).

ii. The Migrant's Cycle of Illegality

To fall into illegality it is not necessary to cross the Mediterranean Sea on a vessel and risk one's life. By travelling on a supposedly completely safe Airbus from America to Europe one could be buying a ticket to an illegal stay. There are five fundamental stages and each will be examined in turn.

a. Stage I: Entry

The first stage concerns mainly clandestine, undocumented entry or breach of national immigration laws. When a migrant enters the EU without a residence permit, they are illegally staying from the initial entry stage. This is the typical and unfortunate example of the migrants arriving on the shores of Lampedusa or Greece, for example.[26] Frontex, the EU borders agency recently enumerated the main routes of irregular migration to Europe, namely:

1. The Central Mediterranean route—migrants coming from Tunisia and Libya to Italy and Malta. This route was the most used in 2014 with 171,000 detected cases of border crossing;[27]
2. The Western Mediterranean route—from Morocco and Algeria to Spain;
3. The Western African route—from the coast of West Africa to the Canary islands;
4. The Eastern borders route—from the countries across the EU's land borders in Eastern Europe into the territory of EU Member States;
5. Western Balkans route—from countries in the Balkans outside the EU into the territory of Member States;
6. The Albania–Greece circular route, and;
7. The Eastern Mediterranean route: from Turkey to Greece by land and sea.[28]

[22] B Vollmer and R McNeil, Briefing: 'Irregular Migration in the UK: Definitions, Pathways and Scale', 3 and Sciortino and Bommes (n 16) 219.

[23] MC Foblets, 'Diversité et Catégories de Personnes dans les Sociétés Contemporaines' in JY Carlier (ed), *L' étranger face au droit, XXes Journées d'études juridiques Jean Dabin* (Brussels, Bruylant, 2010).

[24] See chapter three for more on this issue.

[25] See chapter two for more on this issue.

[26] T Basaran, 'Saving Lives at Sea: Security, Law and Adverse Effects' (2014) 16 *European Journal of Migration and Law* 365.

[27] European Parliament, 'Briefing—Irregular immigration in the EU: Facts and Figures', April 2015, 1 (www.europarl.europa.eu/RegData/etudes/BRIE/2015/554202/EPRS_BRI(2015)554202_EN.pdf).

[28] C Morehouse and M Blomfield, 'Irregular Migration in Europe' (Washington DC, Migration Policy Institute, 2011) 9.

Articles 4 and 5 of the Schengen Borders Code, which determine the conditions for crossing the external borders and for entry for third-country nationals not exceeding three months within a six-month period, illustrate the regulation of the entry stage in the EU.[29] The compulsory character of the fulfilment of the conditions imposed by the Schengen Borders Code in order to avoid falling into illegality can be seen also with regard to the Visa regime, as Article 30 of the Visa Code clearly establishes that the right of entry is not granted automatically through the 'mere possession of a uniform visa or a visa with limited territorial validity'.[30] As such, if a third-country national does not fulfil the conditions imposed in particular by Article 5 of the Schengen Borders Code, their entry is unlawful and can be refused at the border,[31] as set out in Article 13 of the code. The conditions set out in Article 5 (1) of the Schengen Borders Code, for stays that do not exceed three months per six months period, are the following:

i) The possession of a valid travel document or another authorisation for border crossing,[32]
ii) The possession of a valid visa in accordance with Articles 5 (1) b) of the Schengen Borders Code and the Council Regulation (EC) No 539/2001,[33]
iii) There is a valid justification of the 'the purpose and conditions of the intended stay,' and the possession of 'sufficient means of subsistence, both for the duration of the intended stay and for the return to their country into which they are certain to be admitted,'[34]
iv) There is not an alert an alert issued in the SIS for the purposes of refusing entry,[35]
v) Do not represent a 'threat to public policy, internal security, public health or international relations of any of the Member States'.[36]

In addition to those who enter the EU and live in a clandestine way or with no documents, asylum seekers are another group of migrants that may enter the territory irregularly, in accordance with Article 31 of the 1951 Convention on the status of the refugee.[37] Article 31 of the 1951 Refugee Convention protects

[29] European Parliament and Council Regulation (EC) No 562/2006 of the of 15 March 2006 establishing a Community Code on the rules governing the movement of persons across borders (Schengen Borders Code), [2006], amended by OJ L 105 (hereafter Schengen Borders Code).
[30] Art 30 of the Visa Code.
[31] Art 13 (1) of the Schengen Borders Code.
[32] ibid, Art 5 (1) a).
[33] ibid, Art 5 (1) b).
[34] ibid, Art 5 (1) c).
[35] ibid, Art 5 (1) d).
[36] ibid, Art 5 (1) e).
[37] Art 31 (1) of the UN General Assembly, Convention Relating to the Status of Refugees, 28 July 1951 (hereinafter the 1951 Refugee Convention). See also JC Hathaway and M Foster, *The Law of Refugee Status* (Cambridge, Cambridge University Press, 2014) 28–29; G Noll, 'Article 31 (Refugees Unlawfully in the Country of Refuge)' in A Zimmermann (ed), *The 1951 Convention Relating to the Status of Refugees and its 1967 Protocol: A Commentary* (Oxford, Oxford University Press, 2011) 1243–76.

refugees who may have entered and stayed irregularly on the territory of a Contracting State from any penalty imposed for that reason:

> The Contracting States shall not impose penalties, on account of their illegal entry or presence, on refugees who, coming directly from a territory where their life or freedom was threatened in the sense of article 1, enter or are present in their territory without authorization, provided they present themselves without delay to the authorities and show good cause for their illegal entry or presence.

As Goodwin-Gill points out, in order to respect the regime established by the 1951 Refugee Convention the individual claim would have to be dealt with '*before* he or she is affected by an exercise of State jurisdiction'.[38] However, this is not always the case and asylum seekers are all over the world detained in consequence of their irregular entry in violation of the host State's international obligations. In this scenario, although these migrants have not yet fallen into illegality in accordance with international law, they are treated as if they did at a domestic level. The Court of Justice of the European Union (CJEU) has decided that Article 31 of the 1951 Refugee Convention is not under its jurisdiction,[39] arguing that '[i]t is settled case-law that the power, resulting from Article 267 Treaty on the Functioning of the European Union (TFEU), to provide interpretations by way of preliminary rulings extends only to rules which are part of EU law'.[40] For the Court, it 'is undisputed that the Member States have retained certain powers falling within that field, in particular relating to the subject-matter covered by Article 31 of that convention'.[41] This conclusion of the CJEU leaves unaddressed the restrictive interpretation of Article 31 by certain Member States.

Subsequently, such persons may apply for asylum and regularise their stay if granted a refugee status, although this is only one of the possible scenarios. Where the asylum seeker absconds to another Member State while the asylum procedure is taking place the migrant will fall into illegality. The same applies to a rejected asylum seeker who refuses to leave the EU territory. Despite being the most publicised in the media and the most politically debated stage of illegality, illegal entry is also the least significant in terms of quantity of inflows into the EU.[42] However, recently, according to EU Parliament figures, irregular border crossings to enter the EU have risen 'almost threefold, in comparison with 2013, due to a large increase of border crossings by citizens of Syria, Afghanistan and Eritrea'.[43]

[38] GS Goodwin-Gill, 'Article 31 of the 1951 Convention Relating to the Status of Refugees: Non-Penalization, Detention, and Protection', June 2003, available at: www.refworld.org/docid/470a33b10.html, 187.

[39] Case C- 481/13, *Mohammad Ferooz Qurbani*, [2014], EU:C:2014:2101.

[40] ibid, para 21.

[41] ibid, para 24.

[42] F Duvell, 'The Pathways in and out of Irregular Migration in the EU: A Comparative Analysis', (2011) 13 *European Journal of Migration and Law* 245, 247.

[43] European Parliament, Briefing—Irregular immigration in the EU: Facts and Figures, 2015 (n 27) 1.

b. Stage II: Stay or Residence

Whereas a minority of the illegally-staying migrants in Europe incur this illegality at the entry stage, the second stage, that of stay or residence, represents around 50 per cent of the illegally-staying population within the borders of the EU.[44] This second stage of the migrant's cycle of illegality relates to possible irregularities that may occur during the stay of the migrant who has otherwise entered the host country legally. Those who overstay their visa are the most common category of migrants who fall into illegality during their stay in another country. In this context, overstaying is the act of crossing EU borders legally in possession of a valid time-limited visa, whether it be a short-time tourist visa or a longer-term residence visa (such as student or work visa), and *a posteriori* remaining in the host Member State in contravention of their authority (such as staying after the expiry of visa work permit).

With regard to the legal provisions within EU law that regulate this second stage, one example is overstaying a visa by disrespecting, for instance, an annulment or revocation decision of a visa by the national authorities in accordance with Article 34 of the Visa Code. Further, Article 3 (2) of the Return Directive implies what is meant by 'illegal stay' by linking it with the violation of the conditions imposed by Article 5 of the Schengen Borders Code (the conditions to entry as explained in stage I (entry) above). If a migrant violates the conditions imposed they become illegally staying in the host Member State. As such, in the case of an overstayer the migrant would be in violation of Article 5 (1) (b) as a result of not being in possession of a valid visa.

c. Stage III: Dependency

The third stage of the migrant's cycle of illegality—dependency—focuses in particular on the choice of the individual and on the impact of a third actor on the creation of illegality. As Anderson and Ruhs point out, 'illegality may become a strategic choice for some migrants and their employers'.[45] As with the previous stage, the work and employment stage represents a large proportion of migrants living in illegality. Despite legal entry to (and stay within) the territory of the host country, at this stage migrants may cross the line from regularity to irregularity by engaging in illegal employment. Such illegal employment can for example be working or being self-employed in contravention of national immigration law

[44] D Vogel and N Cyrus, 'Irregular migration in Europe–Doubts about the effectiveness of control strategies' Policy Brief No 9, Focus Migration, 2008, 1, for a more detailed study about inflows and outflows onto irregular migrants residents population and the available data: A Kraler and D Reichel, 'Measuring Irregular Migration and Population Flows–What Available Data Can Tell' (2011) 49 *International Migration* 97, 110.

[45] Ruhs and Anderson (n 15) 196 and Anderson and Ruhs (n 6) 175.

through breach of conditions stated in the employment visa. For instance, changing employers without permission, doing work that is not permitted under the work permit or working more hours than allowed are considered to be a different purpose of entry of stay and therefore a violation of the visa.[46] Moreover, employers may also play a significant role in generating illegality. In this scenario the choices of the employer and national legislation regulating it determine scope of illegality. One example is the Italian regularisation programmes that were criticised for giving excessive power to employers and creating a situation of dependency for the migrants in relation to the employers.[47] In those cases the illegality arises out of the actions of a third actor (such as an employer) that directly impacts on the immigration status of the migrant. Dependency is an important feature of the phenomenon illegality as it reveals that the stronger party in the relationship may actively contribute to the creation of the illegality of stay. Not only through a relationship of employment can dependency be generated. The CJEU *NA* case is an example of the creation of dependency through a family relationship.[48] NA, a Pakistan national, married a German national and moved to the United Kingdom in 2004. During their short marriage, two daughters with German nationality were born and NA was the victim of domestic violence. In 2006 the abuser left the United Kingdom and returned to Germany. The divorce proceedings began in 2008 in the UK, two years after NA's German husband left their marital home in the UK. When the question was put to the CJEU whether or not NA would retain her residence after her German ex-husband left the UK in accordance with EU law, the Court's answer was in the negative. The reasoning employed by the CJEU was simple: it applied the 2004/38 Directive and replicated the *Singh and Others* case,[49] which stated that the non-EU citizen would only retain the residence rights until the EU citizen left the Member State, or if the divorce proceedings had begun before that. This was not the case for NA and for that reason she could not retain the right to residence on those grounds. Nevertheless, the CJEU determined that she would be able to stay there as a corollary of her children's EU citizenship-related rights and freedoms, in line with the previous *Zhu and Chen* decision.[50]

However, in terms of the impact that this decision represents for the protection of victims of domestic violence in the EU is problematic. To elaborate, if, in this exact scenario, NA's abuser ex-husband had abducted their daughters when he moved back to Germany, could NA fall into illegality and be deported? Perhaps, given that she would not retain her right to residence, or be granted the right to

[46] ibid, 197.

[47] Amnesty International, 'Italy—The regularisation should protect the rights of migrants workers' (Amnesty International Publications, 2012).

[48] Case C-115/15, *NA* [2016], EU:C:2016:487.

[49] Case C-218/14, *Singh and Others* [2015], EU:C:2015:476.

[50] Case C-115/15, *NA*, para 80 and case C-200/02, *Zhu and Chen*, EU:C:2004:639, para 45.

stay as a corollary of her children's rights. As Advocate General Wathelet stated, this framework

> could be used as a means of exerting pressure to stop the divorce at a time when the circumstances are in themselves enough to wear the victim down psychologically and, in any event, to engender fear of the perpetrator of the violence.[51]

This is a clear example of the problematic issues that may arise in the stage of dependency in cases of domestic violence.

Further, so-called 'bogus students' are also to be considered to be a case of illegality at the stage of dependency. This is the case of the migrant who has a student visa allowing them to stay in the host country and who is found working several hours a week whilst being remunerated as a worker and not a student; thus the initial purpose of their visa no longer applies.[52] Consequently, in such situations, from being a regular student with a valid visa for entering and staying in territory of the State, the migrant loses their legal immigration status and becomes an irregular migrant worker within the conditions of illegality.

d. Stage IV: Departure

The fourth stage concerns the voluntary return of migrants to their country of origin.[53] The Member State's failure to enforce a return decision and the migrant's refusal to respect a return decision are the main paths to irregularity at this stage. Typical examples of individuals falling into illegality at this stage are migrants who, after being denied asylum protection, exercise their agency and do not comply with an order to leave the host country. Migrants who having been issued an order to leave but cannot be returned because of a legal obstacle that protracts their return also fall into illegality, as no legal immigration status has been recognised for these individuals, other than mere toleration status.[54] This latter case is the case of non-removable migrants, a category of migrants that is the focus of chapter three.[55]

Article 7 of the Return Directive contemplates the possibility of voluntary departure of the illegally-staying migrant, a period of time (between seven and 30 days) granted to the migrant to leave the territory voluntarily, if after this period they have not departed the host Member State national authorities may enforce their removal. Member States may refrain from granting a voluntary departure period under Article 7 (4) where there is a 'risk of absconding, or if an application for a legal stay has been dismissed … or if the person concerned poses a risk to public policy, public security or national security'. As such, one may deduce from

[51] Case C-115/15, *NA* [2016], Opinion on Advocate General Wathelet, EU:C:2016:259.
[52] Art 34 of the Visa Code.
[53] Arts 6 and 8 of the Return Directive.
[54] Art 14 of the Return Directive.
[55] For a detailed analysis of the situation of non-removable migrants in the EU see chapter three.

the reading of this provision that once a return decision is issued (under Article 6 of the Return Directive), in principle it is within the migrant's power to exercise their right of voluntary departure which in exceptional circumstances may be limited by the State. Having looked at the migrant's cycle by analysing its four stages, it is now necessary to turns our attention to the State's cycle.

iii. The State's Cycle of Illegality

States are commonly seen as 'membership gatekeepers'[56] because of the control they exercise over the attribution of national citizenship (nationality) and consequently naturalisation and EU citizenship.[57] However, this was not always the case as until the middle of the eighteenth century whether States had the power (under international law) to expel and exclude potential immigrants was not clear.[58] However, State sovereignty and a State's margin of discretion, whilst well established in international law, are today threatened by phenomena such as the illegality of a migrant's stay.[59] Once border control is challenged, state sovereignty is undermined.[60] For some, national immigration law is the best means of examining the concept of illegal immigration.[61] However, in practice there has been considerable reluctance on the part of Member States to commit to a direct and precise definition of who an irregular migrant is, for example. Against this backdrop, we now turn to the first stage of the State's cycle.

a. Stage I: Decision to Grant or Refuse a Residence Permit

The power of granting or refusing residence permits to third-country nationals, a traditional bastion of State sovereignty, is a power that is also responsible for the creation of illegality.[62] At this first stage of the State's cycle of illegality one can distinguish two types of State action that may bring about the illegality of a migrant's stay: a) an active type, granting or denying immigration authorisation

[56] Dauvergne (n 18) 154.

[57] Art 20 TFEU.

[58] B Garth, 'Migrant Workers and Rights of Mobility in EC and USA' in M Cappelletti, M Seccombe and J Weiler (eds), *Integration Through Law Europe and the American Federal Experience*, vol Volume 1 Methods, Tools and Institutions, Book 3 Forces and Potential for a European Identity (Berlin, Walter de Gruyter, 1986) 90, and R Plender, *International Migration Law*, vol 2 (Leiden, Martinus Nijhoff Publishers 1988) 46–47.

[59] K Koser, 'Dimensions and Dynamics of Irregular Migration' (2010) 16 *Population, Space and Place* 181, 189.

[60] Bigo argues that in general all kinds of *nomadic behaviour* undermine the classic conceptions of state capacity to govern. Didier Bigo, 'Criminalisation of "Migrants": The Side Effect of the Will to Control the Frontiers and the Sovereign Illusion' in B Bogusz and others (eds), *Irregular Migration and Human Rights: Theorectical, European and International Perspectives* (Leiden, Martinus Nijhoff Publishers, 2004) 68.

[61] Dauvergne (n 18) 11.

[62] K Groenendijk, 'Introduction: Migration and Law in Europe' in E Guild and P Minderhoud (eds), *The First Decade of EU Migration and Asylum Law* (Leiden, Martinus Nijhoff Publishers, 2012) 18.

to stay and b) a passive type, failing in their bureaucratic duty to process residence and work permits, as well as renewals and appeal procedures in due time. The 'bureaucratic failure', as Duvell labels it, results in avoidable loss of regular statuses and consequently in illegality.[63] With the first stage in particular we can see the traditional power that the host State possesses to define the 'others' within their territory as form of creation of illegality.[64] Kostakopoulou has stated that the 'lack of State authorisation or consent places [migrants] … into the domain of illegality, thereby rendering their presence illegitimate'.[65]

An example of this stage can be seen in relation to the Visa Code rules for Member States to refuse a visa to a third-country national. The main conditions for this discretionary domestic power are enumerated in Article 32 (1) of the Visa Code. The first set of conditions relates to the applicant's:

i) presentation of a false travel document,[66]
ii) lack of justification for the purpose and conditions of the intended stay,[67]
iii) lack proof of sufficient means of subsistence,[68]
iv) having stayed for three months during the current six-month period on the territory of the Member State,[69]
v) being a person for whom an alert within the SIS has been issued for the purpose of refusing entry,[70]
vi) representing a threat to public, internal security or public health,[71]
vii) lack of proof of holding an adequate and valid travel medical insurance.[72]

Alternatively, when there are 'reasonable doubts as to the authenticity of the supporting documents submitted by the applicant or the veracity of their contents, the reliability of the statements made by the applicant or his intention to leave the territory'[73] the migrant's visa shall be refused by the Member State. These provisions create a regime that implies that respect of the conditions imposed on the first stage (entry) by the Schengen Borders Code, is necessary in order to have a legal status in accordance with Article 21 of the Visa Code.

[63] Duvell (n 42) 247.
[64] B Anderson, *Us and Them?: The dangerous Politics of Immigration Control* (Oxford, Oxford University Press, 2013).
[65] D Kostakopoulou, 'Irregular Migration and Migration Theory' in Bogusz Barbara and others (eds), *Irregular Migration and Human Rights: Theorectical, European and International Perspectives* (Leiden, Martinus Nijhoff Publishers, 2004) 43.
[66] Art 32 (1) a) (i) of the Visa Code.
[67] ibid, Art 32 (1) a) (ii).
[68] ibid, Art 32 (1) a) (iii).
[69] ibid, Art 32 (1) a) (iv).
[70] ibid, Art 32 (1) a) (v).
[71] ibid, Art 32 (1) a) (vi).
[72] ibid, Art 32 (1) a) (vii).
[73] ibid, Art 32 (1) b).

b. Stage II: Border Control

The second stage relates to the control of borders traditionally exercised by the State. The control and demarcation of borders is also historically and legally linked to State sovereignty over territory. Specifically, with regard to migration law, it is important to determine whether a migrant has entered the territory of a country (which is different from having a legitimate right to stay).[74] Border control may be defined as 'a multi-layer system aimed at facilitating legitimate travel and tackling illegal immigration'.[75] Enforcing tighter borders is a common strategy used by States to deal with 'illegality', along with 'strict enforcement of immigration and residence controls and, increasingly, cooperation between the state and civil society'.[76]

As this study focuses on the territory of EU Member States, one must take into consideration that both internal and external borders affect the creation of illegality.[77] For instance, the Schengen Borders Code provides a definition of external borders in Article 2 (2): 'the Member States' land borders, including river and lake borders, sea borders and their airports, river ports, sea ports and lake ports, provided that they are not internal border'. Thus, the fact that one lands in the airport of a Member State does not mean that they have crossed the EU's external borders.[78] This matters for the purposes of the creation of illegality because it determines the precise moment when a migrant may cross a border irregularly and is from that moment on illegally staying within the territory of the host country.

Germane to the internal borders of the EU it should be highlighted at this point that the abolition of the controls at the border of Member States that are part of the Schengen agreement (two Member States, the UK and Ireland, are not part) plays a relevant role in shifting the traditional conceptualisation of borders. Illegality depends on the moment when an illegal stay may occur, or where migrants may be asked for identification, and those moments are intrinsically related to where the border is placed. Article 20 of the Schengen Borders Code states that 'internal borders may be crossed at any point without a border check on persons, irrespective of their nationality, being carried out'.[79] The fact that internal borders may be more easily crossed does not have any impact on 'the exercise of police powers by the competent authorities of the Member States under national law,

[74] H Toner, P Boeles, M den Heijer, G Lodder and K Wouters, *European Migration Law* (Antwerp, Intersentia, 2010) 7–8. Boeles gives the example of a migrant who has physically entered the territory of a country, although that entrance and right to stay are denied.

[75] European Council, 2005/C53/01, The Hague Programme: Strengthening Freedom, Security and Justice in the European Union, [2005] OJ C53/1, and Boeles and others, ibid 375.

[76] Anderson and Ruhs (n 6) 175.

[77] For an innovative analysis of the idea to territoriality in the EU: L Azoulai, 'The (Mis)construction of the European Individual Two Essays on Union Citizenship Law, EUI LAW; 2014/14' (http://cadmuseuieu/handle/1814/33293).

[78] Boeles and others (n 74) 8.

[79] Art 20 of the Schengen Borders Code.

insofar as the exercise of those powers does not have an effect equivalent to border checks'.[80] In fact, the CJEU has clarified in recent case law that Articles 20 and 21 Schengen Borders Code:

> [M]ust be interpreted *as not precluding national legislation*, such as that at issue in the main proceedings, *which enables officials responsible for border surveillance and the monitoring of foreign nationals to carry out checks, in a geographic area 20 kilometres from the land border* between a Member State and the State parties to the CISA with a view to establishing whether the persons stopped satisfy the requirements for lawful residence.[81]

In short, this means that despite the abolition of internal borders (for most EU Member States), the control of those borders has not been weakened. Consequently, this affects the control of illegality, given that it is EU law which allows checks 20 kilometres away from the internal land border in accordance with the Schengen Borders Code, for example.

c. Stage III: Registration and Documentation

At the core of the registration and documentation stage is the issue of what it means to be registered in terms of acquiring a migration status. Being registered in the host State is a formality that expresses the State's control over the data on entry and exit of migrants in the territory. Traditionally, thinking about illegality has always been linked to a lack of documentation of the migrant that depended on the host State to formalise the legality of their stay. At first glance the relationship between the acquisition of a migrant's status and the lack or possession of documents may seem straightforward. However in practice, when one looks at the national regulation of this issue, not to mention EU law which is equally applicable, it is clear that the issue is much more complex.[82]

As stated in the literature, 'immigration, as well as tourism, cross-border circulation and all kinds of nomadic behaviour, seem to undermine classic conceptions of state capacity to govern'.[83] Accordingly, the most conventional functions of the State that link sovereignty, migration and registration of migrants evolve and shift with the inclusion of a supranational dimension to the regulation of migration and in particular for this study, the phenomenon of illegality.

A word of clarification about what registration means within the scope of this book must be provided. The idea that underlies illegality is the loss of the

[80] See Art 21 (a) of the Schengen Borders Code.

[81] Case C-278/12 PPU, *Atiqullah Adil v Minister voor Immigratie, Integratie en Asiel*, [2012], EU:C:2012:508 para 88 (emphasis added).

[82] See for example, at the national level Art 9 of the Lei da Assembleia da República nº 23/2007 de 4 de Julho de 2007, aprova o regime jurídico de entrada, permanência, saída e afastamento de estrangeiros do território nacional, Diário da República, 1.a série—N.o 127 and Annex I of the Schengen Borders Code for the supporting documents to verify the fulfilment of entry conditions at a supranational level.

[83] Bigo (n 60) 68.

substance of the right to stay and reside in a certain host country. Conversely, when talking about legality (a scenario where the individual has not lost the right to reside), registration is the stage that follows and deals with those formalities necessary to enjoy that right.[84]

The relationship between being registered in the host country and acquiring a legal status plays an important role in demonstrating that the fact of 'having papers' is not necessarily an indication of legality or vice versa. One may wonder about the real purpose that registration serves and whether it is something that might be used to identify migrants illegally staying in one of the Member States, or if it is a mere formality. There is not one unique answer to this question.

In the case of EU citizens moving to another Member State the Citizens' Directive 2004/38 in Article 8 defines the formalities that may be required for Union citizens to comply for periods of residence longer than three months.[85] This registration with the national authorities by EU citizens does not result in rights of residence—instead it has a declaratory function which has been re-stated by the CJEU in several decisions.[86] In addition, Article 25 of the Citizens' Directive 2004/38 expressly limits national authorities from making registration or other administrative formalities a requirement for the exercise of a right.

In light of the foregoing, the question arises as to the exact link between fulfilling the formalities or, for example, being registered in the host Member State municipality and acquiring a legal status. Is it simply a collection of data or is there a practical agenda behind it? There is not a straightforward answer to this particular question and throughout the book it is shown why 'not having papers' and illegality are not always in a causal relationship.

d. Stage IV: Return Decision and Removal

The final stage of the State's illegality cycle, the regularisation and the return of migrants to their country of origin, is probably the strongest example of a State exercising sovereignty in the area of migration. The power to issue a return decision, similar to the power to grant an authorisation to reside (stage I), represents the core of the State's sovereignty in the area of migration. This stage reinforces the idea that the State makes the illegally-staying migrant deportable. Deportability is, in De Genova's words, the 'possibility of being removed from the space of the nation state' and is a basic feature of the illegality of a migrant's stay.[87] An example

[84] See subsection I.B.i.b of the present chapter for an example of how the lack of registration in the commune may lead to a different type to migrant status.

[85] European Parliament and the Council Directive 2004/38 on the right of citizens of the Union and their family members to move and reside freely within the territory, [2004] OJ L 158/77, (hereafter the Citizens' Directive 2004/38).

[86] Case C-370/90 *Singh* [1992], EU:C:1992:296, para 17; Case C-344/95 *Commission v Belgium*, [1997], EU:C:1997:81, para 22; Case C-459/99 *MRAX* [2002], EU:C:2002:461, para 74; and Case C-215/03 *Oulane* [2005], EU:C:2005:95, paras 17 and 18. See also E Guild, S Peers and J Tomkin, *The EU Citizenship Directive: A Commentary* (Oxford, Oxford University Press, 2014) 144.

[87] Nicholas and Genova (n 3) 439.

of this stage is found in the Return Directive, in particular in Article 6 which establishes that it is within the host Member State's discretion to issue a return decision. Having issued the return decision the Member State has to provide the illegally-staying migrant with a period of time for their voluntary departure (under Article 7) or refuse their application (Article 7 (4)). The Member State's discretion is at the heart of the return procedure, especially if there is no voluntary departure period granted to the illegally-staying migrant or if the 'obligation to return has not been complied with',[88] as in these cases 'Member States shall take all the necessary measures to enforce the return decision'.[89]

III. LEGAL SOURCES

A. EU Law's Role in the Conceptualisation of Illegality

The aim of the previous section was to provide a view of illegality as a phenomenon that results from the combination of factors that may occur at different stages of a migrant's stay in the host State. Another important lesson to take from this schematic analysis is that both the migrant and the State play a role in the creation of illegality. The plurality of sources of illegality and the different possible stages when a migrant may lose their legal immigration status are proof of the dynamic character of the phenomenon of illegality. The dynamic nature of illegality can be seen not only in terms of its various actors and stages but also in relation to the different layers of governance and sources of law which regulate it. Understanding the impact that EU law has on the cycles and aforementioned stages of illegality is a critical step in understanding how illegality is conceptualised in Europe. First of all, it has to be said that nowhere in primary or secondary legislation can one find a definition of illegality. Parts of the definition can be found (such as the meaning of illegal stay or illegally-staying third-country national), but no one complete, uniform definition exists.

However, legislation and jurisprudence do seem to have a commonly agreed definition of what illegality means in EU law. As will be shown, this idea of the concept of illegality is backed up by the traditional binary distinction between legal and illegal migration, which it is argued produces several unwanted effects such as the criminalisation of migrants illegally staying in the EU and an unrealistic categorisation of migrants.[90] In turning to the role of EU law in this area, an overview of EU law's position on illegality as a legal source which is at the origin of the phenomenon is provided first of all in order to clearly determine what part of illegality is covered by supranational regulation and what is left for a Member State's discretion.

[88] Art 8 of the Return Directive.

[89] ibid.

[90] See chapters four and five for more on this issue.

i. EU Law as a Legal Source of 'Illegality'

Firstly, a word of clarification is necessary with regard to what EU law in the area of illegal immigration regulates and what is left to the discretion of Member States. On this issue, Rigo and Karakayali remind us of the fact that the term 'illegal migration' is not technically used.[91] The scholars, nevertheless, conclude that illegal migration is 'undoubtedly considered as an objectified target …, thus implying an already established normative categorisation of people's movements'.[92] Guild reinforces this idea of implicit categorisation of migrants pointing out that even at the Member State level, when the EU leaves much to the discretion of individual States, one cannot always find a definition of illegal entry or presence of a migrant.[93]

Second, EU law's influence in the construction of illegality is felt more strongly within the phases of the aforementioned cycle of State's illegality. The reason behind this is the fact that any interference with the definition of who is living within or outside migration laws interferes with Member State sovereignty.[94] The following section will provide an account of EU legislation approach to illegality as a way of fully understanding where EU law stands with regards to the origin and regulation of this phenomenon.

a. EU Law's Regulation of Illegality

Soft law and legislation on carrier sanctions and facilitation of irregular entry and residence constituted most of the EU initiatives in the area of irregular migration during the beginning of the intergovernmental period. Subsequently, after the Treaty of Amsterdam, a number of Directives structuring the Schengen *acquis* were adopted again in relation to carrier sanctions, facilitation of irregular entry and residence, and mutual recognition of expulsion decisions.[95] The goal of achieving a coherent policy in this area of immigration prompted the Commission and Council to adopt further measures such as a Directive on the legal status of victims of trafficking in persons[96] and a Directive on assistance for expulsions via

[91] S Karakayali and E Rigo, 'Mapping the European Space of Circulation' in N De Geneva and N Peutz (eds) *The Deportation Regime* (Durham NC, Duke University Press, 2010) 125–26.

[92] ibid, 125–26.

[93] E Guild, 'Who is an Irregular Migrant' in C Cholewinski, B Bogusz, A Szyszcak (eds), *Irregular Migration and Human Rights: Theorectical, European and International Perspectives, Immigration and Asylum and Policy in Europe* (Leiden, Martinus Nijhoff Publishers, 2004) 3.

[94] Foblets (n 23) 145.

[95] Council Directive 2001/51/EC on supplementing the provisions of Art 26 of the Convention implementing the Schengen Agreement of 14 June 1985, [2001] OJ L187/45, Council Directive 2002/90, defining the facilitation of unauthorised entry, transit and residence, [2002] OJ L328/17, among other instruments.

[96] Council Directive 2004/81/EC on the residence permit issued to third-country nationals who are victims of trafficking in human beings or who have been the subject of an action to facilitate illegal immigration, who cooperate with the competent authorities, [2004] OJ L261/19.

air transit[97] along with other kinds of measures like the creation of the Schengen Information System, visas and border control initiatives.[98]

However it is the Return Directive and the Directive on Employers Sanctions that represent the most significant measures adopted in this area. The first instrument concerns the detention of irregular migrants, expulsion procedures and standards of treatment during expulsion, whilst the second aims to reduce irregular migration by limiting access to undeclared work. The goals and basic principles of these documents are inferred from the wording of the directives and reveal the path that EU legislation continues to follow in the field of immigration; namely limited recognition of irregular migrant rights and auxiliary measures on border controls, legal migration and asylum.

Before the Treaty of Lisbon, the EC Treaty stated in Article 63(3)(b) that measures should be adopted by the Council in the fields of 'illegal immigration and illegal residence, including repatriation of illegal residents'. Currently, the competence of the EU in relation to illegal migration has a different wording as Article 79(c) TFEU refers to: 'illegal immigration and unauthorised residence, including removal and repatriation of persons'. Guild stresses that the most recent wording reflects the incoherence that dominates the concept of illegal immigration among the EU institutions.[99] Additionally, Bell highlights another important aspect relating to the wording of this article, which is that choosing 'immigration' instead of 'immigrants' may limit the extent of the Union's competence to legislate on issues that are not connected with their entry or exit.[100]

Within the Area of Freedom, Security and Justice (hereinafter AFSJ) there is a notable effort to develop a common EU policy on irregular migration. The Stockholm Programme motto until 2014,[101] in addition to Tampere's agenda of approximation of legal third-country nationals with EU citizen's statuses,[102] stressed the need to 'fight against illegal immigration' efficiently and the 'strengthening of external border controls'.[103] The lack of attention to rights protection of this group of people is explicit from the wording of the aforementioned

[97] Council Directive 2003/110/EC on assistance in cases of transit for the purposes of removal by air, [2003] OJ L321/26.

[98] These initiatives will be the object of analysis of chapter four.

[99] Guild (n 93) 4.

[100] M Bell, 'Irregular Migrants: Beyond the Limits of Solidarity' in Malcolm Ross and Yuri Borgmann-Prebil (ed), *Promoting Solidarity in the European Union* (Oxford, Oxford University Press, 2010) 161.

[101] European Council, 2010/C, The Stockholm Programme—An open and secure Europe serving and protecting citizens, [2010] OJ 115/01.

[102] European Council, Presidency Conclusions, Tampere, 15 and 16 October 1999: III. Fair treatment of third country nationals: '18. The European Union must ensure fair treatment of third country nationals who reside legally on the territory of its Member States. A more vigorous integration policy should aim at granting them rights and obligations comparable to those of EU citizens'.

[103] See 6.1.6. point of the Stockholm Programme: 'Effective policies to combat illegal immigration: The European Council is convinced that effective action against illegal immigration remains essential when developing a common immigration policy'.

multi-annual programme on combating illegal immigration.[104] Furthermore the creation of rights is only discussed if applied to EU citizens or, even if in a rather restrictive way, to third-country nationals legally residing within the EU.

In sum, EU policy that has focused on combating illegal immigration has the clear goal of delimiting a group of citizens that reside outside legality in the EU territory in order to return them.[105] It is not only the apparent lack of EU competence to legislate on rights for persons other than those with a regular migrant status,[106] but also the position adopted by the European Commission and other EU agencies,[107] which reinforces a security-oriented discourse that deals with irregular migration as a category of people that essentially should be fought against.[108]

b. Illegally-staying Third-country Nationals and Illegal Stay in EU Law

In contrast to the situation where an individual legally moves under EU immigration law (where one finds the use of neutral terminology agreed among all Member States to define a legally resident migrant who is a non-EU citizen; third-country national), the task of finding a definition for those who are illegally staying ends up being a more challenging task.[109] It is not easy to find, both at the national and supranational level, a precise term to define illegality, irregular migration or even those who live in a country without a residence permit or legal employment. As mentioned above, definitions normally focus on the scope of legal immigration, as Amaya-Castro has pointed out, reinforcing the fact that 'everybody is potentially illegal'.[110] This potential illegality or irregularity and the thin line that separates it from regular statuses, shows the interchangeability that is typical between illegality and legality in general and in particular in EU law. As Vollmer highlights 'irregular migration points to the changing modalities or the legal *hybridism* of actions and processes and the possible changing status of migratory legality'.[111]

[104] S Carrera and J Parkin, 'Protecting and Delivering Fundamental Rights of Irregular Migrants at Local and Regional Levels in the European Union' (CEPS, 2011). Carrera and Parkin point out in their study that irregular migrants as a category of migrants holder of rights, 'remains an invisible' category in mainstream EU level official discourses and the personal scope of the Area of Freedom, Justice and Security.

[105] Carrera and Parkin, ibid, 2.

[106] Art 79 (2) TFEU.

[107] For example: Frontex (EU borders agency); Europol (European Police Office).

[108] This approach has on the one hand, promoted the adoption of financial policies, laws and frameworks: Framework Programme on Solidarity and Management of Migration flows (2007–2013) and on the other hand, motivated a more intense control of external borders, as well as focused on surveillance technologies, detention and expulsion and criminalisation of solidarity and irregular employment.

[109] K Groenendijk, 'Differential Treatment or Discrimination' in G Elspeth and JY Carlier (eds), *L'avenir de la libre circulation des personnes dans l'UE* (Brussels, Bruylant, 2006) 100.

[110] JM Amaya-Castro, 'Illegality Regimes and the Ongoing Transformation of Contemporary Citizenship' (2011) 4(2) *European Journal of Legal Studies* 140.

[111] Bastian Vollmer, *Policy Discourses on Irregular Migration in Germany and the United Kingdom*, (Basingstoke, Palgrave Macmillan, 2014) 9.

A brief survey of the numerous EU law instruments demonstrates that even at a supranational level there are some gaps and inconsistencies in the definitions provided by the law that relate to the elements of illegality (illegally-staying third-country national, illegal stay and overstayer). The EU has adopted two directives—the Return Directive and the Employers' Sanctions Directive—that deal with this issue. These documents use slightly different expressions to define illegal stay. The Employers' Sanctions Directive defines an 'illegally staying third-country national' as 'a third-country national present on the territory of a Member State, who does not fulfil, or no longer fulfils, the conditions for stay or residence in that Member State'.[112] This wording clearly leaves the definition of those conditions to the discretion of Member States.

In contrast, for the purposes of the Return Directive, an 'illegal stay' is the

> presence on the territory of a Member State, of a third-country national who does not fulfil, or no longer fulfils the conditions of entry as set out in Article 5 of the Schengen Borders Code or other conditions for entry, stay or residence in that Member State.[113]

This definition implies that less discretion is given to Member States. Finally, the proposal for an Entry/Exit System[114] (hereinafter EES) defines 'overstayer' as a 'third country national who does not fulfil, or no longer fulfils the conditions relating to the duration of a short stay on the territory of the Member States,'[115]—a definition that brings us back again to a wider range of possibilities of when one third-country national may fall into illegality.

Interestingly, these three definitions start with the exact same reference to a third-country national who does not fulfil, or no longer fulfils, the conditions of entry. What varies in these definitions are the conditions imposed either by the host Member State or by the Schengen Borders Code, and the level of supranational interference. However in practice, as Karakayali and Rigo argue, 'EU legislation does not define the entry conditions and the residential status of third-country national, nor does it specify the statutory preconditions according to which expulsion decisions are issued'.[116]

Another illustrative case of the role played by EU law in determining the definition of who is illegally staying can be depicted from the meaning of being documented (to accomplish the necessary formalities). The example chosen relates to the Visa Code regime (the possession of a short time visa). Article 30 of the Visa

[112] Art 2 (b) of the Employers Sanctions Directive.

[113] Art 3 (2) of the Return Directive.

[114] Art 5 of the European Commission proposal (COM(2013) 95 final) for a Regulation of the European Parliament and of the Council establishing an Entry/Exit System (EES) to register entry and exit data of third country nationals crossing the external borders of the Member States of the European Union, 2013 and Boeles et al (n 74) 239.

[115] ibid.

[116] S Karakayali and E Rigo, 'Mapping the European space of circulation' in De Genova and Peutz (n 91) 135.

Code establishes that the 'mere possession of a uniform visa or a visa with limited territorial validity shall not confer an automatic right of entry'. From the wording of this Article it can be deduced that fulfilling the conditions imposed by Article 5 of the Schengen Borders Code is a tacit requirement for acquiring a legal migration status,[117] and that consequently the mere possession of a visa (a type of documentation) is not constitutive of the right to stay in the host Member State.

After entering the territory of the Member State the third-country national has the duty to report to the competent authorities, an obligation that is posited in Article 22(1) of the Schengen Implementing Convention:

> Aliens who have legally entered the territory of one of the Contracting Parties shall be obliged to report, in accordance with the conditions laid down by each Contracting Party, to the competent authorities of the Contracting Party whose territory they enter. Such aliens may report either on entry or within three working days of entry, at the discretion of the Contracting Party whose territory they enter.

Boeles highlights that is not obvious whether the right to stay is dependent on the fulfilment of the obligation to report to the competent authorities imposed by the Schengen Implementing Convention.[118] However, if one follows the line of thought that accepts that this obligation is constitutive of the right to stay, a third-country national who fails to comply with the reporting obligation after the three working days deadline (or the one imposed by the Member State) has passed, he or she would be from then onwards illegally staying in that Member State. The expiration of their visa would not be taken into account.

Interestingly, this view does not fit well with the regime of the revocation of visas established in Article 34(2) of the Visa Code which posits that: 'a visa shall be revoked where it becomes evident that the conditions for issuing it are no longer met'. Thus, as the reporting obligation is not one of these conditions, it seems that the lack of such an obligation cannot affect the validity of the visa. The CJEU has recently delivered a decision relating to visa annulment that clarifies that the Visa Code prevents Member States from impeding the movement of visa holders, 'unless the visas have been duly and properly annulled'.[119] As such this decision backs up the argument that in order to, in this particular case, annul a visa, the third-country national must fail to comply with the necessary conditions. In short, the formalities imposed such as the obligation to report are not constitutive of a migration status either legal or illegal, and from here one may conclude that having papers (at an EU and national level) does not equate to being legal just as not possessing them does not straightforwardly mean that person is illegally staying.

Fully aware of the fact that the definitions of this secondary legislation do not cover all potential forms of border crossing illegalities (for example, there is no

[117] *A contrario* an illegal stay, in accordance with Art 3 (2) of the Returns Directive, must violate Art 5 of the Schengen Borders Code, see also Boeles and others (n 74) 383.

[118] ibid, 383.

[119] Case C 83/12 PPU, *Minh Khoa Vo* [2012], EU:C:2012:202, para 45.

particular mention of migrants who become irregular through violation of their work permit) the thesis nevertheless opts to use this terminology and to analyse its scope. The case of EU citizens who are unlawfully staying in the territory of another Member State, proves that the terminology used to refer to illegally-staying migrants is far from being comprehensive as there is no express term in the legislation for EU citizens who are illegally staying within the territory of another Member State.

In short, illegality for the purposes of this study implies a type of migration that is completely or partially in violation of migration rules (whether they are national or supranational), be it visa, work permit or asylum law related. The person who violates these norms is illegally staying within the territory of the host Member State.

ii. National Law as a Legal Source in the Construction of 'Illegality'

A recurring theme of the present chapter in relation to the regulation of the illegality of a migrant's stay in the EU is the combination of different layers of legislation. In Guild's words:

> The complexity of rules at the EU level, applying highly differentiated regimes to persons who seem to be in rather similar situations is complimented by highly elaborate national provisions which create expectations about state action while leaving unresolved the position of substantial numbers of persons.[120]

Having examined the legislative scope of the supranational regulatory layer (EU law) in the preceding subsections, it is necessary to turn to domestic regulation of the phenomenon of illegality. In doing so the exact place that EU law occupies in the construction of national legal regimes of irregular migration in Europe will be elucidated.

The interaction between national legislation and EU law regulation of aspects of illegality varies depending on the issue at hand. For instance, the substance of the social protection granted to illegally-staying third-country nationals and the sanctions and penalties applied in relation to illegal entry or stays are the areas where Member States' power to regulate is greater. Consequently this section examines these parts of the regime of illegality in turn and aims to illustrate the role Member States play in addressing these issues.

First, the TFEU states that Member States have exclusive discretion to determine the 'volumes of admission of third-country nationals coming from third countries to their territory in order to seek work, whether employed or self-employed'.[121] However, not all aspects of the legal regime of illegally-staying third-country nationals in the territory of Member States are so clearly demarcated as falling

[120] Guild (n 93) 17.
[121] Art 79(5) TFEU.

within either national or supranational discretion. For example, if one looks at Article 14 of the Return Directive on the safeguards that should be ensured in relation to third-country nationals awaiting return, it is clear that EU law has a guiding role and that it is for national law to determine the substance of those safeguards.

As such, EU law in this case merely enumerates the principles that Member States should take into account 'as far as possible' whilst at the national level the legislator determines what is covered by that safeguard. The *Abdida* case is illustrative of this type of interaction where EU law plays an indicative role and national law regulates the more concrete aspects. On the one hand Belgian Law (namely Article 9b of the Law of 15 December 1980 on entry to Belgian territory, residence, establishment and removal of foreign nationals) established that:

> A foreign national residing in Belgium who can prove his identity in accordance with paragraph 2 and who suffers from an illness occasioning a real risk to his life or physical integrity or a real risk of inhuman or degrading treatment where there is no appropriate treatment in his country of origin or in the country in which he resides may apply to the Minister or his representative for leave to reside in the Kingdom of Belgium.[122]

However, Article 14(1)(b) of the Return Directive stresses the need to ensure that as far as possible 'emergency health care and essential treatment of illness are provided'. The definition of what amounts to 'emergency health care' and 'essential treatment of illness' are to be interpreted at the domestic level and in the case of Belgian law this meant 'a real risk to his life of physical integrity' or 'real risk of inhuman or degrading treatment'. This example highlights the fact that, in the area of the protection granted to illegally-staying migrants by Member States, EU legislation is responsible for the creation of a threshold, a minimum bundle of rights that (even if not compulsory) should be considered when national legislators address the substance of the status of this group of migrants. In this case EU law plays a residual role whilst national law has a defining function and determines in concrete terms the extent of protection granted.

Second, the entry of irregular migrants into the territory of a Member State may be penalised in a manner other than through the Schengen Borders Code or the Return Directive.[123] It is, in principle, part of the domestic legislative realm and of the 'freedom of Member States to make criminal laws'.[124] The CJEU has been prolific in this area, as will be shown subsequently in subsection IV.A.ii.a, however it has not (yet) gone as far as precluding national legislation that penalises the irregular entrance or stay of a third-country national, as long as they do not compromise the effectiveness of the Return Directive.[125] Consequently, national

[122] Case C-562/13, *Moussa Abdida*, [2014], EU:C:2014:2453, paras 18 and 19.

[123] M Provera, 'The Criminalisation of Irregular Migration in the European Union', CEPS Liberty and Security in Europe, No 80/February, 2015, 16.

[124] Boeles and others (n 74) 389.

[125] Case C 61/11 PPU, *El Dridi* [2011], EU:C:2011:268, para 55.

legislators are in charge of establishing the punishment for irregular entry or stay and as such sanctions may vary from one Member State to another. For example in Germany irregular entry may be sanctioned with a fine or imprisonment whilst in Spain the same offence is not punishable.[126] As in the first example, EU law intervenes by emphasising respect for the object and principles enshrined in the Return Directive, but it is nevertheless at Member State level that the particularities of the penalising regime of irregular entrance and stay are defined. This strengthens the idea that the margin of manoeuvre left for national legislators in this area is in practice stronger and more concrete than the supranational rules included in secondary legislation.

Third, another important example of an aspect of the illegality regime that is left for Member States to legislate has to do with actors assisting illegally-staying third-country nationals and can be found in the 2014 UK Immigration Act.[127] This national legislation requires that landlords carry out a check of their tenant's immigration status prior to making an offer of a tenancy agreement. The purpose of this private immigration control is to verify whether the tenant is illegally staying in the UK. When a landlord finds that the potential tenant does not have the right to rent in the UK and is thus illegally staying, they will be 'liable for a civil penalty if they authorise occupation of accommodation for use as an only or main home by a person who does not have the right to rent in the UK'.[128]

It is worth noting that EU law creates duties akin to the latter duty imposed on UK private landlords, for example in the Facilitation Directive in Article 1(1)(b)[129] which states that Member States shall sanction:

> any person who, for *financial gain, intentionally* assists a person who is not a national of a Member State to reside within the territory of a Member State in breach of the laws of the State concerned on the residence of aliens.[130]

In order to be sanctioned under the Facilitation Directive the express intention of a person to assist an illegally-staying migrant for financial gain is a prerequisite.[131]

[126] Provera (n 123) 16.

[127] UK Immigration Act 2014 (www.legislation.gov.uk/ukpga/2014/22/contents/enacted).

[128] See the Code of Practice on illegal immigrants and private rented accommodation—Civil penalty scheme for landlords and their agents, October 2014. (www.gov.uk/government/uploads/system/uploads/attachment_data/file/376788/Code_of_Practice_on_illegal_immigrants_and_private_rented_accommodation__web_.pdf) 7.

[129] Council Directive 2002/90/EC defining the facilitation of unauthorised entry, transit and residence, [2002] OJ L 328/17 (hereinafter Facilitation Directive). See also Art 6 (1) of the UN General Assembly, Protocol against the Smuggling of Migrants by Land, Sea and Air, Supplementing the United Nations Convention against Transnational Organized Crime, 15 November 2000.

[130] Emphasis added.

[131] Fundamental Rights Agency (FRA), Report on the Criminalisation of migrants in an irregular situation and of persons engaging with them, 2014 (http://fra.europa.eu/sites/default/files/fra-2014-criminalisation-of-migrants-0_en_0.pdf) 8 and 13. See also on the same issue the Fundamental Rights Agency (FRA), Comparative Report on Fundamental rights of migrants in an irregular situation in the European Union, 2011, 62–64.

Despite this, the Directive does not require that Member States refrain from punishing people when there was no intention or financial gain. Consequently, the UK Immigration Act 2014 is not in violation of EU law and landlords may be sanctioned for renting houses to illegally-staying migrants, as Member States are not limited by the Facilitation Directive to sanction exclusively those cases that fulfil the conditions there established.[132] By partially regulating the phenomenon of illegality and leaving a margin of manoeuvre for Member States, EU law allows Member States to design their national legislation in accordance with their own interests and political agendas (such as, in this particular case, by recruiting private actors to play the role of immigration authorities).

It cannot be argued that the relationship between EU law and national law is one of exclusivity. As illustrated above, the extent of Member States' discretion is variable depending on the aspect of illegality that is being regulated. This discretion may have the defining function of legislating on the extent and type of protection granted to illegally-staying migrants, defining the type of sanction to be applied, or may even allow for the dissemination of private actors as immigration authorities. Nevertheless, what can be said about the role of national legislation as a source of illegality is that it is at this level that the core and specificities of the legal regimes that regulate the status of illegally-staying migrants are decided. EU law, thus far, has a crucial role in terms of macro-managing and establishing the guiding principles of the legislation in the area of illegality, but Member States retain substantial discretion to determine, for example, the degree of solidarity granted to an illegally-staying migrant, the type of sanction they may incur and who enforces such sanctions.

iii. National Judicial Interpretation of Supranational Rules on Illegality: The Example of French Courts

The way illegality is conceptualised at the EU level has an impact on domestic court decisions and highlights the relationship between the supranational and national interpretations of that phenomenon. Two contradictory French court decisions are used as examples of possible interpretations of the scope of illegality at the domestic level and are illustrative of the complexity of this exercise. First, in the decision of the Cour d'Appel of Paris No 13/00613 of the 23 February 2013,[133] a national judge applied EU immigration law, namely the Return Directive, to a EU citizen without having taken into account the distinction between third-country nationals and EU citizens. Second, the decision of the Conseil d' État of

[132] Fundamental Rights Agency (FRA) Report on the Criminalisation of migrants in an irregular situation and of persons engaging with them, 2014 (http://fra.europa.eu/sites/default/files/fra-2014-criminalisation-of-migrants-0_en_0.pdf) 8 and 13. See also on the same issue the Fundamental Rights Agency (FRA) Comparative Report on Fundamental rights of migrants in an irregular situation in the European Union, 2011, 62–64.

[133] Cour d'Appel de Paris Nº B-13/00613, 23 février 2013.

22 June 2012 No 347545 produced the contrary result by refusing to equate EU citizens and third-country nationals for the purposes of the application of a more favourable provision of the Return Directive.[134]

The most interesting aspect of the first decision is the way the domestic court interpreted the concept of illegality and simultaneously applied EU immigration law designed for third-country nationals to a Portuguese EU citizen. The fact that the French court was indifferent to the EU conception of illegality, and to the scope of application of the Return Directive, suggests the adoption of another position on illegality at the national level. The Paris Cour d'Appel adopted a broader notion of what can be considered to be an unlawful stay of an EU citizen in its judgment. In this particular case, the broadening of the scope of a norm that was meant for one category of migrants suggests that the national court's perspective of illegality is considerably wider and distinct from that constructed by EU legislation and the CJEU's decisions.

In relation to the second decision, the Conseil d'État in 2012, before the first judgment, delivered a decision validating the refusal to equate a Romanian national with a third-country national even if that would have meant more favourable treatment. Gicquel explains that the disagreement between the Cour d'Appel of Paris and the Conseil d'Etat is based on the fact that the Court d'Appel of Paris considered the division between third-country nationals and EU citizens to be interchangeable.[135] In contrast the Conseil d'État took a more orthodox position and found that an EU citizen cannot be equated with a third-country national in the host Member State. Although the issues discussed in both judgments did not touch upon the issue of the illegality of an EU citizen's stay, one can conclude from the divergent positions of the courts that there is no clear interpretation of the possibility of a citizen of the Union becoming unlawfully staying in another Member State.

These decisions illustrate that both conceptual and implementation levels of the Return Directive are affected by the different national interpretations of the concept and scope of illegality. As such, it is evident from the examples chosen that for domestic courts the supranational concept of illegality in certain situations may not be straightforward. In this particular case, the French courts disagreed on the categorisation of the migrants involved, which had implications not only for the procedural guarantees granted to the individuals but also for the type of legislation applicable to each case. The issue of the unlawfulness of EU citizens will be further explored in greater detail in chapter two. However at this stage it is crucial to highlight that the relationship between the national and supranational judicial interpretations of EU legislation in this area may have implications that are reflected in the way the scope of illegality is determined, and consequently,

[134] Conseil d' État N° 347545, 22 juin 2012.

[135] H Gicquel, 'Citoyenneté européenne, qualité d'étranger et éventualité d'une discrimination à rebours' (2013) *AJDA—L'actualité juridique Droit administrative* 863.

affects the guarantees granted to the migrants who are illegally staying within the territories of the Member States of the EU.

Ultimately, this shows that even if one argues that there is an implicit concept of illegality in EU law that does not mean that the same concept has the same scope and meaning from Member State to Member State or even, as demonstrated, within the judicial authorities of the same Member State.

IV. EU INSTITUTIONAL FRAMEWORK

A. Institutional Balance in the Governance of Irregular Migration

The EU institutional framework in the field of irregular migration is 'evolving' and is a crucial part of the development of the construction of illegality in EU law.[136] The present subsection addresses the shift in the roles played by the three main institutional EU actors (the EU Parliament, the Commission and the Council) in the regulation of illegality as well as the reaction of Member States to those changes.[137] The area of immigration is characterised by a central tension between the powerful influence of Member States' discretion and, simultaneously, the 'Europeanisation' of migration law which acts to dilute that power.[138] National authorities, EU policy documents and some scholars tend to justify the States' loss of sovereignty as the price paid for the establishment of the Internal Market and the abolition of control at the internal borders.[139]

Other commentators such as Groenendijk argue that this situation is more complex. For instance, States may have an advantage to cede sovereignty in this area due to the fact that policy decisions made in the area of migration by individual Member States necessarily have an impact on other Member States, or the fact that there are clear 'highly visible' advantages to common EU rules (such as the fact that the costs are supported by additional organisations and other governments and as such are 'less visible').[140] Regardless of the main reasons which motivate States to voluntarily cede sovereignty, the tension between sovereignty and the need for common rules is a recurring feature of this area of law.[141]

[136] A Balch and A Geddes, 'The Development of the EU Migration and Asylum Regime' in H Dijstelbloem and A Meijer (eds), *Migration and the New Technological Borders of Europe* (Basingstoke, Palgrave Macmillan 2011) 22.

[137] Acosta has referred to these actors as: 'the good, the bad and the ugly in EU migration law', the Council being the bad, the EU Parliament the good and the Commission the ugly. See D Acosta, 'The Good, the Bad and the Ugly in EU Migration Law: Is the European Parliament becoming Bad and Ugly? (The Adoption of Directive 2008/15: The Returns Directive)' (2009) *11 European Journal of Migration and Law* 19.

[138] ibid, 179 and B Melis, *Negotiating Europe's Immigration Frontiers* (The Hague, Kluwer Law, 2001) 11.

[139] Groenendijk (n 62) 10.

[140] ibid, 10 and 11.

[141] ibid, 14.

Before the Treaty of Maastricht, there was 'loose intergovernmental cooperation'[142] in relation to irregular migration. During this period a set of Resolutions and Recommendations without binding force were adopted such as the Recommendation adopted in 1992 on irregular migration.[143] The Maastricht Treaty in 1993 was responsible for the institution of the three-pillar structure as well as EU citizenship. The pillar structure consisted of: the European Community (the first pillar), the Common Foreign and Security Policy (the second pillar) and police and judicial cooperation in criminal matters (the third pillar). The third pillar (Title IV) included measures relating to combating unauthorised immigration, residence and work by nationals of third countries on the territory of Member States.

The period that followed saw continual and significant institutional reorganisation in this area. With the signing of the Amsterdam Treaty in 1997 Member States accepted that the EU Commission, the EU Parliament and the CJEU would play a larger role in this field of EU Law. The introduction of Title IV on the free movement of persons, asylum and immigration is illustrative of the increase in EC competencies in this area. In particular, Article 63(3)(b) EC expressly established the supranational powers for the regulation of certain aspects of 'illegal migration and illegal residence'. With regard to the decision-making procedure, Article 67 of the Amsterdam Treaty established limits in terms of decision-making procedure by imposing the need for unanimity from the Council on a Commission or a Member State's legislative proposal, after the consultation of the EU Parliament.

Subsequently, in 2005 in the area of irregular migration the co-decision procedure entered into force.[144] This meant a stronger role for the EU Parliament and a change with regard to the voting rules: unanimity was no longer required in the Council with the introduction of qualified majority voting (QMV).[145] These changes were seen by some as a prospect of a 'migrant-friendly approach in the European Union',[146] however this was called into question during the negotiations of the Return Directive.[147] In short the institutional evolution during this period is succinctly described by commentators as:

> a gradual erosion of an original intergovernmental logic, with migration and asylum loosely incorporated into the EU at Maastricht (1992) and then from Amsterdam (1997) onwards, brought gradually closer to the supranational core of the EU decision-making.[148]

[142] S Peers, *EU Justice and Home Affairs Law* (Oxford, Oxford University Press, 2011) 501.

[143] ibid, 501 and Recommendation of Immigration Ministers on 30 Nov/1 December 2002 (SN 4678/92, WGI 1266, 16 Nov 1992), published in Elspeth Guild and J Niessen, 'The Developing Immigration and Asylum Policies of the European Union: Adopted Conventions, Resolutions, Recommendations, Decisions and Conclusions' (Alphen aan den Rijn, Kluwer, 1996).

[144] Art 251 of the EC Treaty. See also for more on the co-decision procedure, Acosta (n 137) 24–25.

[145] Council Decision 2004/927/EC providing for certain areas covered by Title IV of Part Three of the Treaty establishing the European Community to be governed by the procedure laid down in Art 251 of that Treaty, [2004] OJ 2005 L 396/45.

[146] Acosta (n 137) 21–22.

[147] ibid, 21–22.

[148] Balch and Geddes (n 136) 24.

When in 2009 the Lisbon Treaty entered into force some described it as the 'culmination of the institutional changes begun at Amsterdam' 10 years previously.[149] The pre-existing pillar structure was abolished with first and third pillar issues becoming part of what was previously the first pillar. The Lisbon Treaty established in Articles 68, 69 and 70 that in the area of freedom, security and justice the main actors are the Union, the European Council, National Parliaments, the European Parliament and the Commission. In relation to the decision-making procedure the Lisbon Treaty kept the same rules (QMV in the Council and co-decision or ordinary legislative procedure in the wording of the Lisbon Treaty[150]) in the following areas:

(a) the conditions of entry and residence, and standards on the issue by Member States of long-term visas and residence permits, including those for the purpose of family reunification;
(b) the definition of the rights of third-country nationals residing legally in a Member State, including the conditions governing freedom of movement and of residence in other Member States;
(c) illegal immigration and unauthorised residence, including removal and repatriation of persons residing without authorisation;
(d) combating trafficking in persons, in particular women and children.[151]

In relation to the evolution of the position of the three main institutions in this area after the Lisbon Treaty, the one that stands out the most is the role of the EU Parliament. The 'Lisbonisation' of the EU Parliament meant that 'parliamentary accountability [was] at the heart of the AFSJ foundations'.[152] This shift can be seen especially with regard to the EU Parliament's role as co-legislator in areas that were previously the exclusive domain of the Council, such as police and judicial cooperation in criminal matters in accordance with Article 81(2) of the Treaty of Lisbon (or in the power of consent that the EU Parliament possesses for the conclusion of readmission agreements).

The complexity of the institutional environment in the area of irregular migration is also a result of the tension that exists between Member States when negotiating the measures to regulate this area at the EU level. In the last 10 years the secondary legislation adopted in the area of migration and asylum has resulted in Member States ceding part of their discretion on the core functions of the State such as determining whose foreigners should stay and whose should leave. For instance, even though the TFEU establishes that the area of freedom, security and justice is a shared competence area,[153] Member States retained power over the

[149] ibid.
[150] Art 79 (2) TFEU.
[151] ibid and 294 TFEU.
[152] S Carrera, N Hernanz, and J Parkin, 'The "Lisbonisation" of the European Parliament: Assessing Progress, Shortcomings and Challenges for Democratic Accountability in the Area of Freedom, Security and Justice' CEPS Liberty and Security in Europe, no 58, 2013, 3.
[153] Art 4 (2) j) TFEU.

'volumes of admission of third-country nationals coming from third countries to their territory in order to seek work, whether employed or self-employed'.[154] This is illustrative of the delicate balancing act between the Union's competences granted by Amsterdam and Lisbon and Member States' will to protect their sovereignty. Balch and Geddes have highlighted in relation to Member States' position that:

> [I]mmigration and asylum are policy areas where older, and relatively larger, Member States (such as Germany, France and the UK) have traditionally been among the main receiving states in the EU, and have been particularly keen to maintain national controls.[155]

The discretion that Member States retain in the areas of migration of asylum in combination with the 'steadily growing'[156] EU powers have been a source of tension in relation to Member States' relationship with the EU institutions and even among each other. This tension has increased recently in the wake of the Mediterranean migration crisis and has affected the EU institutional environment as well as prompting decisions with regard to the dimensions of EU migration that should be prioritised. The European Council meeting that took place in June 2015 highlighted the three key priority areas: 'relocation/resettlement, return/readmission/ reintegration and cooperation with countries of origin and transit'.[157]

It was not without reluctance that some Member States reacted to this agenda, for instance Germany and France sought revision of the plan stating that the situation that these two Member States, along with Sweden, Italy and Hungary, were in was neither fair nor sustainable. In addition Hungary's race to build a 175km fence[158] illustrates perfectly the tension that characterises Member States' responses to the EU strategy on migration.

i. The Court of Justice and the Regulation of Illegality

An account of the impact that the EU institutions have on the construction of illegality would not be complete without looking at the CJEU's influence on this phenomenon. Despite the discussion during the negotiations on the Amsterdam Treaty about the creation of a specialised immigration court or chamber within the CJEU, no such thing ultimately came into being.[159] The threat of a flood of immigration cases that would make the CJEU another forum for asylum cases

[154] Art 79 (5) TFEU.
[155] ibid, 26.
[156] C Barnard and S Peers, *European Union Law* (Oxford, Oxford University Press, 2014) 798.
[157] European Council, Conclusions, EUCO 22/15, 25/26 June 2015 (2015), 1.
[158] See for more on these events, for example: Migrants on Hungary's border fence: Patrick Kingsley, 'This wall, we will not accept it', *The Guardian*, 22 June 2015, (www.theguardian.com/world/2015/jun/22/migrants-hungary-border-fence-wall-serbia.).
[159] Groenendijk (n 62) 5.

and impede the delivery of urgent cases prevented the creation of such a court. However, in practice neither of these threats have materialised in the years that have followed the entry in force of the Amsterdam Treaty.[160] Given the fact that there is no specialised immigration court or chamber at the EU level, the questions that may arise in this field of law, including those issues which are of particular interest for this book relating to illegality, are dealt with under the general rules and jurisdiction of the Court of Justice of the European Union.

With regard to the jurisprudential impact of the CJEU on the regulation of illegality, it is fair to say that to date this impact has been somewhat limited and mostly related to issues that arise from the implementation of the Return Directive. Nevertheless, the influence of the CJEU deserves attention owing to the fact that it has the potential to transform the scope of illegality in EU migration law. Two main trends illustrate the position of the case law of the CJEU apropos illegality.

As such, this subsection looks at the recent role of the CJEU towards illegality especially with regards two types of cases: (i) those related the judicial protection of illegally-staying migrants and (ii) those that influence the creation of a social protection of illegally-staying migrants in the EU.

a. The CJEU and the Judicial Protection of Illegally-staying Third-country Nationals

The Court of Justice's decisions that deal with the phenomenon of illegality have been numerous in recent times. In particular there have been a significant number of cases which touch upon the procedural guarantees granted to third-country nationals during a return procedure in accordance with the Return Directive. In relation to the CJEU's position on the criminalisation of illegally-staying third-country nationals at the domestic level that allows for a conflation of illegality and criminality, it should be noted that chapter four looks at this issue in significant detail by analysing the same type of conflation as a result of the enactment of EU immigration databases. However, as a pre-emptive exercise that highlights another cause for conflation of illegality with criminality the main example of the Court's opposition to the criminalisation of illegally-staying third-country nationals is less than rigorous and deals with the grounds for pre-removal detention.

The case of *El Dridi* is one of the most relevant cases with regard to the interpretation of Articles 15 and 16 of the Return Directive by addressing the relationship between pre-removal detention and criminal detention.[161] Further, this case also deals with the issue of the criminalisation of illegally-staying third-country nationals at the Member State level. The importance of this decision lies in the fact that it shows that EU law may impose limits on the criminalisation of migration at

[160] ibid.
[161] See the *El Dridi* judgment (n 125).

the national level, when protecting the achievement of the objectives of the Return Directive.[162] Nevertheless, the exact scope of Member States' power to criminalise immigration offences is not clear from the judgment.[163]

Similarly, the *Achughbabian* judgment, which was delivered shortly after the *El Dridi* case, confirmed that Member States have to respect EU law when adopting domestic criminal legislation.[164] However, in this case the CJEU stated that the Return Directive is not designed to harmonise the entire regulation of the stay of a third-country national.[165] Additionally, this case is relevant due to its clarification that the Return Directive 'does not preclude the law of a Member State from classifying an illegal stay as an offence and laying down penal sanctions to deter and prevent such an infringement of the national rules on residence'.[166] However, 'mindful of the impact of this ruling on state sovereignty … the Court went on to confirm its finding in *El Dridi* that Member States retain the power to criminalise'[167] whenever the Return Directive return procedure was not applicable.

There have been efforts by the Court to address the issue of the criminalisation of irregular migration. Although these have not proved to be enough to completely prevent the conflation of criminality and illegality, the main aim of these judgments is to protect the effectiveness of the application of the Return Directive, and consequently those situations which fall outside the scope of the Return Directive remain within the retained power of the Member State to criminalise the stay of third-country nationals. While detention on the grounds of a criminal provision must end 'as soon as the physical transportation of the individual concerned out of that Member State is possible',[168] in the words of Costello 'detention for committing a crime is conceptually and legally distinct from immigration detention'.[169] Crucially, this is a distinction which the Court has not made clear to date.

The Court's role in interpreting provisions that deal with aspects of the regulation of illegality is not limited to the issues that were discussed in *El Dridi*, *Achughbabian* and *Sagor*. The CJEU has also ruled on the safeguards of illegally-staying migrants who have been detained during the pre-removal period.

[162] V Mitsilegas, 'The Changing Landscape of the Criminalisation of Migration in Europe: The Protective Function of European Union Law' in Maria João Guia, Maartje van der Woude and Joanne van der Leun (eds), *Social Control and Justice—Crimmigration in the Age of Fear* (New York, Eleven International Publishing, 2013) 105 also see *El Dridi* judgment (n 125) para 55.

[163] Boeles and others (n 74) 389.

[164] Mitsilegas (n 162) 110.

[165] Para 28 of the Case C-329/11 *Achughbabian*, [2011] EU:C:2011:807.

[166] ibid, para 28.

[167] V Mitsilegas (n 162)109.

[168] Case C-430/11, *Sagor*, [2012], EU:C:2012:777, para 43 and *Achugbabian* judgment (n 165) para 45.

[169] C Costello, 'Human Rights and the Elusive Universal Subject: Immigration Detention under International Human Rights and EU Law' (2012) 19 *Indiana Journal of Global Legal Studies* 257, and for the same position see: A Beduschi, 'Detention of Undocumented Immigrants and the Judicial Impact of the CJEU's Decisions in France' (2014) 26 *International Journal of Refugee Law* 2.

From the leeway that is open to the Court of Justice for Member States to impose criminal sanctions on illegal stays,[170] we now turn to another aspect of the judicial protection granted to illegally-staying migrants in which the CJEU plays an important role: the right to be heard. Two particular recent decisions were crucial in highlighting the importance of the right to be heard within EU law in relation to illegally-staying third-country nationals.[171] First, in *Mukarubega* the CJEU stated that even though the right to be heard is not specifically contemplated within the text of the Return Directive,[172] 'such a right is however inherent in respect for the rights of the defence, which is a general principle of EU law'.[173] Second, in *Boudjlida* the Court clarified the content of the right to be heard. As such, the content of the right to be heard is defined in accordance with paragraph 55 of this decision as:

> the right to be heard prior to the adoption of a return decision must be interpreted not as meaning that the authority concerned is required to warn an illegally staying third-country national, prior to the interview organised with a view to that adoption, that it is contemplating adopting a return decision against him, to disclose to him the evidence on which that authority intends to rely to justify that decision, or again to allow him a period for reflection before admitting his observations, but as meaning that that third-country national must have the *opportunity effectively* to submit his point of view on the subject of the illegality of his stay and reasons which might, under national law, justify that authority refraining from adopting a return decision.[174]

As such, the Court of Justice interpreted the content of the right to be heard as limited to providing the third-country national with the opportunity of effectively pronouncing on the issue of the illegality of his stay and on the reasons that may justify the decision of the national authorities not to issue them a return decision. In addition the CJEU states that the aim of the right to be heard is 'to allow the competent national authority to investigate the matter in such a way as be able to adopt a decision in full knowledge of the facts and to state reasons for that decision adequately'.[175] This is a formulation that can be interpreted as being more in line with the well-justified return decisions than granting procedural rights to illegally-staying third-country nationals. Nevertheless, it was also reiterated by the Court in the *Boudjlida* decision that in accordance with Article 13 of the Return Directive the third country national has the right to legal assistance and legal aid (albeit only in the case that a return decision has been issued and an appeal brought, in addition to being able to, at their own expense, make use of these services during the entire return procedure).[176]

[170] ML Basilien-Gainche, 'Immigration Detention under the Return Directive: The Shadowed Lights' (2015) 17 *European Journal of Migration and Law* 104.

[171] ibid, 120.

[172] Case C-166/13, *Sophie Mukarubega* [2014], EU:C:2014:2336, paras 41 and 45.

[173] ibid, para 45. See also Case C-249/13, *Khaled Boudjlida* [2014], EU:C:2014:2431, para 34.

[174] *Boudjlida* judgment, ibid, emphasis added.

[175] ibid, para 59.

[176] ibid, para 65.

In the literature, the CJEU's position in these cases has been defined by Basilien-Gainche as 'vague', 'elusive'[177] and 'particularly upsetting' for effectively 'emptying the right of any substance and limiting the consequences of its violations'.[178] In addition, De Bruycker and Mananashvili point out the fact that one of the perverse outcomes of these decisions is the priority given to 'the interest of States in fighting irregular immigration' over procedural guarantees whilst trying to balance them.[179] Furthermore, these scholars, after conducting a detailed analysis of this block of cases and in particular of the *G and R* case[180] (a decision that deals with the right to be heard in the course of proceedings relating to an extension of the pre-removal detention period) concluded that the judgment is in line with *El Dridi* and *Achughbabian*.[181] This is the case since in all three cases the Court gives priority to the fact that 'Member States effectively take care of the return as a priority in the implementation of the Directive'.[182]

For the purposes of our analysis of the phenomenon of illegality and the role played by the different EU institutions in its regulation, it is important to understand this prioritisation of the 'effet utile' of the Return Directive[183] which De Bruycker and Mananashvili advocate. Consequently, it seems that the position of the CJEU is functionalist, rather than protective, in character, given that the primary goal of granting the right to be heard to a third-country national relates more to trying not to impair the effectiveness of the return procedure than ensuring the fundamental rights of the individual.

Finally, the CJEU's position in relation the judicial protection of illegally-staying third-country nationals can be presented as ambivalent in relation to the criminalisation or penalisation of the sanctions for those falling into an illegal stay, as argued in subsection II.C.ii.a. This position is coherent with the Court of Justice's stance on the protection of the right to be heard, which seems to be mostly functionalist, seeking to guarantee the effectiveness of the return process. As such, one may conclude from this analysis that the supranational concept of illegality for the CJEU implies above all else ensuring the removal of irregular migrants as the main priority for the Member States.

b. The CJEU and the Social Protection of Illegally-staying Third-country Nationals

Second, mention has to be made of the role the Court plays in other areas apart from the return procedure of illegally-staying third-country nationals.

[177] Basilien-Gainche (n 170) 104.

[178] ibid, 120.

[179] P De Bruycker and S Mananashvili, 'Audi alteram partem in immigration detention procedures, between the ECJ, the ECtHR and Member States: G & R' (2015) 52 *Common Market Law Review* 589 and in the same direction Basilien-Gainche (n 170) 122.

[180] Case C-383/13 PPU, *G and R* [2013], EU:C:2013:533.

[181] De Bruycker and Mananashvili (n 179) 589.

[182] ibid, 589.

[183] ibid, 570 and 586, see also Recitals 2 and 13 of the Return Directive, the *Mukarubega*,judgment (n 172), para 70.

In particular, the role of the Court in contributing to expanding the scope of the status of illegally-staying migrants requires examination in relation to EU employment law and social rights. The recent *Tümer* case is one such example of how the CJEU's judgments in this area have potential implications for the concept of illegality.[184] This judgment is an important clarification that EU employment law is applicable to third-country nationals even if they are illegally staying in the territory of the host Member State.[185] In particular, this case focuses on the interpretation of the Insolvent Employers Directive[186] and determines that it:

> Must be interpreted as *precluding national legislation* on the protection of employees in the event of the insolvency of their employer, such as that at issue in the main proceedings, *under which a third-country national who is not legally resident in the Member State concerned is not to be regarded as an employee with the right to an insolvency benefit* ...[187]

Whilst this issue will be examined in greater detail in chapter three, for our present purposes it suffices to reiterate that such cases demonstrate that the jurisprudence of the CJEU outside the area of the return procedure is potentially relevant to the conceptualisation of illegality in EU law. This is so as a result of cases such as (but not limited to[188]) *Tümer* which affirm that EU law is applicable even to those illegally staying in an EU Member State. As such, it cannot be excluded that in the future, in the course of a certain case, the CJEU could influence (either deliberately or otherwise) the concept of illegality, which may have far reaching implications for the status of illegally-staying migrants in the EU especially with regard to the development of a social protection of these migrants.

In the *Abdida* decision the CJEU took a step further towards the expansion of the social rights of illegally staying third-country nationals.[189] In this case the Court interpreted Article 14 of the Return Directive on the safeguards to be 'taken into account as far as possible' whilst a return decision has been postponed, in such a way that requires Member States to:

> Provide to a third country national suffering from a serious illness who has appealed against a return decision whose enforcement may expose him to a serious risk of grave and irreversible deterioration in his state of health the safeguards, pending return, established in Article 14 of Directive 2008/115.[190]

In addition to making access to health care compulsory in situations such as the one Mr Abdida found himself in, the Court requires that Member States provide for

[184] Case C-311/13, *Tümer*, [2014], EU:C:2014:2337.

[185] S Peers, 'Irregular migrants and EU employment law', Analysis—Expert insight into EU law developments, (2014) (http://eulawanalysis.blogspot.pt/2014/11/irregular-migrants-and-eu-employment-law.html).

[186] European Parliament and Council Directive 2008/94/EC of 22 October 2008 on the protection of employees in the event of the insolvency of their employer, [2008], OJ L 283.

[187] See *Tümer* judgment (n 184) para 49, emphasis added.

[188] See the Case C-562/13 *Moussa Abdida* [2014] EU:C:2014:2453, Opinion of AG Bot for a justification of a minimum status for illegally-staying third-country nationals grounded in the right to dignity as contemplated in the European Charter of Fundamental Rights.

[189] See the *Abdida* judgment (n 122).

[190] ibid, para 58.

the 'basic needs' of the migrant.[191] Although this decision represents an important supranational effort to make illegally-staying migrants' social rights stronger,[192] the CJEU leaves the determination of what the substance of those 'basic needs' should be to the discretion of Member States (even if it recognises that providing health care would be rendered redundant if there was no guarantee of other basic needs). As such one may read the consequence of this decision as the recognition by the CJEU of the existence of social protection that certain illegally-staying migrants, in certain circumstances, are entitled to and that the measurement of such solidarity depends solely on the generosity of the Member States.

Having said this, one must not forget that while this recognition by the Court is crucial for the enforcement of the right to be provided with 'basic needs' (whatever those may be), the legal limbo in which the third-country nationals pending return live in was also voluntarily retained by the CJEU, as will be shown later in chapter three. This is so as in the judgment *Mahdi*[193] the Court ruled that no autonomous residence is to be granted by Member States to a third-country national when there is no longer a reasonable prospect of removal in accordance with Article 15(4) of the Return Directive.[194] Nevertheless Member States were not exempted of the obligation to provide these illegally-staying migrants with a 'written confirmation' of their situation.

It is fair to ask then what can one conclude from the recent developments of the CJEU jurisprudence with regard to the social protection of illegally-staying third-country nationals.

Ultimately, one has to acknowledge that there are some signs of change and that the latest decisions *Tümer* and *Abdida* are a reflection of the Court's efforts to recognise the existence of a minimum bundle of social rights (or 'basic needs' in the Court's wording), which in the end is in line with the Commission's initial proposal for the Return Directive.[195] It is nevertheless interesting to point out that the CJEU has not gone as far as making the protection formal and compelling Member States to grant a residence permit to illegally-staying migrants who have their return postponed (non-removable migrants), as *Mahdi* shows. The CJEU ruled that to formalise the social protection of this group of migrants, Member States must provide the third-country nationals with written confirmation for which they possess a 'wide discretion concerning the form and format'.[196] The formal wide discretion of Member States is extended to the substance of that social protection.

[191] ibid, paras 59, 60, 61 and 62.

[192] S Peers, 'Could EU law save Paddington Bear? The CJEU develops a new type of protection', EU Law Analysis—Expert insight into EU law developments, (2014), (http://eulawanalysisblogspotpt/2014/12/could-eu-law-save-paddington-bear-cjeuhtml).

[193] Case C-146/14 PPU, *Mahdi*, [2014], EU:C:2014:1320.

[194] ibid, para 89.

[195] European Commission (COM(2005) 391 final) proposal for a Directive of the European Parliament and of the Council on common standards and procedures in Member States for returning illegally-staying third-country nationals, Brussels, 2005.

[196] Para 88 of the *Mahdi* judgment (n 193).

All in all, even if there is supranational recognition that illegally-staying migrants enjoy social protection to be delivered at the national level, the CJEU only goes so far and leaves Member States to put flesh on the bones of these rights, perpetuating thus far the uncertainty in terms of the legal limbo and the legal protection that irregular migrants (in particular non-removable) live in, which makes illegality such a complex phenomenon to conceptualise.

V. CONCLUSION

Chapter one has provided an analysis of the phenomenon of illegality which is at the heart of the book. The analysis in the preceding chapter answered the question of what illegality entails for the purposes of the present study. Illegality is defined as a phenomenon that is intrinsically linked to a migrant's status and that results from the violation of a legal source (either national or supranational). The first part of the analysis, the conceptual part, examined illegality from a holistic perspective that can be created by two cycles, the migrant's cycle of illegality and the State's cycle of illegality. The second part of the analysis looked at the possible legal sources of illegality that are at the origin of this phenomenon. Last, the third part addressed the dynamics of the EU institutional framework (EU Parliament, Commission, Council and CJEU) in the area of irregular migration and consequently touched upon the construction of a supranational concept of illegality. In the following chapter we turn our attention to the supranational law regulating this phenomenon.

2

The Case of Unlawfully-staying EU Citizens

I. INTRODUCTION

IRREGULAR IMMIGRATION IS commonly associated with boats arriving on the shores of Mediterranean Europe,[1] no documents and to a certain extent even with crime.[2] The illegality of a migrant's stay is produced mainly as an effect of the law, both national and European, as explained in chapter one. If the conditions to enjoy the right to reside in a Member State imposed in law are not fulfilled, then this right may be limited or denied. However, it is not easy to reconcile the concept of illegality with EU citizenship and free movement of people within the Schengen space. This chapter addresses this uncomfortable intersection and examines EU secondary legislation and the jurisprudence of the Court of Justice (CJEU) in relation to the EU interpretation of the unlawfulness of an EU citizen's stay.

Recently, free movement of people and potential restrictions to this cornerstone of EU integration have become targets of heated political debates that aim to reconfigure the EU as we know it and as it was originally designed. This challenge to the EU legal order has 'been a source of confusion, surprise and frustration for many EU lawyers'[3] and for the EU generally. Chapter two intends to clarify part of that confusion by providing a detailed analysis of the phenomenon of illegality and EU citizens. This exercise requires a closer look into the restrictions to the freedom of movement of the Union citizens that are at the origin of the creation of the unlawfulness of stay of EU citizens.

The present chapter starts by addressing, at the conceptual level, who are unlawfully-staying EU citizens in terms of EU law. Next, a systematic examination of the sources and causes of this unlawfulness is provided. The chapter then moves on to, first. analyse the concept of unlawfully-staying EU citizen from the

[1] The media plays a crucial role in the creation of this general idea, see for example: Miguel González and Ignacio Fariza, 'Rajoy gets illegal immigration at top of EU-Africa summit agenda', *El País*, April 2014, (http://elpais.com/elpais/2014/04/03/inenglish/1396519020_176450.html).

[2] J Parkin, 'The Criminalisation of Migration in Europe: A State-of-the-Art of the Academic Literature and Research', CEPS Liberty and Security in Europe, no 61, October 2013.

[3] Editorial Comments, 'The Free Movement of Persons in the European Union: Salvaging the Dream while Explaning the Nightmare' (2014) 51 *Common Market Law Review* 731.

perspective of the CJEU. Second, this part of the book examines the jurisprudence of the Court that touches upon this matter in three thematic blocks of analysis: (i) the neutralisation of supranational illegal stay, (ii) a tougher approach towards legal residence, and (iii) supranational 'legal residence' as a condition for solidarity. The purpose of this analysis is to understand in which ways has the CJEU has interpreted the unlawfulness of the stay of EU citizens at the supranational level and by going through these different stages understand the jurisprudential evolution of the concept and highlight the gradual shift of the meaning of legal residence for the purposes of the access to solidarity in another Member State.

The third and last part of chapter two is dedicated to the procedural, substantive and political consequences of EU citizens' supranational unlawful stay. This reveals a clear division between the status of EU citizens who are living in unlawfulness in the territory of another Member State, which invokes the narrative of the 'good citizen' and 'bad citizen',[4] and the existence of a category in between that is simply present with no access to solidarity, however not expelled most of times.

The importance of this chapter goes beyond the pure black and white analysis of the supranational unlawfulness of stay of citizens of the Union. More than illegality or unlawfulness it is the degree of stability of the right to reside (and the factors that influence it) that affects the enjoyment of the rights in relation to EU citizenship. As such the role that EU citizenship plays in reconfiguring the concept of illegality of the EU is at the heart of this analysis.

II. ILLEGALLY-STAYING THIRD-COUNTRY NATIONALS AND UNLAWFULLY-STAYING EU CITIZENS

Restrictions on an EU citizen's right to move and reside in another Member State have been addressed elsewhere in the literature,[5] to a certain extent in the jurisprudence and are the subject of secondary EU legislation.[6] However, the CJEU, scholars and EU legislation have thus far failed to approach derogations on free movement and the right to reside in another Member State from the perspective of the unlawfulness of one's residence status. It is important to remember that the combination of illegality or unlawfulness of stay and EU citizenship is unexplored, although it can and in fact frequently does happen in practice. As we will see, the CJEU has not dealt with this combination in an altogether straightforward manner and EU legislation restricts available means for deportation of EU citizens.

Before addressing what may cause the unlawfulness of an EU citizen's stay, one aspect must be clarified: the existence of a concept of 'illegal stay' for third-country nationals and the fact that EU citizens are *a priori* excluded from its scope.

[4] L Azoulai, 'The (Mis)construction of the European Individual Two Essays on Union Citizenship Law, EUI LAW, 2014/14 (http://cadmus.eui.eu/handle/1814/33293) 12–16.

[5] N Nic Shuibhne, 'Derrogating from the Free Movement of Persons: When can EU Citizens be Deported?' (2005–06) 8 *CYELS* 187.

[6] Citizens Directive 2004/38.

The terminology used by EU legislation to refer to the illegal nature of the stay of a third-country national is coherent. However, the same cannot be said in terms of the substance of the concept, as there is no such coherence with regards to the illegality of what a third-country national means.

The aforementioned provisions mention the individual necessarily as a third-country national, which excludes EU citizens from the scope of this legislation. As such, at first sight one could ask: does this EU legislation exclude EU citizens from becoming illegally staying altogether? However, the answer to this question is quite straightforward and finds its legal basis in the Citizens' Directive 2004/38. As a result of this Directive there is no doubt that an EU citizen who violates the conditions imposed by that particular piece of legislation (for example Article 7 (1) b)) to stay in another Member State is illegally staying within that territory. After answering this initial query, one may go further and question whether there is another type of illegality into which EU citizens may fall. The premise that the designations of 'illegal stay', 'illegally staying' and 'overstayer' are exclusive to third-country nationals living within the EU territory has not been challenged so far at the CJEU. In fact, the Court uses this terminology in relation only to third-country nationals and not to EU citizens.[7] Although this issue is clearly more complicated than mere consideration of different terminology, it is important nevertheless to take a closer look at the substance of the phenomenon.

As Thym has stated in relation to the mobility of EU citizens: 'intra-European mobility is treated similarly to a Scotsman moving to London'.[8] This idea of ease of movement is rooted in the freedom of movement which is one of the very foundations of EU law and the most treasured right of citizens of the Union.[9] Furthermore, as this commentator also points out, EU citizens do not have to deal with two core features that define EU migration rules for third-country nationals. First, after transitional periods for new Member States have passed there is no restriction of access for low-skilled workers or for part-time employment for EU citizens living in another Member State, and second no linguistic or cultural integration test may be imposed on EU citizens moving within the EU.[10] This is in line with the idea that Union citizens move more swiftly between legality and illegality of stay, and as such there is an easier way out of illegality in comparison to third-country nationals.

In short, the illegality of a stay of a third-country national is terminology commonly used in EU legislation, although the content of the conditions are mostly left to the Member State's discretion which leaves a significant margin of manoeuvre

[7] See for example a comparison between the terminology used in the cases: Case C-357/09 PPU *Said Shamilovich Kadzoev*, [2009], EU:C:2009:741, Case C-61/11 PPU, *El Dridi* [2011], EU:C:2011:268, Case C- 145/09, *Land Baden-Wurttemberg v Panagotis Tsakouridis*, [2010], EU:C:2010:708.

[8] D Thym, 'EU Migration Policy and its Constitutional Rationale: A Cosmopolitan Outlook' (2013) 50 *Common Market Law Review* 711 and 712.

[9] EUROPA—Press Releases—Special Eurobarometer: Right to Move and Reside Freely in the EU and Right to Good Administration Are the Most Important Citizens' Rights, July 7, 2011.

[10] Thym (n 8) 711 and 712.

in terms of their exact definition, apart from excluding EU citizens from its scope. Let us now look at the sources, framework and consequences of the illegality of EU citizens and discuss whether this is another type of illegality distinct from third-country nationals.

A. Sources and Causes of EU Citizens' Unlawful Stay

There are three types of causes that can result in an EU citizen acquiring the status of being illegally staying in another Member State to which they have migrated. The first are specific causes such as the unreasonable burden criteria and the loss of worker status. The second are general causes relating to public policy, public security or public heath codified in the Citizens Directive 2004/38.[11] The third cause is a stand-alone cause, namely, abuse of rights under EU law. Each will be addressed in turn.

As derogations from the free movement of persons, these causes are rarely conceptualised as causes of EU citizens' illegality, which makes this analysis even more topical and challenging. Moreover, Nic Shuibhne explains that even though one can normatively distinguish between express derogations to free movement of people and the extinction of the right to reside in another Member State on the grounds of the lack of financial resources, the consequence will inevitably be the same: 'the host state can impose its own immigration preference notwithstanding the supranational presumption of free movement'.[12] Thorough analysis of reasons for deportation has been provided in the literature and as such it is not the aim of this chapter to go over this ground again but rather to consider the conceptual legal consequences of non-compliance with the conditions imposed by EU law to reside in the host Member State.

i. Specific Causes: The Loss of the Status of Worker and the Lack of Sufficient Resources

The Citizens' Directive 2004/38 distinguishes three types of residence status based on the criteria of temporality: a) up to three months of residence,[13] b) more than three months of residence[14] and c) after having resided legally and continuously for five years in the host Member State.[15] The first type is granted to every EU citizen who wants to live in another Member State for up to three months: in this case he or she should be granted the right of residence 'without any conditions or any

[11] Arts 27 to 33 of the Citizens' Directive 2004/38 and see also *Tsakouridis* judgment and Case C- 348/09, *PI v Oberburgermeisterin der Stadt Remscheid* [2012], EU:C:2012:300.
[12] Nic Shuibhne (n 5) 188.
[13] Art 6 of the Citizens' Directive 2004/38.
[14] ibid Art 7.
[15] ibid Art 16.

formalities other than the requirement to hold a valid identity card or passport'.[16] These migrating EU citizens are less likely to lose their right to reside in another Member State as there is not any financial requirement imposed on them and they enjoy an almost unconditional right of residence.[17] Only the grounds of public policy, public security, or public health may limit their right to reside in the host Member State for the first trimester.[18]

After the first three months, in order to guarantee the enjoyment of the right to reside in another Member State an EU citizen must either be a worker or self-employed, or have sufficient resources for themselves and their family members to avoid becoming a burden on the social assistance system of the host Member State and have comprehensive sickness insurance cover in the host Member State.[19] To maintain their right of residence an EU citizen could, alternatively, be enrolled in a vocational training programme as well as being in possession of comprehensive sickness insurance cover and sufficient resources for themselves and their family members.[20] If an EU citizen fails to comply with these conditions they consequently lose their right to reside in another Member State for more than three months and can thus be expelled to their Member State of origin. These are specific causes of the illegality of a stay of an EU citizen given that they apply only to certain categories of individuals, who, having lived for more than three months and not more than five years in another Member State, do not fulfil the conditions set out in Article 7 of the Citizens' Directive 2004/38.

Traditionally, the wording of Article 7 of the Citizens' Directive 2004/38 distinguishes three types of regimes to regulate the right to reside in another EU Member State: (i) economically active citizens,[21] (ii) economically independent or inactive citizens[22] and (iii) students.[23] Economically active citizens are granted the widest of the three forms of residence in terms of rights and the strongest protection against expulsion.[24] The definition of economically active EU citizens is intrinsically related to the definition of 'worker' as extensively developed in the case law and the evolution of the free movement of workers under Article 45

[16] ibid, Art 6 (1).

[17] AA Dashwood and others, *Wyatt and Dashwood's European Union Law* (Oxford, Hart Publishing, 2011) 472.

[18] See Art 14 (1) of the Citizens' Directive 2004/38 for the retention of the right of residence of this group of migrants when they become an 'unreasonable burden on the social assistance system of the host Member State', Art 24 (2) of the Citizens' Rights Directive for the Member States' power of limiting the access to social assistance on the first three months and E Guild, S Peers and J Tomkin, *The EU Citizenship Directive: A Commentary* (Oxford, Oxford University Press, 2014) 123.

[19] Art 7 (1) a) and b) Citizens' Directive 2004/38.

[20] ibid, Art 7 (1) c).

[21] ibid, Art 7 (1) a).

[22] ibid, Art 7 (1) b).

[23] ibid, Art 7 (1) c). The scope of this chapter does not include the analysis of the 'students' category.

[24] ibid, Art 14 (4) a). Dashwood and others (n 17) 473. P Dollat, *La citoyenneté européenne: théorie et statuts* (Brussels, Bruylant, 2008) 167. Dollat categorises type of migrant EU citizens as 'bénéficiaire privilégié' emphasising the idea that they enjoy from the widest form of right to move and reside in another Member State.

Treaty on the Functioning of the European Union (TFEU). The loss of the status of worker, if not complemented with the conditions imposed on economically inactive citizens, may, in principle, be a cause of illegality of the stay of a Union citizen. The Citizens' Directive 2004/38 offers a reinforced protection against the loss of worker status to certain categories who fall under Article 7 (3)—in practice a protection that means a wider right to reside in another Member State and for that reason a protection against illegality of stay in another Member State.

The scope of Article 7 (3) of the Citizens' Directive 2004/38 on the retention of the status of worker is currently not completely clear. In accordance with Article 7(3) one has the right to retain their worker status whenever, for instance, he or she is temporarily unable to work due to an illness or accident (among other more peripheral circumstances).[25] A striking example of the lack of clarity of the scope of this protection is the situation of Jessy Saint Prix in a judgment that was delivered by the Court of Justice.[26] The question referred to the CJEU disputes whether the worker status is retained by a mobile EU citizen who had to give up work temporarily at the late stages of pregnancy and due to the illness of her baby was delayed to return to work. Although the question is posed in relation to the right to be granted income support and not with regards to the claimant's right to reside, a narrow interpretation of the worker status could have led to the loss of the right to reside in the host Member State.

On this topic O'Brien concludes that from the wording of Citizens' Directive 2004/38 it can be said that 'women's free movement rights and choices are to be curtailed, *on becoming pregnant* ...'[27] This aspect is relevant because it shows that the derogations to free movement and the right to reside are not exhaustive and there are still specific categories of migrants who have a weaker right to reside in the host Member State and therefore they are more liable to fall into illegality. Wahl, the Advocate General responsible for delivering the Opinion in this case, explained that 'the mere fact that a Union citizen has lost his or her status as a worker does not mean that all rights attaching to that status automatically and immediately disappear'.[28] The CJEU ruled in the same vein as the Advocate General, stating that:

> a woman who gives up work, or seeking work, because of the physical constraints of the late stages of pregnancy and the aftermath of childbirth retains the status of 'worker', within the meaning of that article, provided she returns to work or finds another job within a reasonable period after the birth of her child.[29]

[25] Art 7 (3) b) to d) of the Citizens' Directive 2004/38 for the other circumstances that may prevent a EU citizen from losing their worker status, and for a detailed overview, see Guild, Peers and Tomkin (n 18) 134–41.

[26] Case C-507/12, *Jessy Saint Prix v Secretary of State for Work and Pensions*, [2014], EU:C:2014:2007.

[27] C O'Brien, 'I Trade, Therefore I Am: Personhood in the European Union' (2013) 50 *Common Market Law Review* 1666.

[28] (n 26) Opinion of AG Wahl, para 45.

[29] ibid, para 46.

So what do the particular facts of this case mean to the more general question examined in this book? In short, in this particular case the Court made it clear that a woman who finds herself in this situation retains the status of worker. However, ambiguity with regard to other categories of Union citizen migrants still exists.

The second category under Article 7 are economically inactive or independent citizens residing in another Member State for more than three months. This group of people are obliged to comply with the requirements of possession of 'sufficient resources' to avoid becoming an 'unreasonable burden' on the social assistance of the host Member State and a comprehensive health insurance at being illegally staying. Much could be said about the scope of this criterion, but for our purposes it is only necessary to stress the main points. Crucially for our purposes regarding the condition of owning sufficient resources to avoid becoming an unreasonable burden to the host Member State, the Court has in the past seemed to be reluctant to make this ground a source of illegality of EU citizens' stay. As a result some commentators have described its scope as 'virtually meaningless as a Member State instrument for deportation'.[30]

Having said this, the landscape has changed with regard to the meaning of this source of illegality for the purposes of deportation, as can be seen for example by the Belgian immigration statistics and the grounds for expulsion of intra-migration in 2013. As such, 2,712 people had their Belgian residence permits withdrawn of those '816 were Romanians, 393 were Bulgarians and 323 were Spaniards'.[31] Further, specifically with regard to the Spanish citizens, Spain's Secretary of State for Immigration and Asylum explained that the reason for the expulsion of these EU citizens was 'on the grounds of their constituting an excessive burden on Belgium's social security system'.[32]

In the literature some have stressed that the regulation of free movement of inactive people is not 'crystal clear'.[33] Becoming an 'unreasonable burden' is directly related with being unlawfully staying within the territory of the host Member State and as such what is covered by the concept of 'unreasonableness' dictates the scope of this source of illegality. The unreasonableness test helps establishing whether or not an ordinary citizen of the Union may lawfully enjoy the freedom of movement.[34] However, as Thym argues, even though this test offers some clarity in the abstract, 'the definition of (un-) lawful presence and the application of non-discrimination rules remain ambiguous'.[35]

[30] Nic Shuibhne (n 5) 210.

[31] EU Parliamentary question for written answer to the Commission, 15 January 2014, www.europarl.europa.eu/sides/getDoc.do?type=WQ&reference=E-2014-000335&language=EN, OJ C 288.

[32] ibid.

[33] D Thym, 'The Elusive Limits of Solidarity: Residence Rights of and Social Benefits for Economically Inactive Union Citizens' (2015) 52 *Common Market Law Review* 21.

[34] ibid, 49.

[35] ibid, 49.

The CJEU delivered its decision in the *Brey* case, a judgment that deals directly with the definition of the concept of unreasonableness.[36] *Brey* also raises questions with regard to the relationship between Social Security Regulation 883/2004 and the 2004/38 Citizens' Directive, although they are now put aside, as they were already addressed by Verschueren,[37] and belong to a different forum of analysis. The relevance of the *Brey* decision is based on the fact that it leaves the decision on the unlawfulness of the residence of inactive EU citizens who may be an unreasonable burden to the social assistance system of the host Member State more uncertain and does not give the clarity that the unreasonability test needed.[38]

This is so as the Court states that to measure unreasonableness of the burden imposed on the host Member State's social assistance system the test should take into account the individual burden caused by the national of the other Member State by assessing:

> [T]he amount and the regularity of the income which he receives; the fact that those factors have led those authorities to issue him with a certificate of residence; and the period during which the benefit applied for is likely to be granted to him.[39]

Furthermore, the national authorities competent to assess the extent of the burden on the national social system of the host Member State (in accordance with the position taken by the Commission during the *Brey* proceedings) should determine the proportion of the burden of all EU citizens who are beneficiaries for that specific benefit as a whole.[40] As such, to test whether the burden was unreasonable the CJEU created a 'double test'[41] to be applied by the host Member State, which takes into account, on the one hand, the individual circumstances and, on the other, the social assistance system as a whole. In short, the Court established criteria that, in respect to the 'limits imposed by EU law',[42] attempt to balance the right to free movement of EU citizens and the integrity of the social assistance system of the host Member State. Nevertheless the question of the extension of the degree of solidarity that exists between the Member States of the EU is not clearly answered by the *Brey* test, which consequently leaves the situations of illegality originating out of a lack of sufficient resources and becoming a so-called 'unreasonable burden' an uncertain legal consequence, dependent on the national implementation of the unreasonableness test.

This reading of the unreasonableness test must be combined with what the Court boldly said in *Alimanovic*[43] in relation to the existence of an objective

[36] Case C-140/12, *Pensionsversicherungsanstalt v Peter Brey*, [2013], EU:C:2013:565.

[37] H Verschueren, 'Free Movement or Benefit Tourism: The Unreasonable Burden of Brey' (2014) 16 *European Journal of Migration and Law* 147.

[38] ibid, 177.

[39] Para 78 of the judgment *Brey* (n 36).

[40] Para 78 of the judgment *Brey* (n 36) and Verschueren (n 37) 171 and 172.

[41] Verschueren, ibid 179.

[42] Para 70 of the judgment *Brey* (n 36).

[43] Case C-67/14, *Jobcenter Berlin Neukölln v Nazifa Alimanovic and Others*, [2015], EU:C:2015:597, paras 59–60.

'gradual system' that exclude the need for the individual assessment as regards the situation of jobseekers and access to social benefits, which made clear that no individual assessment was necessary in that case. The CJEU case law has dealt with the topic of unlawfulness and has intertwined the development of its regime on EU citizenship and access to social assistance, as will be shown below.[44]

ii. General Causes: Public Policy, Security and Health Grounds

The second type of cause that can result in the unlawfulness of the residence status of an EU citizen relates to public policy, security and health. With regard to the free movement derogations on these grounds the Citizens' Directive 2004/38 qualifies them as 'exceptional circumstances' and offers a high level of protection against expulsion to Union citizens and their family members in accordance with their degree of integration in the host Member State.[45] These are termed 'general causes' since they apply (even if at different levels) to the freedom of movement and residence of all categories of migrants covered by the Citizens' Directive 2004/38. The TFEU includes two provisions establishing the derogation of free movement of workers, establishment and free movement of services by reasons of public policy, public security and public health, namely Articles 45 (3) and 52 (1) and although there is no equivalent provisions for Article 21 TFEU (citizenship) the derogations contained in the Treaty and secondary legislation apply to EU citizens.

The Citizens' Directive 2004/38 also restricts free movement on the grounds of public policy, public security or public health in Article 27 which states that:

> Member States may restrict the freedom of movement and residence of Union citizens and their family members, irrespective of nationality, on grounds of public policy, public security or public health. These grounds shall not be invoked to serve economic ends.

Interpreting the meaning and scope of public policy, public security within a process of expulsion of an EU citizen became a herculean task for the CJEU and for some has led to the incoherence of 'the law and undermining legal certainty through confusing the notions of public order and public security'.[46] A factor that contributes to the complexity of the interpretation of the expressions 'public policy' and 'public security' is the fact that they may vary from Member State to Member State.[47] The use of these grounds must respect a set of limitations: first, they may not be invoked to serve economic grounds;[48] second, the principle of proportionality must be respected;[49] third, the decision must be based exclusively

[44] See subsection I.B.iv.

[45] See Recital 24 and Art 28 of the Citizens Directive 2004/38.

[46] D Kochenov and B Pirker, 'Deporting the Citizens within the European Union: A Counter-Intuitive Trend in Case C-348/09, PI V Oberburgermeisterin der Stadt Remscheid' (2013) 19 *The Columbia Journal of European Law* 369, 389.

[47] Guild, Peers and Tomkin (n 18) 253.

[48] Art 27 (1) of the Citizens' Directive 2004/38.

[49] ibid, Art 27 (2).

on the personal conduct of the EU citizen;[50] fourth criminal convictions alone may not be the reason to decide under those grounds,[51] and the personal conduct of the individual concerned must represent a genuine, present and sufficiently serious threat affecting one of the fundamental interests of society.[52]

Prior to any expulsion decision based on these grounds, Member States must respect the considerations imposed by Article 28 (1) of the Citizens' Directive, such as 'how long the individual concerned has resided on its territory, his/her age, state of health, family and economic situation, social and cultural integration into the host Member State and the extent of his/her links with the country of origin'. These considerations are taken into account in combination with the protection threshold granted to EU citizens as a result of their integration in the host society.[53] This threshold for individuals in possession of a permanent residence means that they can only be expelled if there are 'serious grounds of public policy or public security'.[54] In the case of EU citizens who are minors or who have been residents in the host Member State for more than 10 years' expulsion may only happen whenever there are 'imperative grounds of public security'.[55]

The interpretation of the derogations to free movement gains importance when compared to the rules applied to illegally-staying third-country nationals in accordance with the Return Directive. The scope of the reasons that justify a migrant's unlawfulness of residence reveals the core of the phenomenon illegality as it is the objective criteria that determines who deserves a legal migration status and who does not. Advocate General Sharpston has highlighted this issue in her Opinion on the case *Z Zh and O v Staatssecretaris van Veiligheid en Justitie*.[56] The impact of the interpretation of the grounds for derogations to free movement is obvious. It is particularly interesting to look at the observations presented by some Member States in this case with regard to the interpretation of 'public order' within the scope of Article 7 (4) of the Return Directive[57] and the derogation on grounds of public order under the Citizens' Directive.[58]

The general view of Member States was that:

> [T]he derogation on grounds of [public order] under the Citizenship Directive should be interpreted more narrowly than that in the Returns Directive; and the concept of 'risk' or 'danger' to [public order] under the latter should be interpreted less strictly than the notion of 'grounds of [public order]' in each of the three directives.[59]

[50] ibid.
[51] ibid.
[52] ibid.
[53] ibid, Art 28 (2) and (3). See also on this matter: N Nic Shuibhne, 'Limits Rising, Duties Ascending: The Changing Legal Shape of Union Citizenship' (2015) 52 *Common Market Law Review* 889, 921–26.
[54] Art 28 (2) of the Citizens' Directive 2004/38.
[55] Art 28(3) of the Citizens' Directive 2004/38.
[56] Case C-554/13 *Z.Zh and O v Staatssecretaris van Veiligheid en Justitie* [2014], EU:C:2015:94, Opinion of AG Sharpston.
[57] Belgium, the Czech Republic, France, Greece, the Netherlands, Poland and ibid, para 24.
[58] ibid, para 53, 54 and 55.
[59] ibid, para 55 final.

In short, Member States argued that the notion of public order should be interpreted differently (in other words more narrowly) when applied to EU citizens than to illegally-staying third-country nationals. This view implies the existence of a hierarchy which means that falling into illegality at the national level could present more or less of an obstacle depending on the migrant's country of origin.[60]

Advocate General Sharpston did not share the same position in her Opinion. Sharpston clarified that even though EU citizens and illegally-staying third-country nationals 'cannot be assimilated and they are governed by different rules', the criteria for assessing whether a right should be limited must not be interpreted less rigorously in any case.[61] In the Opinion it is argued that illegally-staying third-country nationals are covered by the EU Charter of Fundamental Rights and that the same rigour should be respected in relation to the application of those rights, whether the individual is a third-country national or a Union citizen.[62] As such, the examination of the risk that a migrant represents to the public order of a host Member State is based on the personal conduct of the individual.[63] The methodology used to make decisions under the Citizens' Directive is the same as that used with regard to the Return Directive Article 7 (4) and those 'decisions should be adopted on a case-by-case basis according to objective criteria'.[64]

This debate illustrates how the interpretation of the scope of the general causes of unlawfulness of EU citizens (or illegally-staying third-country nationals) may play a defining role in determining who is covered by illegality and who is not. The importance of this discussion lies especially in understanding that the criteria used to determine what is a derogation is objective and neutral and applied to mobile people within the EU equally without a distinction being made between EU citizens and third-country nationals.

iii. Stand-alone Clause: Abuse of Rights under EU Law

Last, the third possible cause of illegality of the stay of an EU citizen is the abuse of rights under EU law. Article 35 of the Citizens' Directive 2004/38 states that it is within the Member State's discretion to take measures to refuse, terminate or withdraw any of the rights that could be granted by the Directive when there is an abuse of rights or fraud, such as a marriage of convenience.[65] The connection made between abuse of rights and marriages of convenience is also stated in

[60] ibid, para 58.
[61] ibid, para 59.
[62] ibid, para 59.
[63] ibid, para 60 and C-48/75 *Royer*, [1976], EU:C:1976:57, para 71.
[64] (n 56) Opinion of AG Sharpston, para 60.
[65] Other designations often used are 'sham' or 'bogus marriages', 'fraudulent marriages'. For a more comprehensive analysis on marriage migration with a special focus on the UK see: H Wray, *Regulating Marriage Migration into the UK: a Stranger in the Home* (Farnham, Ashgate Publishing Ltd, 2011), and H Wray, 'An Ideal Husband? Marriages of Convenience, Moral Gate-keeping and Immigration to the UK' (2006) 8 *European Journal of Migration and Law* 303 or B De Hart, 'Introduction: The Marriage of Convenience in European Immigration Law' (2006) 8 *European Journal of Migration & Law*.

Recital 28 which clarifies that 'any other form of relationships contracted for the sole purpose of enjoying the right of free movement and residence' are against EU law. This last source of illegality is categorised as stand-alone cause of illegality because it is enshrined in a separate Article in the final provisions of the Directive. The abuse of rights is yet another cause of Union citizens' illegal stay that has an unclear scope and seems difficult to invoke.[66]

The Court dealt first with abuse of rights in *Singh* in which it stated that marriages of convenience are those which are contracted only with the purpose of securing residence rights and this represents an abuse of rights in EU law.[67] In *Akrich* the CJEU clarified that to be granted a privileged status as a result of making use of EU law is not automatically abuse of rights:

> [T]here would be an abuse if the facilities afforded by Community law in favour of migrant workers and their spouses were invoked in the context of marriages of convenience entered into in order to circumvent the provisions relating to entry and residence of nationals of non-Member States.[68]

Later in *Metock* the Court has stated that Member States:

> [M]ay adopt the necessary measures to refuse, terminate or withdraw any right conferred by that directive in the case of abuse of rights or fraud, such as marriages of convenience, it being understood that any such measure must be proportionate and subject to the procedural safeguards provided for in the directive.[69]

In order to understand the stand-alone cause of the illegality of an EU citizen's stay in another Member State one has to look at what is meant by 'abuse of rights', as its scope determines what is covered by the abuse of rights as a source of unlawfulness. The definition of abuse for the purpose of the Citizens' Directive 2004/38 is a concept that 'was derived from EU law',[70] as such Member States must be able to demonstrate a 'well-founded suspicion of abuse' to proceed to the investigation of individual cases.[71]

In this respect, the national reports within the FIDE Report highlight that there remains one question unanswered by the CJEU: does Article 35 of the Citizens Directive 2004/38 preclude the right to free movement or are the derogations to be examined under the premises of the abuse of rights? The report moves on to highlight that there are examples of national practices distinguishing the application of Article 35 and Articles 27 and 28 of the Citizens' Directive 2004/38, for

[66] Dashwood and others (n 17) 288, and Nic Shuibhne (n 5) 208. See als, *Zhu Chen v Secretary of State for the Home Department* case, paras 34–41 for an example of the Court denying invoking the argument of abuse of rights.

[67] Case C-370/90, *R v Immigration Appeal Tribunal and Singh, ex parte Secretary of State for the Home Departement*, [1992], para 24.

[68] Case C-109/01, *Akrich*, [2003], EU:C:2003:491, para 57.

[69] Case C-127/08, *Metock*, [2008], EU:C:2008:449, para 75.

[70] Guild, Peers and Tomkin (n 18) 300.

[71] Ibid, 300.

the purposes of expulsion of an EU citizen.[72] In addition, looking at the CJEU decisions on dealing with abuse of rights, there is an unequivocal link between those grounds and marriages of convenience. As such, one should question what fits within the scope of abuse of rights for the purposes of the Citizens Directive 2004/38. Costello, for example, argues that the concept of abuse of rights has a 'limited role' in the case law on EU citizenship in comparison with other free movement provisions.[73]

Consequently the analysis of the grounds that justify a derogation to free movement and that are causes (specific, general grounds and stand-alone) of the unlawfulness of EU citizens residing in another Member State, highlighted two aspects of the regulation of illegality. First is the tendency to narrow down the concept of worker, and second, the objectivity of the criteria applied to decide if certain conduct falls within the meaning of a risk to public order in relation not only to EU citizens, but also to third-country nationals.

The impact that causes of unlawfulness have on the scope of that phenomenon depends greatly on the interpretation of the terms in secondary legislation, both by the CJEU and by national courts. Turning from the factors contained in secondary legislation that may be responsible for the illegality of an EU citizen's stay in the host Member State, it is necessary to examine the position taken by the CJEU on the illegality of an EU citizen's stay in order to elucidate the reasoning behind that supranational concept.

B. Rethinking the Court of Justice's Jurisprudence on the Unlawful Residence of EU Citizens

i. The Unlawfully-staying EU Citizen

The introduction of the notion of European citizenship in the Maastricht Treaty caused what has been termed 'conceptual metamorphosis', especially in the area of the EC rights of free movement and residence.[74] As Kostakopoulou argues, EU citizenship has a 'transformative potential'; potential that can be seen for example in the way the CJEU has used this notion.[75] What role does citizenship play when the Court deals with the unlawful stay of EU citizens in another Member State? It is relevant to analyse the CJEU's role on this matter because of the trend 'of

[72] N Nic Shuibhne and J Shaw, 'General Report' in U Neergaard, C Jacqueson and N Holst-Christensen (eds), *Union Citizenship: Development, Impact and Challenges, The XXVI FIDE Congress in Copenhagen, 2014, Congress Publications Vol 2* (2014), 133.

[73] C Costello, 'Citizenship of the Union: Above Abuse? in Rita de la Feria and Stefan Vogenauer (eds), *Prohibition of Abuse of Law: A New General Principle of EU Law* (Oxford, Hart Publishing, 2011) 321 and 353.

[74] D Kostakopoulou, 'The Evolution of European Union Citizenship' (2008) 7 *European Political Science* 285, 288.

[75] ibid, 293.

incorporating directly into legislative proposals extracts from judgments of the Court'[76] even if it has been pointed out that this is not an effective way of regulating EU citizens' rights to move and reside.

As an introductory remark before we turn our attention to the analysis of some of the most relevant decisions for this issue, is it interesting to mention that the CJEU, when referring to a potentially illegal stay of a EU citizen in another Member State, uses the terms 'lawfully resident' but never 'illegally staying' in the English translation of its judgments. Meanwhile the French version of the case law opts for 'séjourne légalement' or 'résidant légalement'.[77] However in both cases there never seems to be any reference to the possibility of an illegally-staying EU citizen and in the English version there is a differentiated choice of terminology for EU citizens and third-country nationals.[78] This may be solely an issue of translation or mere semantics, but nevertheless it shows that the definition of an illegal stay of a citizen of the Union does not have well-defined contours even within the CJEU's lexicon and decision-making process.

The following sections provide an overview of some of the most relevant cases involving the potential unlawfulness of an EU citizen's stay in a host Member State, which reveals an evolution of the CJEU's approach on this issue in different phases. The first two cases concern the right to be granted social benefits in another Member State, which is the most common way in which questions that touch upon the illegality of EU citizens come before the Court. Both cases required that the EU citizen fulfilled the conditions for being considered a 'worker' in accordance with EU law and being lawfully resident within the host Member State, in order to be granted the social benefit. In general the first stage of such cases deals with access to social benefits and (indirectly) the lawfulness of the residency of these EU citizens in the host Member State, whereas it is only at the second stage that the definition of legal and illegal residence in another Member State for the purposes of the Citizens' Directive 2004/38 is addressed.

There is a gradual shift in the Court's approach to the cases where an EU citizen is illegally staying in the territory of the host Member State. This shift in the jurisprudence moves towards a tougher approach in relation to the access of unlawfully-staying EU citizens to social benefits.

ii. The Neutralisation of Supranational Illegal Stay

The *Martinez Sala* decision is a notorious example of a potentially unlawfully-residing EU citizen in another Member State. In terms of the facts of this case, although Mrs Martinez Sala's compliance with the condition of sufficient resources imposed by EU law was dubious, the Court ruled that as long as she was lawfully

[76] Editorial Comments (n 3) 738.

[77] See para 37 of the French and English version of the Case C-456/02 *Trojani* [2004], EU:C:2004:488, para 52 of the French and English version of the Case C-85/96, *Martinez Sala*, [1998], EU:C:1998:217.

[78] Illegally staying is used for third-country nationals and unlawful residence for EU citizens.

resident within the host Member State she would be entitled to the child-raising allowance under national law.[79] The CJEU's reasoning was grounded in the principle of non-discrimination on the grounds of nationality.[80] It is interesting to note how in this case the lawfulness of the applicant's stay in Germany led the Court to apply the principle of non-discrimination at the supranational level, instead of going through the conditions for residence imposed by the EU, in particular that of not becoming a burden on the social assistance scheme of the state.

In *Trojani* the situation was similar in some important respects. In this case the applicant's status in the host Member State was similarly unclear, as was the fulfilment of the requirements imposed by Article 1(1) of Directive 90/364.[81] Mr Trojani was lawfully resident in Belgium, however when the Court compared his situation with the clauses limiting Articles 20 and 21 TFEU the legality of his stay was uncertain at the EU level. The way in which the Court turned a blind eye to that fact and focused solely on the applicant's lawful stay in accordance with the national framework of the host Member State and on the fulfilment of the requirements to be categorised as a worker at the EU level is noteworthy.[82] It could be said that in this case the supranational illegality of the stay was neutralised by national lawfulness in order to grant the allowance (the minimex) to Mr Trojani. The Court in *Trojani* held that once a Union citizen resides lawfully in a Member State, even independently of EU law, they are entitled to equal treatment.[83]

Another decision which dealt with the same type of scenario in relation to the situation of students in EU law is the *Bidar* case.[84] This case once more centres on access to social benefits, namely the right to be granted a student loan in the host Member State, and did not directly deal with the right to reside in another Member State. Mr Bidar, a French national, moved to the UK where he completed secondary school sponsored by his grandmother. Subsequently Mr Bidar's application for a student loan was refused on the grounds that he was not settled in the host Member State—a position which Mr Bidar contested.[85] The Court reiterated its statements from *Trojani*[86] (and the later *Grzelczyk*[87] case) in paragraphs 47 and 48 of the *Bidar* decision: students who are *lawfully resident* in the host Member State 'fall within the scope of application of the Treaty for the purposes of the prohibition of discrimination laid down in the first paragraph of Article 12 EC'.[88]

[79] Germany granted her the right of residence based on Council of Europe Convention on social and medical assistance, see para 14 of the *Martinez Sala* judgment (n 77).

[80] See para 61 of the *Martinez Sala* judgment (n 77).

[81] Para 35 of the *Trojani* judgment (n 77), and P Craig and G De Búrca, *EU Law: Text, Cases, and Materials* (Oxford, Oxford University Press, 2011) 836.

[82] Paras 37 and 40 of the *Trojani* judgment (n 77).

[83] ibid, para 40.

[84] Case C-209/03, *Dany Bidar* [2005], EU:C:2005:169.

[85] ibid, para 22.

[86] Para 45 of the *Trojani* judgment (n 77).

[87] Case C-184/99 *Grzelczyk v Centre public d'aide sociale d' Ottignies- Louvain-la-Neuve*, [2001], EU:C:2001:458, para 42.

[88] Para 37 of the *Bidar* judgment (n 84).

As such, the CJEU assumed the lawful residence of the applicant in this case by making a passing reference to the fact that Mr Bidar's resources or sickness insurance were not questioned.[89] Interestingly, in these cases it is the period of time that the individual was lawfully staying in the host Member State (or possessing a residence permit as Mr Trojani did), that the Court relied upon to justify access to social assistance. Once more, the Court made a brief reference to the right to reside in another Member State, even mentioning the supranational requirements for the lawful exercise of this right to grant access to a social benefit; in Mr Bidar's case a student loan for maintenance.

These cases highlight the dynamics between EU and national law concepts before the entry into force of the Citizens' Directive 2004/38 (and its early stages), which were characterised by a neutralisation of supranational illegality in favour of the principle of non-discrimination.[90] These CJEU decisions relied on citizenship in an unclear way, perhaps even deliberately; making no attempt to illuminate the issue of when an EU citizen is unlawfully staying in the host Member State on financial grounds. What one may conclude from these cases is that by neutralising the EU law conditions to live in another Member State, the Court was able to confer the benefit of access to social assistance in the host Member State.

There are three potential bases that may justify an EU citizen's right to reside in another Member State: national law, EU law, or a combination of both.[91] As mentioned above, the decisions in *Martinez Sala*, *Trojani* and *Bidar* privileged national authorisation of residence and turned a blind eye to the supranational conditions imposed by EU law to reside legally in another Member State. Olsen illustrates this idea very clearly, stating that 'while the nation-state clearly is no longer the sole provider of individual rights, the mode of inclusion and exclusion is still strongly attached to it'.[92] The neutralisation of supranational illegal stay to reside in another Member State can be seen as being related to the idea of municipal or urban citizenship.[93]

An interesting idea that is historically related to the first stage of the CJEU approach to the unlawfulness of the stay of an EU citizen is the concept of municipal or urban citizenship. Municipal or urban citizenship is a membership conception that is found in late medieval Europe, such as the old regime of the Dutch town of Bois-le-Duc, or even before that in ancient Greece.[94] Municipal citizenship is a conception of belonging that emphasises the fact that citizenship has

[89] ibid, para 36.

[90] Paras 35 and 36 of the *Trojani* decision (n 77), and Dashwood and others (n 18) 211.

[91] ibid, 216.

[92] E DH Olsen, 'European Citizenship: Toward Renationalization or Cosmopolitan Europe?' in E Guild, CJ Gortázar Rotaeche and D Kostakopoulou (eds), *The Reconceptualization of European Union Citizenship* (Leiden, Brill Nijhoff, 2014) 357.

[93] This book uses municipal and urban citizenship interchangeably.

[94] M Prak, 'Burghers into Citizens: Urban and National citizenship in the Netherlands during the Revolutionary Era (c. 1800)' (1997) 26 *Theory and Society* 403 and R Baubock, 'Reinventing Urban Citizenship' (2003) 7 *Citizenship studies* 139.

its origins in the city and that cities are 'the battleground through which groups define their identities, stake their claims, wage their battles and articulate citizenship rights and obligation'.[95] This is an idea that one may find influences in some of the cases brought to the Court that deal directly or indirectly with the right to reside in another Member State. In short, examples of the idea or spirit of municipal citizenship can be found in judgments where migrants, both EU citizens and third-country nationals, enjoy a particular status within the city which is not recognised at the national level (or in some cases at the EU level).

With regards to examples of municipal citizenship of EU citizens, one could recall the aforementioned cases: of *Martinez Sala* and *Trojani*. It was clear that in these cases there was some form of recognition by the host Member State's authorities of the integration of Mrs Martinez Sala and Mr Trojani into society. This recognition resulted in a national residence permit being granted despite the dubious fulfilment of the requirements imposed by EU law to live in another Member State.

The idea of urban citizenship becomes even more interesting when put together with the status of illegally-staying third-country nationals. Urban or municipal citizenship is not exclusive to EU citizens and the *Zambrano* decision shows us how a third-country national living in Belgium may acquire municipal citizenship.[96] Mr Zambrano, a non-removable migrant (a category of migrants that is the focus of chapter three[97]) received an order to leave Belgium which included a *non-refoulement* clause. Leaving aside the question of the non-removability of Mr Zambrano, what is relevant for the issue of urban citizenship is that despite being illegally staying and not being granted a work permit for several years, he enjoyed a certain status in the municipality. In terms of signs of this municipal citizenship enjoyed by the applicant, one can enumerate his registration in the municipality of Schaerbeek.[98] Furthermore the fact that Mr Zambrano signed an employment contract for an unlimited period to work full-time and that 'his work was paid according to the various applicable scales, with statutory deductions made for social security and the payment of employer contributions',[99] reinforces the idea of Mr Zambrano's integration in the host society.

The practice of cities rather than nation States granting residents and citizens legal statuses was a common practice until the nineteenth century in certain parts of Europe. This idea of the city as a provider of a certain rights is (even implicitly) still alive in the some of the cases brought to the Court where illegally-staying migrants (whether they be EU citizens or third-country nationals) enjoy some kind of status in the city and not at the national level. Furthermore, it is argued

[95] E Isin, *Being Political: Genealogies of Citizenship* (Minneapolis, University of Minnesota Press 2002) 283–84.

[96] Case C-34/09, *Gerardo Ruiz Zambrano* [2011], EU:C:2011:124.

[97] For a more detailed analysis of non-removability see chapter three.

[98] Paras 18 to 20 of the *Zambrano* judgment (n 96).

[99] ibid.

that there is a connection between the privileging of national lawfulness when analysing the neutralisation of the supranational requirements for an EU citizen to reside within the territory of another Member State discussed above. For this reason, it seems difficult to apply Holton's view on the impact of citizenship that 'citizenship thus erodes local hierarchies, statuses, and privileges in favour of national jurisdictions and contractual relations in principle on an equality of rights'.[100] In these particular cases EU citizenship seems to have a different consequence and implicitly accepts that there may be another implicit means by which an individual can be granted citizenship-related rights and duties that is rooted in the idea of municipal membership.

iii. A Tougher Approach to Legal Residence

Although the emphasis on national lawfulness was clear in the judgments mentioned above, it is important to contrast these decisions with more recent cases that deal more directly with the meaning of 'illegal residence' in EU law and that do not seem to privilege the national dimension in the same way. In the *Jipa* decision the Court addressed the definition of 'illegal residence'—a definition used at the national level by Romania. Subsequently the CJEU was asked whether previous 'illegal residence' in another Member State could be interpreted as falling within the grounds of 'public policy' or 'public security' to restrict an individual's freedom of movement in accordance with Article 27 of Citizens' Directive 2004/38.[101]

The Court decided that in Mr Jipa's situation this was not the case. Mr Jipa is a Romanian national who was repatriated after having illegally stayed in Belgium before the 2007 enlargement when Romania joined the EU—as such Mr Jipa was not an EU citizen at the time.[102] In 2007 Mr Jipa was prohibited from travelling to Belgium by the Romanian authorities on the grounds of his previous repatriation from the latter Member State on account of his 'illegal residence'. Significantly, however, the CJEU stated that the Romanian authorities could not restrict an EU citizen's freedom of movement based solely on his previous illegal residence.[103]

The relevance of the *Jipa* case lies in the fact that the CJEU expressly addressed the significance of the concept of 'illegal residence'. The Court additionally distinguished the concept of 'illegal residence' from the situations covered by Article 27 of Citizens' Directive 2004/38. The CJEU posited that 'illegal residence' could only be considered a justification for a restriction if there was personal conduct of that national constituting a genuine, present and sufficiently serious threat to one of

[100] J Holston, *Cities and Citizenship* (Durham NC, Duke University Press, 1999) 1.

[101] Case C-33/07, *Jipa*, [2008], EU:C:2008:396.

[102] DM Sandru, CM Banu and D Calin, 'The Preliminary Reference in the Jipa Case and the Case Law of Romanian Courts on the Restriction on the Free Movement of Persons' (2012) 18 *European Public Law* 625.

[103] Paras 27 and 30 of the *Jipa* judgment (n 101).

the fundamental interests of society, which was not the case in respect of Mr Jipa. In doing so the CJEU excluded the possibility of defining previous 'illegal residence' as a reason for restriction of free movement. The CJEU did not delve deeper into the legal definition of 'illegal residence', leaving it as a matter of national discretion, but the fact it was mentioned acknowledges that an EU citizen may be illegally staying within the EU, as well as fitting in with the Court's practice of privileging the national dimension on this matter.

However, later in 2011 the CJEU delivered the *Ziolkowski* judgment.[104] This case concerned a Polish national who had moved to Germany before Poland's accession to the EU. The Court was asked precisely about the significance of the fact that Mr Ziolkowksi had resided legally for more than five years in another Member State under national law, although he had not fulfilled the conditions as set out in Article 7 (1) of the Citizens' Directive for the purposes of acquiring a right of permanent residence as set out in Article 16 (1) of the same Directive.[105] The CJEU in this case clarified the scope of the meaning of having 'resided legally' for the purposes of Article 16 of the Directive by stressing that it refers only to 'a period of residence which complies with the conditions laid down in the directive' and that compliance with national law alone, not satisfying the conditions imposed by EU law, cannot be considered a legal period of residence within the meaning of Article 16 (1).[106]

One of the striking questions is what to make of *Trojani*, given that Mr Trojani's situation fit perfectly into what the Court considered *a contrario* an illegal period of residence in *Ziolkowski*—was *Trojani* an anomaly? Or does *Ziolkowski* mark a break from the Court's practice of privileging Member States' rules on legality of stay? In fact, in this decision there seems to be a clearer articulation of the regime which governs EU citizens who are unlawfully staying in the host Member State. This could be due to the fact that this case relates directly to the definition of what can be considered illegal residence for the purposes of the Directive and does not address the attribution of a benefit to a EU citizen which then incidentally raised the issue of residence, as was the case in *Martinez Sala*, *Trojani* or *Bidar*.

This tougher (or more literal) approach of the CJEU to the meaning of 'legally residing' within the scope of Article 16 of the Citizens' Directive 2004/38 is an attempt to keep everybody happy in the 'difficult balancing act between the ambitious objectives behind EU citizenship and Citizens' Directive 2004/38 on the one hand, and the Member States and their tougher approach to immigration on the other'.[107] The same balancing act is also clear in the next line of cases that deals with access to social benefits and the right to reside in another Member State.

[104] Case C-424/10, *Ziolkowski*, [2011], EU:C:2011:866.

[105] Para 28 of the *Ziolkowski* judgment, ibid.

[106] ibid, paras 46 and 47.

[107] A Łazowski, 'Children of the Lesser Law: Comment on Ziolkowski and Szeja' (2013) 38 *European Law Review* 404.

iv. Supranational 'Legal Residence' as a Condition for Solidarity

Finally, turning to the CJEU decision in *Dano*,[108] this case deals with the issues of free movement of people and access to benefits and impacts on the determination of when a Union citizen is unlawfully staying within the territory of the host Member State. It is important to highlight the fact that the access to social benefits may shape the illegality of the stay of EU citizens, or the degree of the right of security of residence. The main difference between the latter line of cases and the *Jipa* and *Ziolkowski* cases is the fact that *Dano* answers questions related to the right to access social benefits and equally, incidentally, touches upon the question of legal residence, whilst *Jipa* and *Ziolkowski* directly address this matter. As mentioned previously, the implications of these cases (*Jipa* and *Ziolkowski*) in terms of the definition of what 'legal residence' entails in accordance with the provisions of the Citizens' Directive 2004/38 do not fit comfortably with what the Court has said about residing lawfully in the territory of the host Member State in the initial jurisprudence about the access to social benefits, such as the *Martinez Sala* and *Trojani* decisions.

The CJEU has, however, recently reduced (or attempted to reduce) these differences on the interpretation of the scope of the conditions to be fulfilled for 'legal residence' at supranational level. When the Court delivered the decision in *Dano* (later confirmed by *Alimanovic*) it overruled the *Martinez Sala* and *Trojani* line of thought in several important aspects. The challenge that the *Dano* judgment poses to the *Martinez Sala* and *Trojani* cases can be seen in two parts of the decision. The first challenge relates to the formal argument in relation to the facts and the importance of Ms Dano's residence permit, to which the CJEU turned a blind eye as opposed to what has happened to Mrs Martinez Sala who arguably was in a weaker position with regards the type of residence permit she possessed.[109] In *Dano* the possession of a 'residence certificate of unlimited duration'[110] did not allow Ms Dano to support her claim with the principle of non-discrimination laid down in Article 18 TFEU, as Mrs Martinez Sala had done with her residence permit based on the European Convention on Social and Medical Assistance of 11 December 1953.[111] Given that Ms Dano was not considered to be lawfully residing in Germany she did not enjoy the protection of equality under Article 18 TFEU and 24 (1) of the Citizens' Directive 2004/38.[112]

Turning from this formal argument, the most relevant part of the *Dano* decision is the clear challenge to *Baumbast* and *Trojani* in not taking into account the principle of proportionality when examining the limitations to the right to reside

[108] Case C-333/13, *Elisabeta Dano, Florin Dano v Jobcenter Leipzig*, [2014], EU:C:2014:2358.
[109] Compare para 36 of the judgment *Dano*, ibid with para 14 of the judgment *Martinez Sala* (n 77).
[110] Para 36 of the judgment *Dano*, ibid.
[111] Para 14 of the judgment *Martinez Sala* (n 77).
[112] Para 69 of the judgment *Dano* (n 108).

in another Member State for more than three months.[113] In *Dano* the CJEU discarded proportionality from its reasoning and placed the requirement of EU 'legal residence' as the main condition to access social assistance:

> To accept that persons who do not have a right of residence under Directive 2004/38 may claim entitlement to social benefits under the same conditions as those applicable to nationals of the host Member State would run counter to an objective of the directive, set out in recital 10 in its preamble, namely preventing Union citizens who are nationals of other Member States from becoming an unreasonable burden on the social assistance system of the host Member State.[114]

After an analysis of the jurisprudence it can be said that there is a 'teleological twist underlying the *Dano* judgment'[115] which is revealed in the adaptation of the objective of the Citizens' Directive 2004/38 to fit the purpose of the decision. For example, in *Ziolkowski*[116] and in *Brey*[117] the Citizens' Directive 2004/38 aimed to facilitate and strengthen 'the exercise of the primary and individual right to move and reside freely within the territory of the Member States'. However, in *Dano* the Directive, and in particular Article 7 (1) (b) 'seeks to prevent economically inactive Union citizens from using the host Member State's welfare system to fund their means of subsistence'.[118] In relation to this adaptation of the objective of the Citizens' Directive 2004/38, O'Brien highlights that 'the *Dano* judgment transformed Directive 2004/38 from an instrument to promote free movement into one to prevent benefit tourism'.[119]

At this stage it is necessary to link the *Dano* reasoning with the case of the unlawful stay of EU citizens residing in another Member State. As has been shown, there has been a gradual shift in the legal landscape and in the reasoning that the CJEU has resorted to in order to address the meaning of the unlawful stay of EU citizens. In earlier judgments (such as *Martinez Sala* and *Trojani*) the fact that there was uncertainty about the fulfilment of the supranational conditions for a legal stay was not enough to prevent the claimant from being covered by the principle of non-discrimination and consequently from being granted the benefit they claimed. In contrast, more recently this approach has changed and EU legal residence determines access to social assistance. As such, the CJEU has clearly taken a tougher approach and clarified that the conditions imposed by EU law to reside legally in another Member State are essential.

The combination of that approach with the Court's reasoning in the cases about access to social benefits, such as *Dano*, has made 'legal residence' a *conditio sine*

[113] Para 34 of the judgment *Trojani* (n 77) and para 91 of the Case C-413/99 *Baumbast and R. v Secretary of State for the Home Department*, [2002], EU:C:2002:493.
[114] Para 74 of the judgment *Dano* (n 108).
[115] Thym (n 33) 25.
[116] Para 37 of the judgment *Ziolkowski* (n 104).
[117] Para 53 of the judgment *Brey* (n 36).
[118] Para 76 of the judgment *Dano* (n 108) and Thym (n 33) 25.
[119] C O'Brien, 'Civis Capitalist Sum: Class as the New Guiding Principle of EU Movement Rights' (2016) 53 *Common Market Law Review* 951.

qua non in order to enjoy equality under EU law. To return to the central question, namely what this says about the unlawfulness of the stay of EU citizens in another Member State, a number of implications of this approach are significant as we will see in the following section. The most relevant has to be the fact that this reasoning of the Court leaves open the possibility of the existence of a category of Union Citizens who are 'simply present' within the territory of the host Member State. As Shuibhne points out this allows for the proliferation of '*tolerated* citizen[s] who [are] not expelled from a host State but [are] not supported there either'.[120]

In other words, the Court's jurisprudence does not cure the situation of those EU citizens who move freely within the Schengen Area, without residing lawfully within the territory of the host Member State and instead are 'simply present',[121] who have limited access to solidarity and to equality on the grounds of the burden that they may, theoretically, represent. The Court's case law produced a qualitative shift from a Treaty-based residence right, for example in the *Baumbast* decision to the 'generalization and hardening of the conditions, limits, and duties of Union citizenship',[122] in the most recent decisions such as *Dano.*[123]

C. Procedural, Substantive and Political Consequences of EU Citizens' Supranational Illegal Stay

Situations of unlawfulness of an EU citizen's stay in a host Member State are regulated by a combination of norms and governance levels. Treaty provisions and secondary legislation on citizenship, free movement and national legislation transpose these rules and impose conditions to be granted a residence permit or access a social benefit, without becoming an 'unreasonable burden' as shown above. EU legislation and the Court dealing with the unlawful stay of EU citizens have left considerable discretion for Member States to shape their view of this type of illegality. A particularly relevant aspect is the special interplay between national laws and EU immigration law. One commentator has recently labelled the interplay between EU and national law as 'colliding legal worlds'.[124] When two legal systems function in parallel, it is not surprising that areas of friction arise and the implementation of EU immigration law at the national level is one such area.[125]

The following analysis focuses on the consequences of a Union citizen's unlawful stay at three levels: (i) the procedural consequences of unlawfulness of EU citizen's

[120] Nic Shuibhne (n 53) 926.

[121] Nic Shuibhne and Shaw (n 72) 90.

[122] Nic Shuibhne (n 53) 926.

[123] O'Brien (n 119) 946.

[124] J Shaw and N Miller, 'When Legal Worlds Collide: An Exploration of What Happens When EU Free Movement Law Meets UK Immigration Law' (2013) 38 *European Law Review*.

[125] ibid, 9 and for an example of the aftermath of the *Zambrano* case at the national level see O'Brien (n 27) 1652.

stay in another Member State; (ii) the substantive consequences of unlawfulness of EU citizen's stay in another Member State and (iii) the political consequences of unlawfulness of EU citizen's stay in another Member State.

i. Procedural Consequences of Unlawfulness of EU Citizen's Stay in another Member State

The procedural implications that arise from EU citizens exercising their free movement rights are intertwined with the level of protection they are granted in the host Member State, as mentioned above in relation to the causes of unlawfulness.[126] The four most relevant procedural moments are now interrelated with the unlawfulness of a Union citizen, each will be considered in turn.

a. Administrative Formalities

When an EU citizen's residence in another Member State has a duration of more than three months the host Member State has the option to require the registration of that individual with the national authorities in accordance with article 8(1) of the Citizens' Directive 2004/38. Within the scope of this Directive compulsory administrative formalities required of EU citizens who migrate to another Member State have a purely declaratory role and 'may no under circumstance be made precondition for the exercise of a right …'.[127] This has been stressed in the early jurisprudence of the CJEU[128] and is clear from the wording of the relevant articles of the Citizens' Directive 2004/38 such as Articles 5(5), 8(2) and 9(3).

As such, the main aim of the fulfilment of these formal requirements imposed by domestic law is to prove the existence of rights granted to EU citizens by EU law.[129] National authorities may carry out checks in order to guarantee compliance with registration or other administrative formalities[130] and to resolve issues of evidence that may arise regarding one's right of residence in another Member State.[131] Proportionate sanctions may be imposed whenever there is a violation of such administrative formalities.[132]

b. Detention

The right to free movement and residence enjoyed by all EU citizens implies that any detention of an EU citizen with a view to subsequent expulsion is an *a priori*

[126] See subsection i. Sources and Causes of EU Citizens' Unlawful Stay, this chapter.
[127] Art 25 of the Citizens' Directive 2004/38.
[128] *Royer* judgment (n 63), para 33.
[129] For example see: ibid, paras 31–33, Case C-215/03, *Oulane*, [2005], EU:C:2005:95, paras 17–18.
[130] Art 26 of the Citizens' Directive 2004/38.
[131] See *Oulane* judgment (n 129) para 22, and Case C-459/99, *MRAX* [2002], EU:C:2002:461, para 79. See also Guild, Peers and Tomkin (n 18) 242–43.
[132] *Oulane* judgment (n 129) para 38.

violation of that fundamental freedom.[133] The lack of a valid identity card or passport may not be used as a reason to detain an EU citizen as the CJEU highlighted in the *Oulane* and *MRAX* cases.[134] In the *Oulane* decision the Court stressed that detention could only be justifiable:

> on an express derogating provision, such as Article 8 of Directive 73/148, which allows Member States to place restrictions on the right of residence of nationals of other Member States in so far as such restrictions are justified on grounds of public policy, public security or public health.[135]

If national authorities do not prove that the restriction on free movement is based on a threat to public policy, public security or public health the detention of an EU citizen would not be in conformity with EU law. This does not mean that Member States may not impose other penalties 'comparable to those which apply to similar national infringements and are proportionate'.[136]

There are two values that guide the application of penalties to unlawfully-staying EU citizens: respect for their freedom of movement and the proportionality of the sanctions applied. This balancing exercise has an impact with regard to the regulation of illegality in the sense that it contributes to the creation of a category of EU citizens who are unlawfully staying in the host Member States. To elaborate, a person who is unlawfully staying in another Member State, for instance due to lack of sufficient resources, may have their access to social benefits restricted (especially since the Court's ruling in the *Dano* case[137]) but this person may not be detained for expulsion if they do not represent a threat to public policy, public security or public health.

c. Expulsion

In the context of EU law and in particular with regards to intra-EU migration, expulsion is considered to be a 'measure that can seriously harm persons who … have become genuinely integrated into the host Member State'.[138] An expulsion decision is the legal consequence for illegally-staying third-country nationals[139] as it is for unlawfully-staying EU citizens although not automatically and only in exceptional circumstances.[140] Taking into consideration that free movement of persons is a cornerstone of the EU the Commission and the CJEU have clarified that 'provisions granting that freedom must be given a broad interpretation,

[133] Art 45 TFEU.
[134] Para 44 of the *Oulane* judgment (n 129).
[135] ibid, para 41 and Case C-388/01 *Commission v Italy*, [2003], EU:C:2003:30, para 19.
[136] Para 38 of the *Oulane* judgment (n 129) and see also Case C-378/97 *Wijsenbeek* [1999], EU:C:1999:439, para 44.
[137] See subsection I.B.iv.
[138] Recital 22 of the Citizens Directive' 2004/38.
[139] Art 6 of the Return Directive.
[140] Arts 27 and 28 of the Citizens' Directive 2004/38.

whereas derogations from that principle must be interpreted strictly'.[141] This illustrates that expulsions of EU citizens are designed to be exceptional measures acceptable only in exceptional circumstances. Whilst Member States retain the power to expel individuals from their territory, EU law and the CJEU have not left Union citizens residing in a host Member State completely unprotected.[142]

The Citizens' Directive 2004/38 introduced expulsion on the grounds of public policy, public security and public health of the host Member State and a proportionality test included in Article 28 (1) to avoid unlawful expulsions from host Member States.[143] When an EU citizen or their family members are permanently residing in the host Member State the threshold for expulsion is higher, being only possible 'on serious grounds of public policy or public security'.[144] After having resided for 10 years in the host Member State, or if the individual is a minor, an expulsion decision may only be taken if that decision is based on imperative grounds of public security, which represents an even higher layer of protection against expulsion.

The general regime of expulsion established by the Citizens' Directive 2004/38 includes the prohibition on expelling an EU citizen whose identity card or passport has expired even if that was the document which served the purpose of registration.[145] Furthermore, the mere fact that an EU citizen or their family member applied to the social assistance system of the host Member State should not automatically mean the expulsion of that citizen of the Union.[146] Interestingly, this mention in Article 14 (3) of the Citizens' Directive of the recourse to the social assistance system of the host Member State not having as an automatic consequence the expulsion of the person is the only mention of expulsion based on the lack of sufficient resources that can be found in the general expulsion regime of the Directive. The absence of a clear regime for the expulsion of EU citizens who became a burden to the social assistance system of the host Member State,[147] and who lose their right to reside on the territory of another Member State for more than three months, raises interesting questions. For instance, questions arise as to whether there exists a harmonised regime for the expulsion of these EU citizens or whether they are to be tolerated within the host Member State.

Neither the wording of the Citizens' Directive 2004/38 nor the Commission Communication on guidance for better transposition and application of the

[141] Commission, Communication to the European Parliament and the Council on guidance for better transposition and application of Directive 2004/38/EC on the right of citizens of the Union and their family members to move and reside freely within the territory of the Member States, COM(2009) 313 final, Case C-139/85 *Kempf* [1986], EU:C:1986:223, para 13 and *Jipa* judgment (n 101), para 23.

[142] D Kostakopoulou, 'When EU Citizens become Foreigners' (2014) 20 *European Law Journal* 457.

[143] JS Gehring, 'Roma and the Limits of Free Movement in the European Union' in Willem Maas (ed), *Democratic Citizenship and the Free Movement of People* (Leiden, Martinus Nijhoff Publishers, 2013) 159.

[144] Art 28 (2) of Citizens' Directive 2004/38.

[145] Art 15 (2) of the Citizens' Directive 2004/38.

[146] ibid, Art 14 (3).

[147] ibid, Art 7 (1) b).

Directive include a provision that expressly states the procedure for expulsion of EU citizens who have become an 'unreasonable burden' on the social assistance system of the host Member State.[148]

Whilst the Directive is not straightforward regarding the consequences of an unlawfully-staying EU citizen (in terms of financial burden) in a Member State, the Court in recent jurisprudence on the interpretation of Article 28 of the Citizens' Directive provided some clarification.[149] Recent decisions have dealt with the interpretation of concepts included in the Citizens' Directive 2004/38 such as 'imperative grounds of public security' and 'serious grounds of public policy and public security'.[150] Given that the Directive clarifies that these grounds shall not serve economic ends they are irrelevant in the context of expelling an EU citizen who before being granted permanent residence has become unemployed and, for example, does not have sufficient resources to live in the host Member State.[151] Furthermore, if one compares the cases on expulsion and the aforementioned cases of *Bidar* and *Trojani*, there is no mention in the latter to the general expulsion regime.

The way the expulsion regime is designed to operate correlates directly with the degree of stability of the right to reside. In fact, the Citizens' Directive 2004/28 addresses the expulsion of EU citizens from the view of the protection that they are granted, which is increasingly stronger depending on the period of time that the migrant has lived in the host Member State, their age, health, family and economic situation, social and cultural integration and the links with the country of origin, in accordance with Article 28 of the Citizens' Directive 2004/38. Recent CJEU jurisprudence has tolerated the deportation of EU citizens from one Member State to another, for example in the *PI* and *Tsakouridis* cases, which some commentators have described as undermining the 'core of EU citizenship'.[152]

This notwithstanding, when one looks at the rules for the expulsion of EU citizens who have become an unreasonable burden for the Member State it is clear that there is not yet such a regime implemented in these cases. In fact expulsions may occur on these grounds but the practical implications are questionable. The FIDE Report highlights this, stating that there is 'little evidence that ready recourse to expulsion occurs where Union citizens cannot demonstrate compliance with the conditions in Article 7—whatever current political and media rhetoric

[148] Communication from the Commission to the European Parliament and the Council on guidance for better transposition and application of Directive 2004/38/EC on the right of citizens of the Union and their family members to move and reside freely within the territory of the Member States, COM(2009) 313 final, Brussels, 2009.

[149] See, eg: the *Tsakouridis* judgment (n 7) and the *PI* judgment (n 11).

[150] See *Tsakouridis* judgment, ibid, paras 39 and 40. See also on this topic Craig and De Búrca (n 81)756–59 and L Azoulai and S Coutts, 'Restricting Union Citizens' Residence Rights on Grounds of Public Security. Where Union Citizenship and AFSJ meet' (2013) 50 *Common Market Law Review*.

[151] S Peers, 'Can Unemployed EU Citizens be Expelled and Banned from Re-entry?', EU Law Analysis, http://eulawanalysis.blogspot.pt/2014/03/can-unemployed-eu-citizens-be-expelled.htm, (2014).

[152] Kochenov and Pirker (n 46) 390.

might suggest'.[153] This is illustrative of the creation of a legal liminal space where EU citizens are unlawfully staying in the host Member State and depend on the national authorities' interpretation of the EU procedural rules to either be granted a residence permit or be issued an expulsion order. The creation of this limbo position by EU and national law is also motivated by the fact that no exclusion orders may be issued in this case as will be shown in the following section.

d. Exclusion Orders

'Exclusion orders' are equivalent to the Return Directive's 'entry bans'[154] for the purposes of the Citizens' Directive 2004/38. After an expulsion decision is taken against an EU citizen who was unlawfully staying, on the grounds of public policy, public security or public health,[155] the host Member State may also issue an exclusion order to prevent that person from re-entering the country for a certain period of time. The Citizens' Directive 2004/38 in Article 32 only regulates the right to ask for their termination and leaves its definition for national discretion. Article 32 also leaves to national authorities the authority to interpret whether a 'reasonable period' has passed for the Union citizen excluded to submit an application for lifting the exclusion order.

The relevance of this procedural step relates to the absence of borders in the Schengen area. For instance, one may ask how, in an EU mostly without internal borders, can the current regime expulsion of Union citizens who become an unreasonable burden on the host Member fit with the non-existence of exclusion orders for these cases. Let us illustrate this with a practical example. Mrs May is a British national and has been living in the Algarve in Portugal for more than three months without sufficient resources and without sickness insurance cover, in violation of Article 7(1)(b) of the Citizens' Directive 2004/38. On the grounds of having become an unreasonable burden on the Portuguese social assistance system the national authorities issue Mrs May an expulsion order. However, there is no legal basis to simultaneously issue an exclusion order. As such, Mrs May could potentially move to Andalucía in Spain temporarily and move back to the Algarve as her right to entry to the Portuguese territory would not be limited by an exclusion order. This example shows how the expulsion regime of EU citizens unlawfully staying in other Member States is designed and implemented and how it contributes to the proliferation of limbo situations of migrants who may simply stay within the territory of other Member States without a clear status or procedural consequences.

The procedural dimension of the unlawfulness of residence of an EU citizen is characterised by the declaratory role of 'having papers' as well as registration and

153 Nic Shuibhne and Shaw (n 72) 93.

154 Art 3 (6) of the Return Directive: '"Entry ban" means an administrative or judicial decision or act prohibiting entry into and stay on the territory of the Member States for a specified period, accompanying a return decision.'

155 Arts 27 and 29 of the Citizens' Directive 2004/38.

by the discretion of national authorities in particular with regard to the interpretation and definition of certain terms included in the Citizens' Directive 2004/38. By contrasting these findings with the regulation of unlawfulness within EU citizenship, it is clear that the procedural regime of expulsion allows for the multiplication of liminal statuses of Union citizens who may stay in another Member State without a legal status, a clear expulsion process and, as we shall see next, access to social assistance.

ii. Substantive Consequences of Unlawfulness of an EU Citizen's Stay in another Member State

With regard to the substance of the status of unlawfully-staying EU citizens living in another Member State, it is crucial to assess what part of the EU citizenship is more affected by the illegality of one's stay, in particular the stability of the right to reside (and the enjoyment of social benefits) in another Member State. The conditions necessary to legalise a migrant's stay are imposed both nationally and supranationally and are thus respected at both levels of governance. The dynamics that result from this shared responsibility for EU citizenship and its effects raise important questions.[156] One of the most topical issues is that of what makes the right to reside in another Member State stable. Free movement of people and EU citizenship-related rights (for example the implementation of the Citizens' Directive) have contributed to a more stable right to reside in another Member State, however as Kostakopoulou points out 'the security of residence of EU citizens remains insecure'.[157]

The right to reside somewhere is, with few exceptions, granted to those who are living legally within the territory of the EU. With regard to the right to reside in the territory of an EU Member State it is important to distinguish the right per se established by law and the degree of stability of the enjoyment of that right. The stability of the right to reside is directly related to the issue discussed above in relation to supranational legal residence being a condition for solidarity in section I.B.iv.

The status of an EU citizen from the perspective of the stability of their right to reside ranges from being legally staying on the territory of the host Member State (and as such having the most stable right to reside) to being unlawfully staying with unstable residence and liable to expulsion. The aforementioned instability can be caused by different factors such as: (i) lack of financial resources, (ii) recourse to social benefits, (iii) the temporary nature of the presence of the migrant within the Member State and (iv) a criminal record.

The stability of the right to reside in another Member State, or the lack of it, is responsible for creating 'in-between' statuses: EU citizens who are unlawfully

[156] Nic Shuibhne and Shaw (n 72) 66.
[157] Kostakopoulou (n 142) 458.

staying in the host Member State but who are not issued an expulsion decision. The FIDE reports, and in particular the report that focus on the UK case, has raised concerns about the issue of the stability of residency of an EU citizen national of another Member State in the UK.[158] It was clear from this report that there was a category of Union citizens who were 'simply present' in the UK as a result of their lack of resources and not fulfilling Article 7 of the 2004/38 Directive.[159] The report goes further and explains that:

> That status does not confer any right of residence in the UK under either EU or national law. Such persons are deemed subject to UK immigration control and, therefore, liable to removal by the Secretary of State.[160]

Although these migrants' right to reside is not stable their de facto deportability is doubtful as the Report shows. This is so for two reasons; first these cases are only rarely dealt with in court.[161] Second, even when such cases are dealt with by national courts, such 'simply present' migrants are usually left in legal limbo without a formal protection status. In the words of the FIDE report with regard to the situation in the UK these migrants are most often granted 'a non-status without any rights attached to it and in a position which is liable for expulsion by the Secretary of State'.[162] The idea of a 'non-status' mentioned in the FIDE report is similar to the atypical status of non-removability of third-country nationals which is the object of the analysis of chapter three.[163] In both cases (in most Member States), the migrants in these situations are simply present with no rights granted, liable to expulsion, but not actually expelled in the majority of the cases. However, in the case of EU citizens there is no obstacle to removal contrary to non-removable migrants. Unlawfully-staying EU citizens are in this scenario: EU citizens within the EU with an unstable right to reside in the host Member State, a precarious social status and an unlawful stay.

The case law discussed in the previous section highlighted the fact that this category of migrants has become more evident since the *Dano* and *Alimanovic* decisions which have brought a clear shift in the reasoning of the early cases that dealt with unlawfulness of stay for lack of resources such as *Martinez Sala* and *Trojani*. As such, since the *Dano* decision the liminal legal space where 'present but not lawfully resident in the host State, under EU or national law'[164] has increased. In addition to the national practice of allowing the simple presence of certain

[158] T Horsley and S Reynolds, 'The United Kingdom—Citizenship within Directive 2004/38 EC—Stability of Residence for Union Citizens and their Family Members)', in Neergaard, Jacqueson and Holst-Christensen (n 72) 839.

[159] ibid, 846.

[160] ibid, 846.

[161] ibid, 846 and *Chief Adjudication Officer v Wolke* (HL) [1997] 1 WLR 1640.

[162] ibid, 846 and *Kaczmarek v Secretary of State for Work and Pensions* [2008] EWCA Civ 1310. See here also *Abdirahman v Secretary of State* [2007] EWCA Civ 657.

[163] See Nic Shuibhne (n 53) 934, for more on the concept of liminality and status-less in relation to EU citizens.

[164] Nic Shuibhne and Shaw (n 72) 92.

unlawfully-staying EU citizens by virtue of Article 7 of the 2004/38 Directive, the Court has made legal residence a *conditio sine quo non* to enjoy equality in access to social assistance. These EU citizens may then be left to live within this non-status created not only by national legislation and decisions but also by the supranational interpretation of the Citizens' Directive 2004/38.

The easier deportability of EU citizens from the host Member State of residence is the most significant impact on the fundamental status of EU citizenship, creating the risk of this status turning into 'just an abstraction'.[165] In the words of Kochenov: '[t]he essential issue to consider in this context is not where one is removed, but residence security as a citizen at the place where one's life-project evolves'.[166]

It is important for the analysis of the unlawfulness that EU citizens may fall into to understand the in-between statuses such as the 'simply present' categories of migrants as they define what illegality is within EU citizenship: a legal phenomenon that affects the stability of residence of Union citizens and impacts upon the enjoyment of their rights in another Member State.

The de facto expulsion of EU citizens in the case of lack of sufficient resources seems to be secondary for some Member States and the primary sanction is the denial of access to social benefits. Consequently, perhaps in trying to protect the very essence of that status that was meant to be the fundamental status of citizens of the EU, the way the unlawfulness of the stay of these migrants is addressed results in more fragmentation within citizenship and the creation of liminal legal statuses.[167] The next chapter is devoted to the analysis of another liminal legal space created by both EU and national law, relating to third-country nationals. This illustrates one of the premises which is transversal to the entire book, that of the traditional legal binary of legal and illegal not being the most suitable for the conceptualisation of illegality adopted in EU law.

iii. Political Consequences of Unlawfulness of EU Citizens' Stay in another Member State

Another important aspect that characterises the dynamics between supranational and national views on an EU citizen's unlawful stay relates to the problematic national transposition and interpretation of the Citizens' Directive 2004/38 and its political impact at a Member State level.[168] This is a point to be addressed as '[l]egal discussions of major social phenomena cannot proceed merely by reference to trends in laws and court decisions. The law provides an interesting picture,

[165] Kostakopoulou (n 142) 462.
[166] Kochenov and Pirker (n 46) 378.
[167] Nic Shuibhne (n 53) 934.
[168] S Carrera and A Faure Atger, 'Implementation of Directive 2004/38 in the context of EU Enlargement' A proliferation of different forms of citizenship, CEPS Special Report, 9 April 2009, 1.

and it is necessary to understand what that picture tells us'.[169] That having been said, consideration of the specifically political consequences generated requires particular attention and expertise which fall outwith the scope of this book.

Nevertheless, a number of striking examples of this phenomenon can be cited as being illustrative of the kind of political consequences generated. First, the case of the discriminatory evictions and expulsions from France of Romanian and Bulgarian Roma shows us that the discomfort in associating EU citizens with illegality does not apply to all the citizens of the EU. Sigona reminds us that the Roma may be citizens of the EU 'much like the Swedes or the Danes (including numerically), and not some kind of alien body from a remote elsewhere'.[170]

Notwithstanding the fact that in 2010 the French Government received an ultimatum from the Vice-President of the Commission Viviene Reding to adapt its national law in this regard, in practice it does not appear to have changed considerably. In fact these practices have continued and increased under President Hollande's government.[171] Whilst the Citizens' Directive 2004/38 has been formally transposed, the main issue lies with administrative and law enforcement practices relating to evictions and expulsions of migrants which have not changed.[172] The expulsion of Roma who are Union citizens is an example which proves that the illegality of EU citizens may not be avoided as the CJEU did in early cases such as *Martinez Sala* and in fact the lack of clarity regarding what it encompasses allows, at the national level, Member States to construct their own view of illegality. This potentially threatens the bases and the normative assumptions that define EU citizenship.[173] Futhermore, there are important legal issues that arise from this scenario. The violation of non-discrimination on the grounds of nationality and race[174] and no collective expulsion[175] are both violations of EU law and international human rights law.

[169] B Garth, 'Migrant Workers and Rights of Mobility in EC and USA' in Cappelletti M, Seccombe M and Weiler J (eds), *Integration Through Law Europe and the American Federal Experience*, vol 1 Methods, Tools and Institutions, Book 3 Forces and Potential for a European Identity (Berlin, Walter de Gruyter, 1986), 87.

[170] N Sigona, 'EU Citizenship, Roma Mobility and Anti-Gypsyism: Time for Reframing the Debate?' in Bridget Anderson and Michael Keith (eds), *Migration: The COMPAS Anthology* (Oxford, COMPAS, 2014) 146.

[171] S Carrera, 'The Framing of the Roma as Abnormal EU Citizens—Assessing European Politics on Roma Evictions and Expulsions in France' in Guild, Gortázar Rotaeche and Kostakopoulou (n 92) 33.

[172] ibid, 48 and H O'Nions, 'Roma Expulsions and Discrimination: The Elephant in Brussels' (2011) 13 *European Journal of Migration and Law* 361, 369.

[173] Carrera (n 171) 60.

[174] See: Arts 18 TFEU and 21 of the EU Charter of Fundamental Rights, the Council Directive 2000/43/EC of 29 June 2000 implementing the principle of equal treatment between persons irrespective of racial or ethnic origin, [2000] OJ L 180 (Racial Equality Directive) and Art 14 of the ECHR and Art 1 of the Protocol No 12 to the Convention for the Protection of Human Rights and Fundamental Freedoms.

[175] See: Art 19 of the Charter of Fundamental Rights of the European Union, and Art 27 of the Citizens Directive 2004/38 and Art 4 of Protocol No 4 to the Convention for the Protection of Human Rights and Fundamental Freedoms.

Second, the right to free movement has recently been threatened by the domestic policies of some Member States. In an attempt to tackle the unemployment caused by the financial crisis of 2008 and the risk of benefit tourism Member States such as the UK, Germany and Belgium have been taking measures to more narrowly define the concept of 'worker' and have deported higher numbers of EU citizens who have migrated to their territories.[176] These policy choices are relevant for the purposes of this chapter because they show that despite the significant discretion that Member States have in determining the conditions of the right to reside, in recent times this discretion has pushed the limits of EU law. Such domestic practices risk affecting the essence of EU citizenship rights and *in extremis* may result in the position that O'Brien has recently described, namely that in which market citizenship and the 'worker-commodity' is becoming increasingly more widely accepted in the context of EU law in this area,[177] and '[w]elfare nationalism is washing away the traces of EU citizenship.'[178]

Finally, with Brexit the optimistic 'EU–take' on the status and rights-enhancing potential of EU citizenship has come under pressure. There appears to be a 'push-back' driven by national political elites and apparently absorbed by the CJEU in certain cases.[179] The UK's political decision of leaving the EU will directly impact on the development of the concept of EU citizenship and will, necessarily, develop the contours of the status of unlawfully-staying EU citizens.

III. CONCLUSION

Although illegality is not commonly thought of in relation to EU citizens' residence status, it is without doubt a possible legal status for mobile EU citizens living in another Member State. Secondary legislation, case law and the literature focus on the derogations to free movement but do not elaborate the consequences for the legal status of intra-EU migrants. In fact the concept of citizenship and principles such as non-discrimination have allowed the Court to focus on urban or municipal citizenship, leaving significant discretion to Member States to define who is illegally staying. The lack of a supranational definition of what illegality of stay means for EU citizens has consequences at the national level: contradictory judicial decisions, and the possibility of targeting certain nationalities who are affected by tougher implementation of EU rules, making them more liable to become illegally staying in another Member State, such as Romanian and Bulgarian nationals.

Two concepts were examined in chapter two. The first is EU citizenship and the second is illegality, which, in the words of Menjívar is peculiarly powerful but at

[176] See the EU Parliamentary question for written answer to the Commission, 15 January 2014.

[177] O'Brien (n 27) 1681.

[178] O'Brien (n 119) 937.

[179] Case C-308/14, *European Commission v United Kingdom of Great Britain and Northern Ireland*, [2016], EU:C:2016:436.

present an 'amorphous legal concept'.[180] The definition of illegality in relation to EU citizens challenges the very bases of EU law such as free movement—a right that strives to avoid situations where an EU citizen can be expelled. This chapter questioned whether this concept is broad enough to include EU citizens that violate the conditions to live in another Member State. At the EU level the lack of clarity of the reasons that would effectively lead to the expulsion of EU citizens, other than those stated in Article 27 of the Citizens' Directive 2004/38, 'remains a deficiency'[181] and may have an impact on the development of the concept of EU citizenship. The contradictory decisions at the European level are repeated at the domestic level and the uncertainties about the scope of an EU citizen's illegal stay give plenty of discretion to Member States to implement policies and legislation that affect one of the biggest assets of being a citizen of the Union: free movement and residence rights.

[180] C Menjívar and D Kanstroom (eds), *Constructing Immigrant "Illegality"—Critiques, Experiences and Responses* (Cambridge, Cambridge Univervisty Press, 2014) 1.
[181] O'Nions (n 172) 371.

3

Non-removable Migrants in the EU

I. INTRODUCTION

THE 'HIGHLY AMBIGUOUS relationship between the individual and the state as regard to legality'[1] is a corollary of the undetermined distinction between regular and irregular status. In practice the distinction between legality and illegality in EU law is not so clear-cut.[2] The first subsection of this chapter addresses the core aspects of the issue of non-removability of irregular migrants within the EU, which is a phenomenon that demonstrates the unsuitability of the traditional binary of legal and illegal. The chapter then examines what is a 'non-removable migrant' before the causes of the aforementioned legal limbo that results from the lack of a clear distinction between legality and illegality are assessed. Last the chapter reflects on whether, from an EU law perspective, there already exists a status for migrants that fall in a legal limbo as the one addressed here.

This chapter first analyses this complex category of migrants whose status is not defined or regulated under EU law; the heterogeneous category of non-removable migrants. Regulation of non-removable persons raises several concerns and poses a number of questions in need of an urgent answer. One such question relates to the absence of a mechanism at the EU level to directly address these grey areas (where the distinction between legality and illegality is unclear), whether despite this absence there is an EU law protection status for these migrants. Further, the national responses to the same phenomenon vary widely from Member State to Member State. In a nutshell the following subsection poses the questions; is there a link between EU law and the creation of these legal grey areas? And how do national laws fill the gap left open by EU law?

[1] E Guild, 'Who is an Irregular Migrant' in B Bogusz, A Szyszcak (ed), *Irregular Migration and Human Rights: Theorectical, European and International Perspectives, Immigration and Asylum and Policy in Europe* (Leiden, Martinus Nijhoff Publishers, 2004), 16.

[2] F Duvell, 'Paths into Irregularity: The Legal and Political Construction of Irregular Migration' (2011) 13 *European Journal of Migration and Law* 275, 292.

II. THE DEFINITION AND THE CAUSES OF THE NON-REMOVABILITY OF IRREGULAR MIGRANTS IN EU LAW

A. The Definition of Non-removability of Irregular Migrants in EU Law

Non-removable migrants are third-country nationals who, despite their status as irregular migrants, cannot (yet) be removed from EU territory as a result of legal, humanitarian, technical or even policy-related reasons. Non-removable migrants are a diverse group of persons with one common feature: whilst national immigration authorities acknowledge their presence, no measures are taken to deport them. Non-removable migrants possess a transitory and indeterminate status which can last for as long as the impediment to removal lasts. Non-removability is a consequence of stretching the category of people who fall within the category of illegality or irregularity.[3] 'Semi-legal',[4] 'liminal',[5] and 'a-legal'[6] are some of the terms that have been expressed in the literature to describe this unclear legal status. All of these perceptions have their merits in trying to understand such a complex phenomenon from various angles, however there is not yet a study that focuses solely on EU law, non-removability and its articulation with the concept of illegality. The present chapter attempts to fill this gap.

An analysis of the category of non-removable migrants is necessary in order to clarify some of the many half-truths that characterise the discourse regarding deportation, legality and illegality. As Basilien-Gainche has stated:

> the 'unmovable-returnees' are numerous, revealing the 'deportation gap' that exists between the number of migrants detained in order to be removed, and the number of those who are actually eventually deported.[7]

Furthermore it is important to distinguish between illegality and non-removability as two different concepts, even if the latter is included in the former. Non-removable migrants are illegally-staying third-country nationals, though national authorities tolerate their stay in the host Member State. In contrast not all illegally-staying third-country nationals are non-removable. Non-removability is a less broad concept that shares the same, although delayed, possible legal consequences as illegality: regularisation or return to the country of origin. The proliferation of statuses of irregular migrants is part of the process of 'illegalization of people's

[3] C Costello, *The Human Rights of Migrants and Refugees in European Law* (Oxford, Oxford University Press, 2015) 66.

[4] A Kubal, 'Conceptualizing Semi-Legality in Migration Research' (2013) 47 *Law & Society Review* 555, 556.

[5] C Menjívar, 'Liminal Legality: Salvadoran and Guatemalan Immigrants' Lives in the United States1' (2006) 111 *American Journal of Sociology* 999.

[6] H Lindahl, 'A-Legality: Postnationalism and the Question of Legal Boundaries' (2010) 73 *The Modern Law Review* 30.

[7] ML Basilien-Gainche, 'Immigration Detention under the Return Directive: The Shadowed Lights' (2015) *European Journal of Migration and Law* 17 104, 125. See also D Acosta Arcarazo, 'The Charter, Detention and Possible Regularization of Migrants in an Irregular Situation under the Returns Directive: *Mahdi*' (2015) 52 *Common Market Law Review* 1361–78, 1368.

movement' that Rigo and Karakayali correctly consider to have been ignored compared to the evolution of the rights of legally-residing migrants.[8]

Both EU and national law, alone or combined, may generate the situations of non-removability. However, the effects of this scenario are not foreseen or comprehensively regulated by EU legislation (thus far), falling essentially within the scope of domestic law. It should be noted that migrants in this situation are partially included and partially recognised in the administrative and economic life of the host Member State.[9] Most of the time, even though they are ordered to remain within a certain territory, non-removable migrants live without formal authorisation to stay or reside within that territory, thus between the irregularity of their de facto status and the regularity of their tolerated presence in the host Member State's territory. Despite their tolerated (formal or de facto) and officially known presence on EU territory they are part of the category of illegally staying third-country nationals.[10]

Irregular migration is a type of migration status that is irregular due to violation of migration rules (having no regular status in the host country of residence), be it visa, work or residence permit or asylum law-related. It must also be noted that the term illegal relates to a situation or condition under which migrants are living (such as illegal working conditions or the illegality of their stay) rather than defining the status of immigrant.[11] Thus, in short, an irregular migrant is someone who has no legal residence status.[12] The non-removable migrant status fits in the irregular migration category just described, however the situation changes if national authorities grant them a temporary residence permit which, consequently, also grants them a legal status.[13]

B. EU Law as a Source of Non-removability of Irregular Migrants

Non-removability may be a consequence of the fact that EU law does not comprehensively regulate this issue, rather this is left to Member States to address in their own domestic laws. Nevertheless, it is crucial to understand the origins of

[8] S Karakayali and E Rigo, 'Mapping the European space of circulation' in N De Genova and N Peutz (eds), *The Deportation Regime* (Durham, Duke University Press, 2010) 138.

[9] L Azoulai, 'A comment on Ruiz Zambrano judgement: A genuine European integration', European Union Democracy Observatory on Citizenship, (2012), (http://eudo-citizenship.eu/search-results/457-a-comment-on-the-ruiz-zambrano-judgment-a-genuine-european-integration).

[10] ibid.

[11] A Triandafyllidou, *Irregular Migration in Europe: Myths and Realities* (Farnham, Ashgate Publishing Company, 2010) 3.

[12] For example: to work with a tourist visa or an EU citizen who does not comply with the Citizens' Directive 2004/38 conditions.

[13] As happens for example in Cyprus, where migrants who cannot yet be removed enjoy a temporary residence permit, entitled the 'pink card', European Union Agency for Fundamental Rights, *Fundamental rights of migrants in an irregular situation in the European Union, Comparative Report* (http://fra.europa.eu/en/publication/2012/fundamental-rights-migrants-irregular-situation-european-union, 2011) 37.

non-removability and to what extent EU legislation is responsible for the creation of this category of migrants. Non-removability occurs when a return decision is delayed for exceptional reasons resulting in an irregular migrant who should have been returned being prevented from doing so by the host immigration authorities of the Member State. The REGINE study pointed out that non-removability is closely linked to the asylum system, as many asylum seekers who have had their claims rejected or subsidiary protection end up living in a protracted situation of non-removability.[14] Non-removability is a consequential situation from the point of view of EU law. The Return Directive is the main, but not the only, EU framework dealing with returning illegally-staying third-country nationals and plays a central role in the issue of non-removability.

Irregular migrants, removable or otherwise, are essentially a 'by-product of the laws made to control migration and of labour market exigencies',[15] and that is why examination of EU legislation on these matters is an important step towards understanding the causes of non-removability. The mechanism of postponement of removal of irregular migrants contemplated in the Return Directive is a major cause of non-removability situations. Additionally, the same Directive does not contemplate effective solutions to put an end to these protracted 'legal limbo' situations, apart from the attribution of an autonomous residence permit for compassionate, humanitarian or other reasons, given at any moment to Member States.[16]

The negotiations stage of the Return Directive has been the focus of controversy and discussion in relation not only to the European Institutions involved, but also among several scholars who consider it to lack transparency.[17] The Return Directive, which was adopted on 16 December 2008, primarily aims to set out common standards and procedures for returning illegally-staying third-country nationals.[18] Member States had two years to transpose the Directive and consequently by 24 December 2010 it should have already been implemented nationally. The central rule of the Return Directive is that Member States shall issue a return decision to any third-country national staying illegally on their

[14] M Baldwin-Edwards and A Kraler, 'Study on Practices in the Area of Regularisation of Illegally Staying Third-country Nationals in the Member States of the EU' in M Baldwin-Edwards and A Kraler (eds), *REGINE Regularisations in Europe* (Amsterdam, Pallas Publications, 2009) 55.

[15] D Kostakapoulou, 'Irregular Migration and Migration Theory: Making State Authority Less Relevant' in B Bogusz and others (eds), *Irregular Migration and Human Rights: Theorectical, European and International Perspectives* (Leiden, Martinus Nijhoff Publishers, 2004) 42. See also S Castles and M Miller, *The Age of Migration: International Population Movements in the Modern World* (London, Macmillan, 1993) 96.

[16] Art 6 (4) of the Return Directive.

[17] For a detailed view on the negotiations procedure: Fabian Lutz, *The Negotiations on the Return Directive* (Nijmegen, Wolf Legal Publishers, 2010) and Fabien Le Bot, 'La Directive "Retour": Directive de la Honte ou Progrès dans la construction d'une politique européenne en matière d'immigration?' in D Thym and F Snyder (eds), *Europe: Un continent d´immigration? Défis juridiques dans la construction de la Politque européenne de migration* (Brussels, Bruylant, 2011) 347–76.

[18] Recital 5 and Art 1 of the Return Directive.

territory.[19] The return decision shall provide an appropriate period for voluntary departure from seven up to 30 days, with some exceptions.[20] Once the period for voluntary departure expires or if it was not granted, Member States shall take the necessary measures to enforce the return.[21] In the text of the Directive there are, however, some exceptions to this rule, and it is these exceptions, which postpone removals, which are the causes for several cases of non-removability in the EU.[22]

The analysis focuses on the exceptions to the central rule in the Return Directive which are causes of non-removability: reasons for postponement of the removal of irregular migrants. Article 9 of the Return Directive concerning postponement of removal states that Member States shall postpone removal: a) when it violates the principle of non-refoulement or; b) for as long as a suspensory effect is granted in accordance with Article 13 (2). These are the only circumstances where a Member State has the duty to suspend a removal order and consequently they necessarily cause protracted cases of non-removability of irregular migrants. The content of Article 9 of the Return Directive was the object of discussion during the negotiations of the Directive.

Despite the Council's attempts to transform this article into a set of non-binding 'may' clauses,[23] as a result of the European Parliament's refusal to accept this approach the article is composed of two 'shall' clauses. Hence, as mentioned above, Member States are obliged to postpone an irregular migrant's removal in two situations; when it would violate the principle of non-refoulement,[24] and where there is a duty to delay the removal for as long as suspensory effect is granted in accordance with Article 13 (2) of the Return Directive, these are the compulsory causes of non-removability.[25] In addition, Member States may postpone removal taking into account the 'specific circumstances' of the individual case.[26] Physical state or mental capacity shall be taken into account in this latter case as well as technical reasons such as lack of transport capacity or failure of the removal for lack of identification, which are the optional causes of non-removability.[27]

With regard to the compulsory reasons to protract a third-country national's stay in the EU, in particular the prohibition on disrespecting the principle of non-refoulement, it is important to note that (when read together with Articles 5 and 4(4)(b) of the Return Directive) there is an express duty to respect the right of non-refoulement as interpreted as a principle of Community law. Articles 4(4)(b) and 5 Return Directive state that when implementing the Directive, Member States shall take due account of the best interests of the child, family life, the state

19 ibid, Art 6 (1).
20 ibid, Art 7.
21 ibid, Arts 7 (4) and 8 (1).
22 ibid, Art 9.
23 Lutz (n 17) 52.
24 Art 9 (1) a) of the Return Directive.
25 ibid, Art 9 (1) b).
26 ibid, Art 9 (2).
27 ibid, Art 9 (2) a) b).

of health of the migrant and shall respect the principle of non-refoulement. Whilst this obligation was already part of the EC asylum *acquis* regarding asylum seekers, what is the novel about the Return Directive regime is that it extends it to all illegally-staying irregular migrants living in the EU. As Lutz points out, the CJEU will have a margin of manoeuvre to develop its case law under this notion as the Directive does not address the definition of the non-refoulement principle.[28]

The principle of non-refoulement is generally defined as the 'cornerstone of international asylum law'.[29] The prohibition on refoulement binds States not to forcibly or indirectly return a person to their country of origin, or another country where there is a serious risk of becoming a victim of human rights violations. In recent times the protection of non-refoulement has been expanded beyond the scope of refugee law providing human rights protection to migrants under a removal procedure when there are 'substantial grounds' to believe that removal to a country would represent torture or 'irreparable harm' to the migrant.[30] The Return Directive expressly establishes the duty to comply with the UN Refugee Convention, the European Convention of Human Rights (hereafter ECHR) and the Charter of Fundamental Rights of the European Union.[31]

The UN Refugee Convention in Article 33 prohibits the return of refugees when their life or freedom would be at risk on the grounds of his race, religion, nationality or membership of a particular social group or political opinion. Nevertheless, whenever the refugee represents a danger to the security of the host country, or was convicted by a final judgment of a serious crime, they are no longer covered by the protection of Article 33 of the UN Refugee Convention. The European Court of Human Rights (hereafter ECtHR) interprets Article 3 ECHR concerning the prohibition of torture, degrading or inhuman treatment or punishment as covering the prohibition of refoulement.[32] This ECHR provision has a wider scope than the aforementioned provision of the UN Refugee Convention, provided that the activities practised by the migrant are not a criteria to determine whether she or he can benefit of the protection[33]

Furthermore, the ECtHR has expanded the interpretation of this principle to a certain extent. Article 2 ECHR (right to life) and Protocol no 6 (partial abolition

[28] Lutz (n 17) 53.

[29] Pieter Boeles, Maarten Den Heijer, Gerrie Lodder, Kees Wouters, *European Migration Law* (Antwerp, Intersentia, 2010) 253.

[30] S Grant, 'The Recognition of Migrants' Rights within the UN Human Rights System, The First 60 Years' in Marie-Bénédicte Dembour and Tobias Kelly (eds), *Are Human Rights For Migrants? Critical Reflections on the Status of Irregular Migrants in Europe and the United States.* (Abingdon, Routledge, 2011) 31. and UNHRC, 'General Comment 31: The Nature of the General Legal Obligation Imposed on States Parties' (29 March 2004) UN Doc CCPR/C/21/Rev.1/Add.13, para 12.

[31] Recitals 22, 23 and 24 of the Return Directive. UN General Assembly, Convention Relating to the Status of Refugees, 28 July 1951, Council of Europe, European Convention for the Protection of Human Rights and Fundamental Freedoms, as amended by Protocols Nos 11 and 14, 4 November 1950, Charter of Fundamental Rights of the European Union, 26 October 2012, 2012/C 326/02.

[32] *Soering v the United Kingdom*, ECHR (1989) App No 14038/88.

[33] *Saadi v Italy*, ECHR, (2008), App No 37201/06, para 138.

of death penalty), as well as Article 6 (right to a fair trial) are interpreted by the Court as containing a prohibition on refoulement. However in practice most of these claims are ultimately analysed under Article 3 ECHR.[34] The freedom of religion contemplated in Article 9 ECHR does not yet cover protection against return, unless there is a flagrant violation of this provision and its seriousness would imply a consequent violation of the prohibition of torture, degrading or inhuman treatment (Article 3 ECHR), and thus the Contracting States would have to comply with the protection. This notwithstanding, complete clarification of the extent of this principle is not provided. It will be interesting to see how the ECtHR interprets the new non-refoulement obligations and whether they will affect the application of the Return Directive.[35]

The second compulsory reason to postpone a return decision is the Member State's duty to delay the removal for as long as suspensory effect is granted in accordance with Article 13 (2) of the Return Directive.[36] Third-country nationals are entitled to appeal against or seek review of decisions that concern their return before a competent, impartial and independent body.[37] The decision to temporarily not enforce a return is taken by the same authority deciding the appeals or reviews.[38] Once the removal is suspended the third-country national cannot be removed from the territory of the EU and as she or he is not entitled to a temporary residence permit for that period of time, they will find themselves in a situation of non-removability.

Turning to the non-compulsory reasons for protracting a return decision, physical state or mental capacity may be taken into account by the Member State as well as technical reasons such as lack of transport capacity or failure of the removal for lack of identification. In this case, Member States are not bound to delay the return decision, however they may do so if the specific circumstances of the individual case demand it. Pregnancy, no identification available or impossibility to determine the migrant's nationality, non-existent travel documents or absence of safe travelling or secure arrival are examples of the set specific circumstances that may be taken into account by a Member State's authority when deciding whether or not to postpone a migrant's return.[39]

[34] Such as the prohibition to *refouler* a migrant under Art 6 ECHR (the right to fair trial) when there is a risk of flagrant denial of rights that article that protects. However, concerning the freedom of religion established on Art 9 ECHR the Court's reasoning seems to indicate that the article per se cannot protect someone against removal although if there is a sufficiently flagrant violation of Art 9 ECHR, may represent a violation of Art 3 ECHR that impose a duty of protection of persons in this situation upon States.

[35] M Marleen, 'The Implementation of the Return Directive in Belgium: Focus on Suspension of Removal' in Karin Zwaan (ed) *The Returns Directive: Central Themes, Problem Issues, and Implementation in Selected Member States* (Nijmegen, Wolf Legal Publishers 2011), 91.

[36] Art 9 (1) b) Return Directive.

[37] ibid, Arts 13 (1) and 12 (1).

[38] ibid, Art 13 (2).

[39] Fundamental Rights Agency (FRA), Comparative Report on Fundamental rights of migrants in an irregular situation in the European Union, 2011, 37.

Last, Article 15 (4) contains the rules for detention of third-country nationals who are the subject of a return decision. The Return Directive determines that Member States may only detain a third-country national if no other less coercive measure can be applied effectively and only in order to prepare the return or carry out the removal process.[40] The existence of risk of absconding and avoidance of the preparation of return by the irregular third-country national are compulsory requirements to proceed to detention.[41] Nevertheless, if there is not 'reasonable prospect of removal' for legal considerations or the reasons for detention are no longer verifiable, the illegally staying third-country national must be released immediately. The Directive gives no further indication apart from the immediate release for how to deal with these migrants after they are released. Therefore, although these third-country nationals may be removed, they were not (yet) at the time of their release from detention, and once freed they will still be irregular migrants living between legality and illegality within the EU. This situation is another perfect example of non-removability of irregular migrants, which is a consequence of the application of the Return Directive provisions.

C. Typology of Non-removability Situations in the EU

A recent study of the situation of third-country nationals awaiting a return decision in EU Member States suggested that three main categories of non-removable migrants could be identified: 1) those who have had a decision on their stay postponed due to factors outwith their control; 2) those who have had a decision on their stay postponed due to acts committed by the individual themselves; and 3) 'unwanted' third-country nationals.[42] Although this an interesting and most of all useful exercise, the fact that this study does not clearly consider the origins of the migration situation makes it somewhat incomplete and the choice of terminology with regard to 'unwanted' third-country nationals is far from satisfactory as it has negative connotations in relation to their legal status. Thus, another typology is proposed that considers the origins or sources, the forms of protection and the consequences of the legal status of migrants. The following typology is divided into different perspectives that can be used to examine the phenomenon of non-removability:

1. Sources of non-removability: i) EU law: Return Directive, ECHR (right to private and family law and non-refoulement) and Asylum System; ii) National legislation: the specific Spanish example of the case of domestic violence victims (Articles 131 and 132 of Real Decreto 557/2011).

[40] Art 15 of the Return Directive.
[41] ibid, Art 15 (1) a) b).
[42] European Commission, *Study on the situation of third-country nationals pending return/removal in the EU Member States and the Schengen Associated Countries*—HOME/2010/ RFXX/PR/1001, 11/03/2013, 91.

2. Forms of protection: i) protected migrant for humanitarian reasons, ii) neglected for technical and bureaucratic reasons and iii) 'unavoidable' migrant who is simply granted the delay to be removed.
3. Consequences: i) granted a status (even if is a toleration status, iii) acquired a 'municipal status' ii) not granted any status.

i. Sources of Non-removability

First, situations of non-removability can be distinguished by their sources. Both the Return Directive and the ECHR can be potential sources of non-removability of migrants which are analysed in detail in this chapter. However, a reference must be made to the EU asylum system which does not address the situation of refused asylum seekers. The Qualification and the Receptions Directives[43] only mention the existence of a right to reside after the asylum procedure is concluded, leaving situations in which there was an unsuccessful application for asylum unregulated at the supranational level.[44] Recently the CJEU clarified in the *Arslan* case that an asylum seeker has the right to remain in the territory of the Member State 'at least until his application has been rejected at first instance, and cannot therefore be "illegally staying" within the meaning of Directive 2008/115.'[45]

Additionally, the Receptions Directive in Article 6 posits that asylum seekers pending return are entitled to 'a document issued in his or her own name certifying his or her status.' This document is not a residence permit and its legal value is purely declaratory and certifies the temporary situation of asylum seekers awaiting a determination of their asylum application. As such one may question what is the legal status of those who are awaiting a decision as to asylum, given that a residence permit is not granted to them. These individuals seem to be left in the same situation as non-removable migrants. However, in contrast, this legal limbo relates more to the type of documentation they are granted rather than their legal status as the Receptions Directive is more comprehensive in terms of protection and access to fundamental rights than the Returns Directive is.

Furthermore, there are other scenarios where asylum systems produce irregularity and non-removability. One example is the case of unrecognised

[43] European Parliament and Council Directive 2011/95/EU of 13 December 2011, on standards for the qualification of third-country nationals or stateless persons as beneficiaries of international protection, for a uniform status for refugees or for persons eligible for subsidiary protection, and for the content of the protection granted, [2011] OJ L 337/9 (hereinafter Qualification Directive) and the Council Directive 2003/9/EC of January 2003 laying down minimum standards for the reception of asylum seekers, [2013], OJ L31/18, respectively, Arts 7 to 10, Art 15 and Arts 17 to 20. After the 21 July 2015 European Parliament and Council Directive 2013/33/EU of 26 June 2013 laying down standards for the reception of applicants for international protection (recast), [2013] OJ L 180/96 becomes applicable (hereinafter Reception Conditions Directive)

[44] See Art 24 (1) of the Qualification Directive. For more on irregularity of the asylum seekers status see: Costello (n 3) 65.

[45] Case C-534/11, *Mehmet Arslan v Policie ČR, Krajské ředitelství policie Ústeckého kraje, odbor cizinecké policie*, [2013], EU:C:2013:343, para 48.

refugees among rejected asylum seekers. This is where an asylum seeker has a strong claim for international protection, however, asylum procedures fail to recognise it. Also, asylum procedures only grant protection against refoulement on some of the grounds covered by human rights law.[46] Consequently, there are non-removable third-country nationals who may have a human right to stay and, simultaneously, are not recognised as a refugee or as a subsidiary protection beneficiary.

National legislation may also be responsible for the creation of non-removability situations. Although the last section of this chapter is exclusively dedicated to that issue (using the particular example of Portuguese legislation) the Spanish scenario is another interesting example of a situation in which national laws can be the origin of non-removability.[47] Articles 131 and 132 of the Real Decreto 557/2011 state that whenever a victim of domestic violence has an irregular immigration status any measures of return taken should be suspended and the individual may apply to be granted temporary residence and a work permit. As such, this is an example of a purely internal ground generating a situation of non-removability; this exceptional situation is analysed further below from the perspective of the national responses to the grey areas under analysis.

ii. Forms of Protection

Second, the forms of protection are clearly heterogeneous. Some migrants enjoy a 'protected status' normally grounded in humanitarian concerns as shown by the ECtHR case law on the right to private and family life (Article 8 ECHR) or on the prohibition of torture and degrading treatment (Article 3 ECHR), as will be shown below. To give one example of the first set of cases, the Court expressly emphasises the protection of applicants and considers the individual's refusal of a residence permit to be a violation of Article 8 ECHR. Another example of protected migrants is the aforementioned Spanish case. In this case, the fact the national legislation contemplates not only a temporary residence permit but also a work permit with the possibility of applying for a long-term residence permit is a clear expression of the protected form of dealing with non-removable migrants.

In other cases the form of protection leads to a case of a migrant merely tolerated rather than lawfully staying for technical and bureaucratic reasons. The de facto toleration scenario exemplifies this type of protection as we will see in the subsequent examination of the Portuguese situation at section IV.D of the present chapter. In this case there is no domestic immigration law provision addressing the issue as suggested by European legislation and proposals.

[46] For example, on health grounds: Case-542/13 *Mohamed M'Bodj v État Belge*, [2014], EU:C:2014:2452 and the *Abdida* case.

[47] Real Decreto 557/2011, de 20 de abril, por el que se aprueba el Reglamento de la Ley Orgánica 4/2000, sobre derechos y libertades de los extranjeros en España y su integración social, tras su reforma por Ley Orgánica 2/2009.

Another category of non-removable migrants are so-called 'unavoidable migrants' who also find themselves in a situation in which they are awaiting a decision on their stay and formal toleration. Here a reference, for instance, to the way the Return Directive deals with a compulsory reason not to remove an individual is a good example of how this group can be defined. In non-refoulement or suspensory effect cases of postponement of stay (Article 13 (2) of the Return Directive) Member States are obliged to provide individuals with written confirmation in accordance with national legislation that the period for voluntary departure has been extended.[48] These migrants are unavoidably granted a delay of their removal and may even be granted written confirmation of their situation which may in fact be a simple declaratory document of their status. Clearly, the level of protection these individuals enjoy varies in comparison with the situation in which they are granted a temporary residence permit or the Court declares that their removal violates the protection of human rights. The way in which domestic laws implement these different levels of protection is an interesting query to be answered, but one which will be addressed in more detail in subsection IV.D apropos the Portuguese example of protection of non-removable migrants.

iii. Consequences

Third, and relatedly, either Member States temporarily grant a regular status or a residence and work permit to these migrants or (even if they are tolerated de facto as non-removable migrants are in Portugal for example) they do not grant any status at all. These are the only two possible consequences: having a legal stay or not being granted one; either you are in or you are out, there is no halfway house in terms of legality. The way the EU conceptualises an illegal stay is responsible for this outcome due to the fact that EU law establishes that 'illegal stay' means the presence on the territory of a Member State of a third-country national who does not fulfil, or no longer fulfils the conditions of entry as set out in Article 5 of the Schengen Borders Code or other conditions for entry, stay or residence in that Member State.[49] This in effect means that no space is left in EU legislation for any other category of migrant which does not fit comfortably with regard to regular and irregular stays.

D. Identification of Concrete Non-removability Scenarios in the EU

As a way of giving concrete examples of some of the most common scenarios of non-removability of irregular migrants in the EU, the facts of two CJEU cases are briefly summarised.

[48] Art 14 (2) of the Return Directive.
[49] ibid, Art 3 (2).

Mr Ruiz Zambrano, a Colombian national, arrived in Belgium in 1999 with his wife. Both applied for asylum in that Member State. Despite the fact that their asylum application was unsuccessful and an order to leave Belgium was issued, that same order was accompanied by a non-refoulement clause determining that they could not be sent back to Colombia.[50] The Zambrano family stayed in Belgium where they continued to reside and where also they were also registered in the municipality. Mr Zambrano signed a full-time employment contract despite the fact he did not have a work or residence permit. During this period the couple had two children, Diego and Jessica, who are Belgian nationals by birth. After another unsuccessful application to obtain a residence permit, Mr Zambrano was granted a special residence permit dependent on the action of review against the previous refusal of residence permit application.[51]

These facts describe the situation faced by a rejected asylum seeker, providing 'an ordinary example of a legal limbo of which thousands are created in Europe every year: deportation is not required and work and reliance on social assistance are prohibited'.[52] This is a classic situation of non-removable persons and will help to illustrate specific problems that grey areas of categorisation raise.

Turning to the next CJEU case, *Kadzoev*,[53] the scenario is substantially different. Nevertheless, it also describes a situation of non-removability and reveals a gap in the EU's asylum and immigration discourse, the lack of attention to the regularisation of irregular migrants at the supranational level.[54] In 2006 Bulgarian law enforcement officials arrested Mr Kadzoev near the Turkish border. A coercive administrative measure of deportation was imposed on him but due to lack of valid identity documents and sufficient funds to travel abroad he could not be removed. The Bulgarian authorities placed him in a detention centre until it was possible to execute the decree. After his detention Mr Kadzoev unsuccessfully applied for refugee status.

The issue raised in this particular case, in terms of non-removability, is that once Mr Kadzoev is released and his removal cannot be enforced, he has no legal status at the national level, without any valid identity documents, no refugee status granted or a residence permit under Bulgarian Law. Hypothetically, if Mr Kadzoev was asked to show his identity documents by Bulgarian authorities after being released he would have been unable to do it and not only he would be arrested again, but also he could not work or reside legally in Bulgaria. In sum, the consequences of Mr Kadzoev's release are an example of the gap that can be found in the domestic legislation of several countries like Bulgaria.[55] The problem is, once again, the lack of regulation and clarity regarding the status

[50] See para 15 of the Case C-34/09, *Gerardo Ruiz Zambrano*, [2011], EU:C:2011:124.

[51] ibid, para 24.

[52] M Olivas and D Kochenov, 'Case C-34/09 Ruiz Zambrano: A Respectful Rejoinder' (2012) *University of Houston Public Law and Legal Theory Series* 2.

[53] Paras 13, 14 and 15 of the Case C-357/09 PPU *Said Shamilovich Kadzoev*, [2009], EU:C:2009:741.

[54] E Mincheva, 'Case Report on Kadzoev, 30 November 2009' (2010) 12 *European Journal of Migration and Law* 361, 362.

[55] ibid, 369.

of people under these circumstances with no recognised status, be it at the domestic or EU level.

In a schematic way, the most relevant and general examples of this group of migrants living between illegality and legality are the following:

1. Rejected asylum seekers whose removal cannot be carried out for legal, humanitarian or practical reasons;[56]
2. Third-country nationals who have appealed a return decision and have had a suspension granted;[57]
3. Third-country nationals who were detained with no reasonable prospect for removal for legal or other considerations, and who were immediately released.[58]
4. Third-country nationals waiting for the renewal of an expired residence permit.

The crucial question to be posed at this stage is: do those third-country nationals who cannot be expelled have a status? If so, what type of status?

Subsequently, the book analyses a number of key issues. The first relates to the fact that there are two levels of protection and categorisation of non-removable immigrants: the EU level and the national level. This raises the question of how these levels interact and furthermore in which situations may or does EU law affect the categorisation of immigration status determined by the national laws.[59]

III. THE ATYPICAL STATUS OF NON-REMOVABLE IRREGULAR MIGRANTS

A. Is there a *Status* for Non-removable Migrants?

If not granted a temporary residence permit, non-removable migrants are and will continue to be irregular while the obstacle to removal remains in place. Considering whether there is a status for non-removable migrants will, inevitably, require discussion of whether there is an irregular migrant protection status from both an EU law perspective and, consequently, from the Member State point of view. The present subsection will focus on the matter of the justification of the existence of a legal status recognised both at an international and European level. As for the preliminary issue of the existence or otherwise of a status for irregular migrants, the first remark to be made relates to what the International Organization for Migration (hereafter IOM) has stated with regards to the definition of irregular migrant. The IOM defines an irregular migrant as someone who, because they have entered a state illegally or overstayed a visa, loses their legal status in the host Member State.[60]

[56] Para 48 of the *Kadzoev* judgment (n 53).
[57] Art 13 (2) of the Return Directive.
[58] ibid, Art 15 (4).
[59] In the *Zambrano* case from refused asylum seeker Mr. Zambrano became a *quasi citizen* with a permanent residence permit accompanied by a work permit.
[60] IOM, *Glosario sobre Migración*, Series de Derecho International sobre Migration, ed OIM, no. 7, 2006, (http://publications.iom.int/system/files/pdf/iml_7_sp.pdf) 43.

The IOM definition refers to the situation in which an irregular migrant who had a legal status has it withdrawn as a result of the irregularity of their actions. From the perspective adopted the legal status may be withdrawn, but the migrant is left with an irregular migration status enabling them to enjoy certain rights, and as such, it is the extension (of that status) that raises several issues, and non-removable migrants as irregular migrants find themselves in this situation.

Irregular migrants are considered to be entitled to a protection status, to have an irregular residence situation and in the case of non-removable migrants an atypical irregular residence status, as a result of the combination of the illegal and legal spheres. The atypicality of this group is claimed since non-removable migrants are not by rule legal third-country nationals, nor typical illegally staying third-country nationals absconding from the national immigration authorities. However, they are still labelled as such. Thus, despite having lost their legal status, once they have crossed the line from legality to irregularity,[61] their stay is known to (and permitted by) national authorities either formally or informally. Irregular migrants are still entitled to a minimum status despite not complying with the conditions for valid residence in the host Member State. For reasons to be further elaborated presently it is argued that there is a recognised status for irregular migrants and in particular those who cannot yet be removed from the EU.

One could argue that someone without a valid residence permit to live or to work in a Member State should not legitimately enjoy a recognised status such as the status of those who live legally in the EU.[62] Nevertheless, it is agreed in various international and European human rights texts that basic standards of rights apply to all human beings irrespective of their immigration status. The following international documents are examples of the recognition of that status. Articles 1 and 2(1) respectively of the Universal Declaration of Human Rights establishes a notion of human dignity applied to everyone whether they are in possession of a regular immigration status or not. Further, the International Convention on the Elimination of All Forms of Racial Discrimination, although making a distinction between citizens and non-citizens, guarantees protection against discrimination of non-citizens.[63] Additionally, Article 9 (1) of the International Labour Organization (ILO) Convention No 143 on migrant workers posits the right to equal treatment for migrants who entered irregularly and cannot be regularised. Another example mentioned above is the 2003 International Convention on the Protection of the Rights of All Migrant Workers and Members of their Families (ultimately, however, without the support of EU Member States, none of whom opted to ratify the Convention).

In order to justify the existence of a status for irregular migrants it is necessary to emphasise that there is a threshold recognised to all irregular migrants based on

[61] For example, someone who has overstayed their visa or has no valid documentation.

[62] R Rubio-Marin, *Immigration as a Democratic Challenge Citizenship and Inclusion in Germany and the United States* (Cambridge, Cambridge University Press, 2000) 86. Also, LS Bosniak, 'Membership, Equality, and the Difference that Alienage Makes' (1994) 69 *New York University Law Review* 1047.

[63] See Art 1(1) (2).

the universalistic protection of personhood in combination with the concept of human dignity enshrined in some national constitutional texts.[64] This view finds support, for instance, in Advocate General's Bot Opinion in the *Abdida* case.[65] Bot grounded his view in the need to grant illegally staying third-country nationals a minimum standard of basic needs at the risk of affecting the Return Directive's *effect utile* and of disrespecting:

> [T]he respect for human dignity and the right to life, integrity and health enshrined in Articles 1, 2, 3 and 35 of the Charter respectively, as well as the prohibition of inhuman or degrading treatment contained in Article 4 of that Charter …[66]

The scope of the 'basic needs' to be provided to a non-removable migrant are the measure of their protection. Advocate General Bot in the same Opinion argues that even though the extent of the 'basic needs' is left to national discretion, the 'subsistence needs' of the illegally-staying third-country national, a 'decent standard of living' adequate for ensuring the migrant's health should be assured through securing a 'secure accommodation' and 'taking into account any special needs' that the migrant may have.[67] The CJEU did not go as far and did not expressly state the specific protection covered by the 'basic needs' of non-removable migrants, however, it has clearly highlighted the fact that providing emergency health care would 'be rendered meaningless if there were not also a concomitant requirement to make provision for the basic needs of the third country national concerned'.[68]

It is thus clear that supranationally an obligation is imposed on Member States to recognise (and secure) a minimum standard of 'basic needs' for non-removable migrants at the risk of affecting the *effect utile* of the provisions of the Return Directive. Nevertheless, the scope of these basic needs is mostly left for Member States to decide,[69] which makes the supranational recognition of the protection of non-removable third-country nationals intrinsically dependent on the host Member State's generosity.

The fundamental role that the implementation of EU law at the national level plays in determining the scope of protection of non-removable irregular migrants is undeniable. In certain Member States' legislation there are some indications that irregular migrants and non-removable migrants as part of this category indeed have a recognised status and the extension of its protection. The example of Spanish legislation provides a snapshot of national constitutional laws and practices and also highlights how some Member States deal with the recognition

[64] For a detailed study of the constitutional status of irregular migrants, with a particular focus on Spain and the United States: CM Rodríguez, and R Rubio-Marín, 'The Constitutional Status of Irregular Migrants, Testing the Boundaries of Human Rights Protection in Spain and the United States' in Dembour and Kelly (n 30) 74.

[65] Case C-562/13 *Abdida* [2014] EU:C:2014:2453, Opinion of AG Bot.

[66] ibid, para 155.

[67] ibid, para 157.

[68] *Abdida* judgment (n 65), para 60.

[69] ibid, para 61.

of this category of migrants.[70] As Giovanetti Ramos has stated, in relation to the Spanish juridical system, an irregular migrant is someone who can enjoy rights in Spain.[71] Every irregular migrant living in Spain has the duty to register at the municipality (empadronarse en el municipio)[72] and that registration enables the migrant to enjoy, for example, the right to education until the age of 18 on equal terms with Spanish citizens. Irregular migrants in Spain can also gain access to housing and health once they have registered in the municipal population census. This is yet another example of the idea of municipal citizenship analysed in chapter two.[73]

Additionally, the Spanish Constitutional Court has confirmed in previous decisions that irregular migrants should be able to enjoy a minimum standard of fundamental rights, those recognised as being the rights of every human being irrespective their immigration status or category.[74] These decisions concerned the recognition of the right of peaceful assembly of migrants in an irregular situation establishing a link between that right and human dignity. Moreover, on the issue of constitutional recognition of irregular migrants' rights in the judgment STC 95/2003[75] concerning the right to free legal assistance,[76] the Court decided that this right was to be conferred on those migrants who complied with the other legal conditions imposed on those not legally residing in Spain in order to accede to free legal assistance. As Izquierdo Sans concludes after the STC 95/2003 decision, every third-country national (regardless of their immigration status) residing in Spain has access to the benefit of free legal assistance in the same terms as Spanish nationals.[77] Certain decisions of the Spanish Constitutional Court were controversial among scholars for not treating equally all the limitations to the rights that can be enjoyed by irregular migrants.[78]

[70] For an overview of the Spanish legislation on irregular immigration, see: G Àngel, S Chueca, *Derechos Humanos, Inmigrantes en situación Irregular y Unión Europea* (Madrid, Lex Nova, 2010), Parte IV, 203–63, and C González-Enríquez, 'Spain: Irregularity as a Rule' in A Trindafyllidou (ed), *Irregular Migration in Europe. Myths and Realities* (Surrey, Ashgate, 2002) 247–66.

[71] G Alberto Ramos, 'Inmigrantes en situación irregular y la Organización Internacional para las Migraciones', in Àngel and Chueca, ibid 98.

[72] Ley Orgánica 4/2000, sobre derechos y libertades de los extranjeros en España y su integración social, known as Ley de extranjería, revised later by Ley 8/2000 and recently in 2011 by the Real Decreto 557/2011, de 20 abril, por el que se aprueba el Reglamento de la Ley Orgánica 4/2000, sobre derechos y libertades de los extranjeros en Espanã y su integración social, tras su reforma por la Ley Orgánica 2/2009, BOE 30 de abril de 2011; Also see Article 15 of Ley de Bases de Régimen Local 4/1996: 'Artículo 15. Toda persona que viva en España está obligada a inscribirse en el Padrón del municipio en el que resida habitualmente'.

[73] Scholars like Rodríguez and Rubio-Marín pointed out the fact that municipalities started challenging this situation recently, in Rodríguez and Rubio-Marín (n 64) 85.

[74] Tribunal Constitucional de Espanã, STC 236/2007 de 7 de noviembre de 2007 and Tribunal Constitucional de Espanã STC 259/2007 de 19 de diciembre de 2007.

[75] Tribunal Constitutional de Espanã, STC 95/2003 de 22 de mayo de 2003.

[76] Art 119 of the Constitución Española 1978.

[77] C Izquierdo Sans, 'Artículo 13.1—Los Derechos Fundamentales de los Extranjeros' in Maria Emilia Casas Baamonde, Rodríguez-Piñero y Bravo-Ferrer (eds.) *Comentarios a la Constitución Española XXX Aniversario* (Alphen aan den Rijn, Wolters Kluwer, 2009) 233.

[78] In particular, the provisions limiting the rights to assembly, association, union activity and the right to strike; Rodríguez and Rubio-Marín (n 64) 89.

International human rights treaties and the universal concept of human dignity conjugated with constitutional case law like the aforementioned Spanish example establish a minimum threshold below which irregular migrants can be expected to not be allowed to fall, of which non-removable migrants are part. However, the specific features of the status of those migrants whose removal has been postponed are not fully addressed at this level. As such, the following sections will analyse how this is tackled at the EU level, and it will be argued that from an EU perspective these migrants enjoy an atypical migration status.

There are many important questions that remain unanswered such as; how can the protection provided to non-removable migrants such as irregular migrants be categorised? Further, what are the elements of this atypical immigration status?

B. Elements of the Atypical Status of Non-removable Migrants

The atypical 'in between' migration status of non-removable migrants can be seen as a laboratory type of legal status, a category that metaphorically can be seen as an incubatory transitory stage that a migrant may fall into while their situation is not either legalised or a return decision issued.

For the purposes of this study a non-removable migrant living within the EU is an irregular migrant, in a transitory and atypical legal situation. These are the main characteristics of the non-removable migrant status. The main focus of the present section will be on drawing out the individual elements of this atypicality to be found in the general regime that regulates non-removability in EU law. The irregularity of a non-removable migrant is based on the fact that they are not automatically regular whenever the national authorities issue a decision of postponement of their removal. Unless the national authorities confer a temporary formal residence permit, or according to Article 6 (4) Return Directive grant an authorisation to stay for compassionate, humanitarian or other reasons, the third-country national will still be irregular, despite the formal delay of their removal, as mentioned in subsection II.C of this chapter.

The transitory nature of a non-removable migrant status is intrinsically linked to the concrete cause for non-removability; until the bar for removal lasts the migrant will be living in this temporary legal limbo. For example, such a legal limbo situation will persist as long as the enforcement of removal has suspensory effect when a third-country national appeals against a decision of return or for any of the reasons above mentioned.[79] The traditional equation of an individual legal status being a bundle of rights attributed to someone who has to comply with certain obligations does not fit perfectly the category of non-removable migrants, as will now be shown below. The elements of the atypical non-removable migrant status at the supranational level will be developed in three parts based in the Return Directive regime: the rights of irregular migrants pending return

[79] Arts 13 (2) and 9 1 (b) of the Return Directive.

(protection offered), the obligations imposed on irregular migrants pending return (duties to comply with) and the written confirmation of that legal situation (eventual formalisation).

i. Rights of Irregular Migrants Pending Return in the EU

With regard to the protection granted through secondary EU sources, the wording of Recital 12 of the Return Directive allows us to conclude that, normatively, the content of the non-removable migrant's status was not yet fully addressed and that it should be tackled as well as it should be formalised at the national level in accordance with the wording of the Directive. However, at this stage Member States are not obliged to comply. Whilst they are advised to do it there is no mandatory element in the wording of the Recital:

> The situation of third-country nationals who are staying illegally but who cannot yet be removed *should be addressed.* The basic conditions of subsistence *should be defined* according to national legislation. In order to be able to demonstrate their specific situation in the event of administrative controls or checks, such persons *should be provided with a written confirmation of their situation* …[80]

The obligation imposed on Member States to ensure basic standards of subsistence was moved from the main text of the Return Directive to the preamble, more specifically to the aforementioned Recital 12. The Commission's original proposal for the Return Directive imposed a limit on the rights given to non-removable migrants by the Member States,[81] namely that they should not be less favourable than the set of rights contemplated in Directive 2003/9/EC, the Reception Conditions Directive, until 21 July 2015 when Directive 2013/33/EU was to become applicable.[82] These rights (in accordance with the new version of the Directive) include the right to residence and freedom of movement (Article 7), family unity (Article 12), medical screening (Article 13), schooling and education for minors (Article 14), employment (Article 15) and health care (Article 17). In short, third-country nationals waiting for a return decision to be enforced were to have equivalent treatment to asylum seekers under the Reception Conditions Directive in accordance with the wording of the Commission's proposal.[83]

[80] Recital 12 Return Directive (emphasis added).

[81] Art 13 of the, European Commission (COM(2005) 391 final) proposal for a Directive of the European Parliament and of the Council on common standards and procedures in Member States for returning illegally staying third-country nationals, [2005].

[82] Council Directive 2003/9/EC of January 2003 laying down minimum standards for the reception of asylum seekers, [2003], OJ L31/18, respectively, Arts 7 to 10, Art 15 and Arts 17 to 20. After the 21 July 2015 European Parliament and Council Directive 2013/33/EU of 26 June 2013 laying down standards for the reception of applicants for international protection (recast), [2013] OJ L 180/96 becomes applicable.

[83] European Commission (COM(2005) 391 final) proposal for a Directive of the European Parliament and of the Council on common standards and procedures in Member States for returning illegally staying third-country nationals, [2005] and A Baldaccini, 'The Return and Removal of Irregular Migrants under EU Law: an Analysis of the Returns Directive' (2009) 11 *European Journal of Migration and Law* 1, 8.

The purpose of the Commission's proposal for Article 13 concerning a minimum level of conditions for irregular migrants whose return decision was delayed and cannot yet be removed was singular: to limit the legal vacuum resulting from these legal grey areas.[84] Nevertheless, the Return Directive proposal was fiercely criticised by many Member States for sending the wrong political message: it was seen as granting an upgrade to the condition of illegally-staying third-country nationals.[85] Hence, what was left of the original draft, apart from the guidelines in Recital 12 of the Return Directive redirecting the definition of basic conditions of subsistence to a national legislation level, was the formulation of Article 14 of the Return Directive of the safeguards pending return.

Another relevant aspect that relates to the scope of the rights enjoyed by non-removable migrants and that was also on the table during negotiation of the proposal is the extent to which these safeguards were binding and their scope. The European Parliament and the Commission suggested a less discretionary version (for the Member States) of the safeguards pending return, alternatively stating that Member States 'shall ensure' the respect for Article 13 of the Commission's Proposal. Nevertheless, in the final version of the Return Directive the safeguards posited on Article 14 (1) are 'taken into account as far as possible' in relation to third-country nationals during the periods for which the removal has been postponed, which implies a less strict level of protection and a greater margin of discretion for Member States to interpret the scope of this safeguards. As such, Article 14 of the Return Directive determines that, 'as far as possible', Member States should take into account the principles of:

> a) Family unity with family members present in their territory is maintained, b) emergency health care and essential treatment of illness are provided, c) minors are granted access to the basic education system subject to the length of their stay and d) the special needs of vulnerable persons are taken into account.[86]

A pertinent question that can be raised is whether these safeguards are a comprehensive answer to the needs of the people who, after having been issued a return decision, cannot be removed from the territory of the host Member State. In order to answer to that question it is necessary to consider the large margin of discretion left to the meaning of the term 'as far as possible'. The lack of legal certainty provided by a set of safeguards supports the thesis that the kind of protection provided to non-removable migrants is atypical. How each Member State interprets and implements this expression into their national laws mirrors the measure of the rights granted to non-removable migrants.

[84] Art 13 of the, European Commission (COM(2005) 391 final) proposal for a Directive of the European Parliament and of the Council on common standards and procedures in Member States for returning illegally staying third-country nationals, [2005].

[85] Lutz (n 17) 64.

[86] The wording of the Return Directive clearly has the purpose of avoiding limits to the margin of manoeuvre of Member State's when tackling the issue of non-removable migrants' status and the rights they are entitled to under their jurisdiction.

For example, the Portuguese legislation implementing the Return Directive was silent on this issue and did not include the expression 'as far as possible'. The reference made in Lei no 29/2012 (the Portuguese Law that implements the Return Directive) suggests that they ought to be taken into account but does not give any indication as to what extent they should be.[87] It is particularly in those cases where the non-removability of a person endures for a long period of time that the question of whether the protection ensured by the Return Directive is sufficient to address the situation of people living in this legal limbo arises. The Fundamental Rights Agency in its report points out that the list of safeguards is not comprehensive, taking into account that it does not cover all human rights that international law confers to irregular migrants, such as the right to access justice or even the right to be registered at birth.[88]

All in all, the fact that Member States have the option of issuing a return decision or granting a residence permit regularising irregular migrants may perhaps at first glance lead us to the conclusion that this feature would help to avoid the legal limbo described above.[89] However, this is not necessarily the case. It may possibly also increase the number of cases in which Member States issue return decisions which in practice cannot be enforced whilst respecting the principle of *non refoulement* or for technical or humanitarian reasons. Clearly, there is a need to regulate the situation of these people waiting to be returned, and in all fairness, Article 14 of the Return Directive's guidelines do address this situation to a certain extent, albeit in less detailed and strict terms than envisioned by the Commission's proposal in 2005. The European Commission has suggested in a recent Communication that these statuses should be harmonised.[90] Nevertheless, European migration law has not yet harmonised the status of non-removable migrants, despite the argument made by Advocate General Bot in the *Abdida* case: 'To have one's most basic needs catered for is, in my opinion, an essential right which *cannot depend on the legal status of the person concerned*'.[91]

The interpretation of the concept of 'basic needs' is at the heart of the discussion of the rights that must be granted to non-removable illegally-staying third-country nationals. Remarkably, the CJEU has made an effort to broaden the interpretation of the safeguards pending return contemplated in Article 14 of the Return

[87] Art 160 (4) (5) of the Lei nº 29/2012 de 9 de Agosto, 2012, primeira alteração à Lei nº 23/2007, de 24 de julho, que aprovou o regime jurídico de entrada, permanência, saída e afastamento de estrangeiros do território nacional. Diário da República, 1ª série—Nº 154. (hereinafter Lei nº 29/2012).

[88] Fundamental Rights Agency (FRA), Comparative Report on Fundamental rights of migrants in an irregular situation in the European Union, 2011, 29.

[89] Art 6 of the Return Directive reflects greatly this discretion of Member States, especially number 4 of the same provision.

[90] Commission, Communication on an area of freedom, security and justice serving the citizen, COM 2009 (262): 'all too often repatriation measures cannot be carried out on account of legal or practical obstacles. In absence of clear rules, we should study national needs and practices and consider the possibility of establishing common standards for taking charge of illegal immigrants who cannot be deported'.

[91] Para 156 of the Case C-562/13 *Abdida* (n 65) Opinion of AG Bot (emphasis added).

Directive in its recent jurisprudence; an effort that seems to be more in line with what was proposed by the Commission in 2005. The *Abdida* decision illustrates that effort, as the CJEU clearly posited that to comply with the requirement of providing emergency health care and essential treatment of illness in accordance with Article 14 (1)(b) of the Return Directive would be 'meaningless'[92] if there was not 'also a concomitant requirement to make provision for the basic need'[93] of the illegally-staying third-country national.

Undoubtedly, this decision represents a considerable step towards the recognition of a protected core of basic needs that Member States are obligated to protect in the case of non-removable third-country nationals. In fact the Court not only recognises the existence of this protection but also makes it interdependent. For the CJEU it would make no sense to provide the most advanced health care in Europe to an ill third-country national if they were left to starve, or other basic needs were left unfulfilled. Despite this important recognition of protection the Court immediately took a step backwards and noted that it is within the Member State's discretion to determine the scope of the basic needs of the non-removable third-country national.[94] As such, the definition of what the basic needs of a third-country national who does not enjoy a right to reside in the EU are and how should they be fulfilled is kept under the wing of the host Member States, meaning that social protection continues to be a lottery for non-removable third-country nationals.

ii. Obligations Imposed on Irregular Migrants Pending Return in the EU

Second, once removal is postponed Member States may demand that the third-country national fulfil certain obligations with the purpose of preventing or avoiding the risk of absconding.[95] The obligations that Member States may impose on a non-removable migrant range from regular reporting to the authorities, deposit of an 'adequate' financial guarantee, submission of documents or the duty to stay in a certain place.[96] The aforementioned set of possible compulsory obligations is another element of the core of the legal status of non-removable migrants. It must be borne in mind that the corresponding obligation, the duty on Member States to guarantee basic standards of subsistence, was moved from the text of the Directive to the Recitals (Recital 12), whereas the duties imposed on migrants are included in the text of the Return Directive. These legislative choices create a more discretionary understanding of Member States' obligation to non-removable migrants. This is also an aspect that reflects the atypical nature of the status of people living in the legal limbo of non-removability, in other words, the status of non-removable migrants, includes a set of indicative rights and safeguards, and more well-defined duties.

92 Para 60 of the judgment *Abdida* (n 65).
93 ibid.
94 ibid, para 61.
95 Art 9(3) and 7(3) of the Return Directive.
96 ibid, Art 7(3).

Similarly an example of national practices can be drawn from the recent Portuguese law implementing the Return Directive (hereafter Lei 29/2012)[97] which establishes, among other obligations, the possibility of imposing a deposit of a financial guarantee (caução) while the decision of return is not enforced and the period for voluntary return had not expired.[98] What is not clear from the wording of this article is whether this obligation is to be imposed only on migrants during the period for voluntary departure or if it also applies to those who have their removal postponed in accordance with the Return Directive, taking into account that there is not any mention of it in national law.[99] Another point to be made concerning this particular obligation is that in accordance with the Return Directive the deposit of a financial guarantee should be adequate whereas the Portuguese implementing legislation does not mention any adequacy condition. It will be interesting to assess how the national courts implement this provision and what is considered to be an adequate financial guarantee imposed on someone not regularly residing within that Member State's territory.

iii. The Written Confirmation of Non-removability

Third, the written confirmation of non-removability, which is to be provided by Member States,[100] or the temporary residence permit for humanitarian or compassionate reasons that can be granted by the Member States, are the main mechanisms provided by the Return Directive to put an end to or formalise limbo situations.[101] However, it is argued that written confirmation is not in fact a way of regularisation, rather it is a formalisation of the status quo of that person. Therefore, if implemented this measure contributes not only to the recognition and legal certainty of the existence of a status for non-removable returnees, but also allows non-removable migrants more effective access to basic fundamental rights. As such, the written confirmation represents the formal element of the atypical migration status at the centre of the analysis of the present chapter.

Written confirmation of the postponement of removal is firstly addressed in the preamble of the Return Directive. The need to provide these migrants with formal confirmation of their situation for the purposes of an administrative control or checks is stressed in Recital 12. Furthermore, in the same Recital it is stated that Member States should enjoy wide discretion with regard to the form and the format of this confirmation. Article 14(2) contemplates the issuance of a written confirmation in accordance with national legislation stating that the return decision is pending and that it will not be enforced. This provision contributes to

[97] Lei da Assembleia da República nº 29/2012 de 9 de Agosto.

[98] Art 160 no 3 d) Lei nº 29/2012.

[99] Art 9 (3) of the Return Directive.

[100] One should always have in mind that this is not a true solution, as it is not a temporary residence permit, but only a document providing a certain level of security and protection to non-removable migrants.

[101] Art 14 (2) of the Return Directive.

providing a status even if atypical to non-removable migrants. As uncommitted and formal it may be, it is still a significant step towards the recognition of these uncertain legal situations.[102] The Directive is not comprehensive on this matter and, apart from the safeguards while a return is pending stated in Article 14(1) of the Return Directive, there is no mention of how non-removable individuals should be treated or how they should apply for this type of formal recognition of non-removability, leaving this matter to the Member State's discretion.

Recently, the CJEU in the *Mahdi* judgment clarified its position on the matter of the written confirmation to be granted to non-removable migrants.[103] The Court stated that whilst Member States have 'wide discretion concerning the form and format of the written confirmation',[104] Member States must provide it to non-removable migrants when 'there is no longer a reasonable prospect of removal within the meaning of Article 15(4) of that directive'.[105] As such, the Court confirms the compulsory nature of the formal obligation imposed by Article 14(2) of the Return Directive that has a purely declaratory effect of non-removability thus it does not grant any rights.

In contrast, the CJEU did not go as far in relation to the possibility given to the Member States of issuing an autonomous residence permit conferring a right to stay to a third-country national as posited in Article 6 (4) of the Return Directive.[106] Most likely given the constitutive effect (of the right to stay) of that residence permit, the CJEU posited that Member States cannot be obliged to grant it, leaving Member States' sovereignty untouched, with the justification that is not the purpose of the Return Directive to regulate the conditions of residence of illegally staying third-country nationals.[107] One may question the practical consequence of this decision in terms of formalising a non-removable migrant's status and the answer is straightforward: as long as it is purely declaratory it is obligatory.

IV. THE REMEDIES FOR NON-REMOVABILITY: NATIONAL AND EUROPEAN PERSPECTIVES

As a way of concluding the present chapter it is important to address the normative dimension of the issue of non-removability in the EU. Non-removability of irregular migrants is, in several cases, created by impediments or obstacles to enforce a return decision stated in legal documents.[108] As argued above, EU law may

[102] Baldaccini (n 83) 1, 8.
[103] See the Case C-146/14 PPU, *Mahdi*, [2014], EU:C:2014:1320.
[104] ibid, para 88.
[105] ibid, para 89.
[106] ibid, paras 86 and 89.
[107] ibid, para 87.
[108] For example, the EU Agency for Fundamental Rights has divided into three blocks of causes: a) Human rights law and humanitarian considerations; b) Technical obstacles and c) Policy-related obstacles in Fundamental Rights Agency (FRA) Comparative Report on Fundamental rights of migrants in an irregular situation in the European Union, 2011.

in some cases generate these types of situations without providing a satisfactory remedy, leaving it to the discretion of Member States to regularise those living in legal limbo, in particular non-removable migrants. The European Convention of Human Rights and the ECtHR may also cause the non-removability of irregular migrants. At first, the approach of this Court may seem to be more proactive with regards to the status of these migrants, leaving open the question posed by some commentators: namely, in contrast to the Return Directive regime, is there a right to regularisation, in particular for non-removable migrants under the ECHR?[109] Articles 8 and 3 of the European Convention of Human Rights are relevant provisions in order to understand to what extent the Convention contributes to the creation of these limbo situations and what type of solution may be provided by the ECtHR to end them.[110]

A. Article 8 of the ECHR and the Non-removability of Irregular Migrants

The right to private and family life is the focus of the first part of this subsection, since first of all it is one of the areas that most affects the life of a migrant, and second since it is the area that covers the most important cases in terms of access to regularisation via judicial decisions. Private and family life rights are protected by human rights law, more precisely by the content of Article 8 ECHR.[111] The ECtHR has through its decisions prevented the deportation of a person from the host country where they enjoy their family life.[112] The *Boultif v Switzerland* case, for instance, established that 'the removal of a person from a country where close members of his family are living may amount to an infringement of the right to respect for family life as guaranteed in Article 8 (1) of the Convention'.[113] The protection of family and private life will be respected generally if the spouses reside together with their children (who are minors) in the host country of the applicant or in another state. A State measure precluding that right constitutes an interference, which demands a justification.[114] Therefore, no infringement of

[109] D Thym, 'Respect for Private and Family Life under Article 8 ECHR in Immigration Cases: a Human Right to Regularize Illegal Stay?' (2008) 57 *International and Comparative Law Quarterly* and from another perspective: MB Dembour, *When Humans become Migrants: Study of the European Court of Human Rights with an Inter-American Counterpoint* (Oxford, Oxford University Press, 2015).

[110] Non-deportability will be used from non-removability, as is the terminology used by the ECtHR.

[111] Judgments such as: *Boultif v Switzerland*, ECHR (2001) App No 54273/00, or on the right to private life *Üner v the Netherlands*, ECHR (2006) App No 46410/99.

[112] The criteria established by the ECtHR case law address the question whether an expulsion is 'necessary in a democratic society' and 'proportionate to the legitimate aim pursued' in paras 46–48 of the Case *Üner v the Netherlands*, ibid. Part of the criteria are aspects like the amount of time the applicant lived in the host country, the existence of children in the marriage and their respective ages, the gravity situation of which the spouse would face in the applicant's country of origin or even the best interest of the children and the solidity of social, cultural and family ties to the host country and to the country of destination.

[113] *Boultif v Switzerland* (n 111) para 39, see also *Moustaquim v Belgium*, ECHR (1991) App No 12313/86, para 36.

[114] Art 8 (2) ECHR.

the right to respect for family life is legitimate unless it 'is in accordance with the law, necessary in a democratic society and proportionate to the legitimate aim pursued'.[115] The most significant contribution of the *Boultif* judgment was the proportionality test guidelines (hereafter *Boultif* criteria) that the ECtHR utilised. The Court established this test in order to assess the extent to which an expulsion of a foreigner after a criminal conviction is 'necessary in a democratic society and proportionate to the aim pursued'.[116]

The ECtHR *Boultif* criteria for the proportionality test included: a) the nature and the seriousness of the offence committed; b) the duration of the applicant's stay in the country from which he is going to be expelled; c) the time which has elapsed since the commission of the offence and the applicant's conduct during that period; d) the nationalities of the various persons concerned; e) the applicant's family situation, such as the length of the marriage; f) other factors revealing whether the couple lead a real and genuine family life; g) whether the spouse knew about the offence at the time when he or she entered into a family relationship; h) and whether there are children in the marriage and, if so, their age. In addition, the Court should also take into account the seriousness of the difficulties that the spouse would be likely to encounter in the applicant's country of origin, although the mere fact that a person might face certain difficulties in accompanying her or his spouse cannot in itself preclude expulsion.[117]

The ECtHR case of *Üner v the Netherlands* added two extra criteria to the proportionality test; i) the best interests and the well-being of the children; and j) the solidity of social, cultural and family ties to the host country of destination.[118] As such, the proportionality test's main aim is to achieve a balance between the protection of family unity and the maintenance of public order.[119]

The following ECtHR case law on Article 8 ECHR developed the content of the scope of the interference of the right to family and private life. The non-removability of an irregular migrant is directly linked first to the existence of an unjustified interference to the right of family, and, second to the way the national courts interpret and apply national immigration law dealing with legal situation of non-removable migrants. The *Berrehab* case was the first decision 'establishing a right to residence as a fundamental human right contrary to the opinion of the state (including the courts state)'.[120] Yet, as Dembour points out, 'by the time *Berrehab* was decided in 1988, ninety applications had been lodged at Strasbourg concerning deportation'.[121] The author explains that *Berrahab* 'managed to interrupt the flow of inadmissibility decisions' as the applicant was for the first

[115] ibid.
[116] *Boultif v Switzerland* (n 111), para 39.
[117] ibid, para 48.
[118] *Üner v the Netherlands* (n 111), para 26.
[119] ibid.
[120] *Berrehab v the Netherlands*, ECHR (1988) App No 10730/84 and E Guild, *The Legal Elements of European Identity: EU Citizenship and Migration Law*, European Law Library (The Hague, Kluwer Law International, 2004) 16.
[121] Dembour (n 109) 161.

time not a criminal.[122] Mr Berrehab was a Moroccan national who, after divorcing his Dutch wife who was the mother of his daughter, was refused a residence permit. However, the court considered this a breach of his right to family life covered by Article 8 ECHR.

Perhaps, however, the most important decision in this area came a couple a years later in the *Rodrigues Da Silva* judgment in the context of irregular migration, especially with regard to the protection that can be provided by Article 8 ECHR and individual regularisations. A description of the facts and judgment will provide a clear example of how the protection of the right to family and private life can bar the removal of an irregular migrant.[123] Ms Rodrigues Da Silva, a Brazilian woman, arrived in the Netherlands in 1994 on a tourist visa that she subsequently overstayed. She had a relationship for three years with Mr Hoogkamer, a Dutch national and the father of her daughter. The relationship ended three years later without Ms Rodrigues Da Silva having regularised her stay in the Netherlands as she had been entitled to. After the relationship ended Mr Hoogkamer was granted custody of their daughter. Even though she did not have a valid residence permit and was issued a decree to return to Brazil, Ms Rodrigues Da Silva stayed in the host Member State and kept very close ties with her daughter.[124] The ECtHR decided that returning Ms Rodrigues would represent a violation of Article 8 ECHR and therefore granted her a right to regularise her stay, given that the economic wellbeing of the country was not harmed by the applicant's right to stay.

In the ECtHR's opinion the Dutch authorities 'indulged in excessive formalism'[125] when they focused on the illegal residence status rather than on the right to family life of the applicant. It must be noted that the respect for Article 8 ECHR can be a safeguard for those whose removal cannot be enforced,[126] and can also represent a reason to regularise illegal stay on a national level, as in the *Rodrigues Da Silva* case.

Having examined this decision of the ECtHR, one wonders whether the ECHR is not only a source of the obligation to not remove an irregular migrant but also if it could be the case that it also is a source for the right to regularisation. Thym considers that the ECtHR in the *Sisojeva*[127] and *Rodriguez da Silva* cases demonstrates its new readiness, in relation to respect for private and family life, to extend the protective reach of Article 8 ECHR in the field of immigration.[128] Certainly, this type of approach raises questions with regard to the interaction of the Convention with national and European immigration law, taking in account the balance between the protection of human rights and the preservation of the

[122] ibid, 162.

[123] *Rodrigues da Silva & Hoogkamer v the Netherlands*, ECHR (2006) App No 50435/99, para 44.

[124] ibid, para 42.

[125] ibid, para 44.

[126] Art 14 (1) a) of the Return Directive: 'family unity with members present in their territory is maintained'.

[127] *Sisojeva v Latvia*, ECHR (2007) App No 60654/00. This case is another example used by Thym to illustrate the potential of the new Strasbourg case law concerning the illegal immigrant's status.

[128] Thym (n 109) 111.

contracting parts margin of appreciation. At the national level a considerable number of Member States' national legislation already see the disruption of one's family life or private life as a reason for preventing the deportation of a migrant from their territory; Spain and Portugal are examples of that national practice.[129] Indeed the Court taking a position on this matter would to a certain extent address the differing national responses creating grey areas where migrants live in acknowledged irregularity.

Thym's view on the potential of Article 8 ECHR is an interesting take on the regularisation of illegal stay since he advocated the human right to regularisation of an illegal stay—a potential remedy for non-removability at the EU level. Costello acknowledges that the 'the failure to provide a secure right of residence' could mean that migrants may invoke Article 8 ECHR to regularise their stay.[130] Desmond has argued in the same vein that, after the Treaty of Lisbon, there is a better chance of linking the 'regularization potential' enshrined in Article 8 of the ECHR and the regularisation mechanism of Article 6 (4) of the Return Directive.[131] This author goes further and states that the case law of the ECtHR will serve as an indication of the situations when an irregular migrant should be regularised through the application of Article 6(4) of the Return Directive. Others, like Acosta, argue that the CJEU could have also imposed an obligation to regularise non-removable migrants grounded on Article 6(4) of the Return Directive and Article 4 of the EU Charter of Fundamental Rights, similar to what it did in relation to asylum procedures.[132] Although in principle this is a remedy that could in fact put an end to certain non-removability situations, it is hard to disregard the fact that there is nothing compulsory in the wording of Article 6(4) of the Return Directive and its interpretation and use is left to the Member State discretion alone despite all the indications, as confirmed by the CJEU in the *Mahdi* case. However, until there is an EU legislative initiative to deal with the regularisation of irregular migrants this argument seems to have nothing more than normative value.

Moreover, it is important to highlight, as Dembour did, that the ECtHR did not recognise a right to be regularised under Article 8 ECHR. Since the *Boultif* decision, the ECtHR could go either way with regards qualifying a removal of a migrant a breach of Article 8 ECHR or not.[133] It is clear that the ECtHR's case law is still strongly influenced by the States' prerogative over the admission the deportation of migrants, embodied by the case *Abdulaziz v UK*.[134]

[129] Art 124 of the Spanish Regulation 2011 and Art 135 b) of the Portuguese Lei 29/2012: 'Tenham a seu cargo filhos menores de nacionalidade portuguesa ou estrangeira, a residir em Portugal, sobre os quais exerçam efetivamente as responsabilidades parentais e a quem assegurem o sustento e educação'.

[130] Costello (n 3) 114.

[131] A Desmond, 'Regularization in the European Union and the United States—The Frequent Use of an Exceptional Measure' in Anja Wiesbrock and Diego Acosta Arcarazo, *Global Migration: Old Assumptions, New Dynamics* (Santa Barbara CA, Praeger, 2015; eBook Collection (EBSCOhost)) 82.

[132] Acosta Arcarazo (n 7) 1376.

[133] Dembour (n 109) 182.

[134] *Abdulaziz, Cabales and Balkandi v UK* (1985), European Court of Human Rights, App No 9214/80, 9473/81, 9474/81.

ECtHR decisions such as *Antwi*[135] and *Omorgie*[136] back up the claim that there is not settled ECtHR case law on when could be inferred from Article 8 ECHR a right to be regularised. Mr Antwi's removal was not considered to be in violation of Article 8 ECHR. Mr Antwi, a Ghanaian national that lived irregularly in Norway, was married to a Norwegian national who was born in Ghana. The couple had a daughter who was also a Norwegian national. In this case the ECtHR considered that the couple kept strong ties with Ghana (unlike their daughter) and that the removal of Mr Antwi would not be an obstacle to his wife taking care of their child.[137] This outcome contrasts for example with the outcome in *Nunez*.[138]

More recently in the *Jeunesse* decision,[139] the ECHR paved the way for another take on the situations that are covered by Article 8 ECHR and those that disrespect it. The Court stated that the main question to be answered in that case was whether the Netherlands had the duty to grant a residence permit to a Surinamese national who was refused the right to reside in that Member State.[140] The applicant was married to a Dutch national and her children also had Dutch nationality, as such being granted a residence permit would allow her to enjoy her family life within the host State. The ECtHR utilised different reasoning than that which the CJEU relied upon in the *Zambrano* case,[141] which was similar to *Jeunesse* in terms of facts although the reasoning was based on EU citizenship rules.[142] It is noteworthy to look at how the ECtHR took into account the de facto tolerance of the presence of the applicant by the Dutch authorities as a factor:

> The tolerance of her presence for such a lengthy period of time, during which for a large part it was open to the authorities to remove her, in effect enabled the applicant to establish and develop strong family, social and cultural ties in the Netherlands. The applicant's address, where she has been living for the last fifteen years, has always been known to the Netherlands authorities.[143]

The ECtHR argued in *Jeunesse* that the fact that the national authorities tolerated the presence of the applicant within the territory of the Member State for an extended period of time contributed to the creation of strong family, social and cultural ties with the host State. One can then conclude that in this case the 15 years of de facto tolerated non-removability played an important role in being granted the right to a residence permit in the Netherlands. Although this was not the only factor to be taken into account in this judgment, the assessment of the best interests of the child was a determining factor for the outcome of this case. The Court considered that it was the applicant who was in charge of the

135 *Antwi and others v Norway*, ECHR, (2012), App No 26940/10.
136 *Omoregie and Others v Norway*, ECHR, (2008), App No 265/07.
137 *Antwi and others v Norway* (n 135) para 99 and Costello (n 3) 126.
138 Costello, ibid, 126 and *Nunez v Norway*, ECHR, (2011), App no 55597/09.
139 *Jeunesse v The Netherlands*, ECHR (2014), App no 12738/10, judgment of the 3 October 2014.
140 ibid para 105.
141 See the *Zambrano* judgment (n 50).
142 ibid, para 42.
143 Para 116 of the *Jeunesse* judgment (n 139).

children and as such 'their interests are best served by not disrupting their present circumstances'.[144] Further, the applicant was considered the primary and constant carer of the children who do not have any direct link with Suriname, the country to which mother would have been relocated.

In fact the Court went further in arguing not only that the Dutch authorities did not proceed to a proper assessment of these circumstances,[145] but also that 'it is questionable whether general immigration policy considerations of themselves can be regarded as sufficient justification for refusing the applicant residence in the Netherlands'.[146] The ECtHR, nevertheless, stated that the Mrs Jeunesse case is one of exceptional circumstances,[147] and that although in this case there was a violation of Article 8 ECHR, it is hard to depict a general solution to remedy these situations of non-removability.

From this analysis one can conclude that although there are some potential solutions for the regularisation of migrants, such as the regularising power of Article 8 ECHR, which some have advocated, these are still far from the stage of enforceability and are not more than normative proposals. Even if one would agree with this position, it is not a comprehensive remedy because, as shown above, not all non-removability cases are under the protection of Article 8 ECHR. As such, one can ask how some non-removable migrants have their status more easily regularised than others.

B. Article 3 of the ECHR and the Non-removability of Irregular Migrants

We turn now to another provision that also has an impact on the creation of non-removability. An irregular migrant's health or a serious illness is similarly liable to prevent their return to the country of origin. This cause of non-removability has its legal basis in Article 3 ECHR. Once more the ECtHR has drawn up guidelines for situations that might constitute a violation of the prohibition of torture or degrading treatment.[148] The case of *N v the United Kingdom*,[149] which concerned the return of a woman from Uganda infected with HIV/AIDS living in the United Kingdom, lists the criteria used by the Strasbourg court to determine when the removal of a migrant who is seriously ill derogates Article 3 ECHR.

Cases like *D v the United Kingdom*[150] and *N v the United Kingdom* are about people who are receiving high quality treatment in the EU and if returned to their countries risk receiving less than adequate treatment for their serious illnesses. The ECtHR stated first that 'ill-treatment must attain a minimum level of severity

[144] ibid, para 119.
[145] ibid, para 120.
[146] ibid, para 121.
[147] ibid, para 122.
[148] Art 3 of the ECHR.
[149] *N v United Kingdom*, ECHR (2008), App no 26565/05 *27*.
[150] *D v the United Kingdom*, ECHR (1997), App no 30240/96 24.

if it is to fall within the scope of Article 3', and, second, that the assessment of this minimum level of severity 'depends on all the circumstances of the case, such as the duration of the treatment, its physical and mental effects and, in some cases, the sex, age and state of health of the victim'.[151] Additionally, the ECtHR clarified that the scope of Article 3 ECHR is mainly intended to prevent deportation or expulsion where the risk of ill-treatment in the receiving country emanates from intentionally inflicted acts of the public authorities there or from non-State bodies when the authorities are unable to afford the applicant appropriate protection.[152] In this particular case, however, the ECtHR did not accept that the applicant was critically ill at the time and as such could be returned to the country of origin where she would be able to obtain access to medical treatment, support and care, including help from relatives.

Issues of non-removability again would arise when the outcome is different and the irregular migrant is considered to be severely ill and unable to receive appropriate protection in their home country. In this scenario there is no duty on the Member States to grant a residence status to migrants who as a result of their severe illness cannot be removed. Member States have the discretion as to whether or not to grant a residence authorisation in their territory to people in these circumstances. If an irregular migrant is simultaneously prevented from returning to their country of origin due to the prohibition on torture and degrading treatment in accordance to Article 3 ECHR and not granted a residence permit at a national level, that individual will be living in the undefined legal limbo of non-removability.

The protection provided by Article 3 ECHR also includes other humanitarian considerations such as the possibility of preventing the removal of persons who are not protected by international means of protection; for example those who are excluded from the scope of the Qualifications Directive. This legal instrument is not comprehensive in relation to all the categories of migrant in need of international protection. In general terms and as defined in the Qualifications Directive, international protection includes refugee and subsidiary protection status.[153] However, there are still categories of people in need of protection who cannot be included in one of these categories. For example, from the wording of Article 15(c) of the Qualifications Directive,[154] one deduces that it only protects a person whose protection needs are a consequence of civil strife or massive violations of human rights, whereas those whose needs do not result from an armed conflict are excluded.[155] Consequently, those who lack the types of international protection contemplated in the Directive can benefit from an impediment to their removal based on Article 3 ECHR, which were already mentioned above. Despite the fact

[151] ibid, para 29.
[152] ibid, para 31.
[153] Art 2 (a) of the Qualifications Directive.
[154] ibid, Art 15 (c): '(c) serious and individual threat to a civilian's life or person by reason of indiscriminate violence in *situations of international or internal armed conflict*'. (emphasis added)
[155] The Statement of the United Nations Commissioner for Refugees (UNHCR) (2008) see: www.unhcr.org/refworld/docid/4799df7472.html.

that these people are granted protection under the ECHR prohibition on torture and degrading treatment, this protection does not result in the granting of a residence permit by the national authorities in charge. Moreover, as in the other situations of non-removable migrants living in between illegality and legality, the lack of a valid temporary residence permit may affect their access to fundamental rights.

Furthermore, Article 3 of the Convention on the Rights of the Child states that 'the best interests of the child shall be a primary consideration' when public or private social welfare institutions, courts of law, administrative authorities or legislative bodies are undertaking actions concerning children.[156] Thus, when a child is returned unaccompanied, his or her best interest shall be of primary consideration, and his or her return shall be suspended if no appropriate reception can be provided by family members, nominated guardian or other reception facilities in the State of return.[157] Even though each Member State's solutions to these cases are different, normally when protection is attributed to a minor the host Member State grants a residence permit valid until the child is 18.[158] As an adult he or she, in the absence of legal residency (and also when no removal occurs), may find themselves in a position of irregularity.

In the preceding sections a snapshot was provided of how the ECtHR deals with non-removability and whether this practice could reveal a remedy for the legal limbo situations in which these migrants live. Similar to the hands off approach of the CJEU with regards the obligation to regularise non-removable migrants, the ECtHR (despite having the tools to achieve a different outcome) addresses the issue of non-removability with a 'highly casuistic (case-by-case) approach'.[159] Consequently, EU law, namely the Return Directive, and the ECHR leave unanswered the question: how much longer will the EU Courts avoid dealing systematically with legal limbos that maybe generated at a supranational level? Given that EU law, namely the Return Directive, and the ECHR leave this case unanswered it is pertinent to take a look at the Member State' responses to non-removability in their territory.

C. Member States' Responses to Non-removability

Member State sovereignty is weakened by phenomena such as irregular migration[160] due to the fact that once border control is challenged state sovereignty is consequently undermined. Rodríguez and Rubio-Marín observe that irregular

[156] Art 3 of the Convention on the Rights of the Child, opened for signature 20 November 1989, 1577 UNTS 3 (entered into force 2 September 1990).

[157] Art 10 (2) of the Return Directive.

[158] Fundamental Rights Agency (FRA) Comparative Report on Fundamental rights of migrants in an irregular situation in the European Union, 2011, 32.

[159] Dembour (n 109) 182.

[160] K Koser, 'Dimensions and Dynamics of Irregular Migration, Population' (2010) 16 *Population, Space and Place* 189.

migration challenges sovereignty 'highlighting the limits of the State's ability to maintain sovereign control over its territory, but in form of a person endowed with dignity and therefore deserving of respect regardless of status'.[161] In relation to the way domestic policies and legislation address situations of non-removability of migrants (an atypical form of illegality); there is no common ground within the EU. Domestic legal responses to such issues are relatively heterogeneous, not only between Member States but also within them. The causes of the suspension as well as different aspects such as the migrant's individual profile or the interests in question affect the sort of responses given at the national level.[162] The responses to non-removability found at the national level can be divided into the three most common scenarios: (i) de facto toleration, (ii) formal toleration and (iii) temporary residence permits. The solutions range considerably, and more importantly, they imply different levels of security of residence and different immigration statuses.

i. De Facto Toleration

De facto toleration occurs when a given Member State simply does not deal with the category of non-removed migrants. Despite issuing the order of removal, and possibly a copy of their release decision, the national authorities may provide non-removable illegally-staying migrants with any documentation in order to prevent them from, for instance, being re-arrested and detained. If the national laws and administrative practices of a Member State, such as Portugal, for instance, do not provide any authorisation to stay or prove of the existence of an obstacle of removal, non-removed migrants will have to face a genuine legal limbo: no authorisation to stay, however, no enforcement of removal.

ii. Formal Toleration

Member States may grant persons who cannot be removed formal authorisation to stay (formal toleration recognition). The classical formal toleration scenario is the provision of a document proving that removal is to be delayed. Formal recognition corresponds to the obligation imposed by the Return Directive in Article 14(2) which refers, as we have seen, to a written confirmation in accordance with national legislation. Nevertheless, recognised toleration status assures a certain degree of protection since it acknowledges the presence of that person in the territory, protecting them from being arrested and detained, and facilitates access to certain fundamental rights. Normally, formal toleration is also temporary, however in

[161] Rodríguez and Rubio-Marín (n 64) 74.

[162] For instance, when there is a suspension of removal for separated children the response would normally lead to the issuance of a residence permit, whereas if the obstacle for removal is difficulty in identifying the nationality of the person, this may lead to a de facto toleration of that person, in Fundamental Rights Agency (FRA) Comparative Report on Fundamental rights of migrants in an irregular situation in the European Union, 2011, 35.

some Member States like in Germany non-removable migrants who were granted a toleration permit (Duldung) may have this transformed into a residence permit if certain conditions are fulfilled.[163]

iii. Temporary Residence Permits

Also within all Member State's discretion are those avenues related to humanitarian, practical or policy issues as previously explained when addressing this issue at the supranational level (in specific Article 6(4) Return Directive). Indeed, certain legislation such as domestic Finnish legislation, contemplates this possibility. In Finland, irregular migrants who cannot be removed for health reasons are issued a temporary residence permit.[164] Once a temporary residence permit is issued non-removable migrants are then legally residing in the EU. In theory, if a case of non-removability is not as temporary as initially expected, and the temporary residence permit is renewed, it would likely mean that migrants under such circumstances could try to obtain a long-term resident status, in accordance with the conditions imposed by the Long-term Residents Directive.[165]

The status granted to an irregular migrant often changes, especially taking into account the fact that migrants' circumstances are constantly changing. For example, as illustrated above, under Spanish law a woman with an irregular status who has been a victim of domestic violence and who has also proceeded to denounce the aggressor cannot be removed from Spain. She would be granted a temporary residence and work permit. If the aggressor were convicted of committing that crime, the victim would be then granted a residence permit of five years, which would allow her to apply for a long-term residence status.[166] This example highlights the heterogeneous character of this category of migrants, and also shows that it is not feasible to give definitive answers to how a non-removable migrant ought to be treated in the European scene, or if obtaining long-term resident status is the most frequent route out of this condition.

The scenarios and responses vary and simultaneously the statuses change: from irregular migrant living in a clandestine manner a non-removable person can become a long-term resident or have an established specific status as in Germany, or merely be de facto tolerated practically living in a clandestine manner within the host Member State's territory with very limited access to basic fundamental rights (or even be granted a temporary residence permit after a period of time). It should also be noted that a Member State granting formal postponement status to non-removable migrants is not the same as granting those third-country nationals a wider range of rights. In fact, the result may even be the opposite and Member

[163] ibid, 37.

[164] ibid, 37.

[165] Council Directive 2003/109/EC of 25 November 2003 concerning the status of third-country nationals who are long-term residents, [2004], OJ L 16/44, (hereinafter 2003/109 Directive).

[166] Arts 131–34 Real Decreto 557/2011, de 20 abril.

States can use the formal recognition of a toleration status as a tool to control and minimise the rights of those covered by migrant protection. As such, the following subsection focuses on the analysis of Portuguese legislation on the matter. Portugal opted for de facto toleration instead of a recognising a formal toleration status as Germany did.

D. Non-removability in Portugal: A Toleration De Facto Case

For the purposes of providing a more accurate and detailed picture of one of the trends that characterise national practices on non-removability the last subsection is dedicated to the analysis of Portuguese immigration law on the matter. The aim of this exercise is to illustrate one of the ways national legislation that deals with the phenomenon of non-removability tolerating de facto these migrants, without taking any direct measure to address the situation as it is suggested on the Return Directive recital, for instance.[167]

The Return Directive was transposed into the Portuguese legal order by the Lei no 29/2012,[168] which amends the previous Portuguese immigration law Lei no 23/2007.[169] The new piece of legislation came into force on 8 October 2012. Despite the late implementation of the Return Directive and the fact that there has not yet been any significant national case law on it, some remarks can be made. First of all, in relation to detention rules the Directive introduced no significant changes to the existing rules. Similar to the corresponding Spanish legislation, detention is limited to a maximum of 60 days after which the person must be immediately released.[170] If the period for voluntary departure has not yet expired, certain obligations may be imposed on a migrant with the view of avoiding the risk of absconding: for example, the deposit of a financial guarantee. The Directive makes reference to an 'adequate' financial guarantee, whereas the Portuguese implementing legislation does not mention any adequacy condition, and one might question the proportionality of this obligation.[171]

In relation to the safeguards pending return,[172] which relate directly to the status that is granted to non-removable migrants have in each Member States, Portuguese law does not make a reference to the need to ensure any such safeguards during the period of postponement of removal and seems to only impose them during the period for voluntary departure.[173] However, this would be a very literal

[167] Recital 12 of the Return Directive.

[168] Lei da Assembleia da República nº 29/ 2012, Art 2 (1) h).

[169] Lei da Assembleia da República nº 23/2007 de 4 de Julho de 2007, aprova o regime jurídico de entrada, permanência, saída e afastamento de estrangeiros do território nacional, Diário da República, 1.a série—No 127.

[170] Art 146 (3) Lei nº 29/2012.

[171] Art 7 (3) of the Return Directive and Art 160 (3)d) Lei nº 29/2012.

[172] Art 14 of the Return Directive.

[173] Art 160 (4) (5) Lei nº 29/2012.

reading of Article 160 (4) (5) Lei no 29/2012, and the safeguards pointed out by the Portuguese immigration law apply to both periods, postponement of removal and voluntary departure. A recent study of the Commission on the situation of third-country nationals pending return highlighted some of rights that were granted in practice to this group of illegally staying third-country nationals, for instance:[174]

a) Family unity: in reception facilities, families awaiting their deportation are granted a private bedroom, with a private bathroom and there are also facilities available for children to play;
b) Healthcare: emergency, primary and secondary care is provided but it is charged to third-country nationals; NGOs may provide help;
c) Education: no higher and vocational education is possible since an official ID is needed;
d) Access to the labour market: no right to access the labour market is granted, however, it is common practice to legally register the third-country nationals pending return with social security;
e) Reception conditions: accommodation is only granted in emergency cases and for third-country nationals in detention centres.

Further, the Return Directive specifically makes reference to the need to take into account 'as far as possible' the principles contemplated in Article 14 Return Directive, and that condition was in part neglected in the wording of the national implementing legislation. The reference made in Lei no 29/2012 suggests that they ought to be taken into account but does not give any indication as to what extent it should be. In addition to the above, there is the obligation imposed on Member States by the Return Directive as mentioned above of providing written confirmation to the migrant to whom the period of voluntary departure was extended. The written confirmation would also formalise the fact that the return decision would not be enforced temporarily, and consequently, it would grant a certain degree of legal certainty to a non-removed migrant. Nevertheless, it was not contemplated in the implementing Portuguese legislation that any variation of this written confirmation will consequently allow third-country nationals to be granted the de facto toleration status with no official proof of the postponement of their return.

Additionally, one of the most significant legal vacuums that can be found in the Portuguese (and also in the Spanish) legislation concerns the regulation of the access to regularisation by non-removable migrants, as it was stressed in the aforementioned EU Commission study on the situation of third-country nationals pending return.[175] The inexistence of rules allowing the access to

[174] European Commission, *Study on the situation of third-country nationals pending return/removal in the EU Member States and the Schengen Associated Countries*—HOME/2010/ RFXX/PR/1001, 11/03/2013, 34–42.

[175] European Commission, *Study on the situation of third-country nationals pending return/removal in the EU Member States and the Schengen Associated Countries*—HOME/2010/ RFXX/PR/1001, 11/03/2013.

regularisation not only is an explanation, to a certain extent, for the de facto toleration of non-removable migrants (the lack of remedies leads to an indifference towards the situation) at the national level, but also complicates non-removable migrants' shift from illegality to legality by protracting the legal limbo to an even greater extent.

V. CONCLUSION

Non-removable migrants are third-country nationals who are illegally staying in the host Member State and have an atypical immigration legal situation. The atypical immigration status results from the combination of legal and illegal dimensions in the same immigration status. Chapter three assessed the atypical nature of this immigration status. The lack of a definition of the legal status of non-removable migrants has resulted in heterogeneous national responses to the same phenomenon. The chapter started by posing the preliminary question of whether there is a legal status for non-removable third-country national illegally-staying migrants at an EU level. After having agreed on the recognition of such a status, the elements (rights, obligations and written confirmation of non-removability) of that atypical status were analysed from an EU law perspective.

The last part of the chapter focused on the remedies provided by EU and national levels. With the aim of illustrating one of the possible Member States' responses to the non-removability of illegally staying third country nationals, the chapter turned to the example of Portugal as a de facto toleration case. The provision of an example of the domestic treatment of non-removable migrants was necessary to demonstrate the heterogeneity that results from the lack of harmonisation with regard to non-removability of third-country nationals. In addition, more uniform among domestic legislative choices is the fact that the regime for granting access to regularisation to non-removable migrants is mostly non-existent within Member States' legislation and instead more often toleration statuses are the first response to remedy these limbo situations.

4

The Potential Effects of Information Technology Vis-à-Vis Illegality

I. INTRODUCTION

RECENT COUNTER-TERRORISM and public security measures have significantly altered EU immigration law.[1] The 9/11 attacks in the US strongly influenced policy in the areas of crime prevention and immigration adopted by the EU. This event also motivated the increased use of new policing technologies and electronic immigration databases. Consequently it has been claimed that 'the EU is turning into an electronic fortress'.[2] Concepts such as border security have gained increasing significance after these events and the exchange of personal data was enhanced with the purpose of allowing better flow of data between the multiple EU databases, EU agencies and other EU bodies.[3] In addition, new tools to more effectively address the phenomenon of illegality have been created in the form of new border surveillance initiatives.

Chapter four assesses, in relation to data protection, what the key features of illegality are by providing an analysis of the recently established EU surveillance systems. This exercise is also meant to help understand in which ways the concept of illegality adopted by the EU, previously explored in earlier chapters, shapes, or is shaped by, these information systems. The chapter is structured in order to argue that the latest developments in the area of data technology contribute to the so-called phenomenon of 'crimmigration' that essentially conflates immigration and criminalisation.[4]

[1] V Mitsilegas, 'The Borders Paradox: The Surveillance of Movement in a Union without Internal Frontiers' in H Lindahl (ed), *A Right to Inclusion and Exclusion: Normative Fault-lines of the EU is Area of Freedom, Security and Justice* (Oxford, Hart Publishing, 2009) 61; A Baldaccini, 'Counter-terrorism and the EU Strategy for Border Security: Framing Suspects with Biometric Documents and Databases' (2008) 10 *European Journal of Migration and Law* 31, 31–32 and F Boehm, *Information Sharing and Data Protection in the Area of Freedom, Security and Justice: Towards Harmonised Data Protection Principles for Information Exchange at EU-level* (Berlin/Heidelberg, Springerverlag, 2012) 1–2.

[2] B Hayes and M Vermeulen, 'Borderline—The EU's New Border Surveillance Initiatives—Assessing the Costs and the Fundamental Rights of EUROSUR and the "Smart Borders" Proposals', A Study by the Heinrich Böll Foundation, June 2012, 4.

[3] Mitsilegas (n 1)54.

[4] JP Stumpf, 'The Crimmigration Crisis: Immigrants, Crime, and Sovereign Power' (2006) Bepress Legal Series, Working Paper 1635, 378: 'I argue that the trend toward criminalizing immigration law has set us on a path toward establishing irrevocably intertwined systems: immigration and criminal law as

First, a brief contextualisation of the visas and border control systems is provided. The main scope and objectives of the Schengen Information System and its second-generation (hereafter SIS/SIS II), the Visa Information System (hereafter VIS) and EURODAC databases are presented before a thematic analysis is conducted to assess what is actually achieved with the latest developments in the area of data collection and exchange of information. Second, this chapter assesses the necessity and proportionality of the EU's new surveillance initiatives such as the European External Border Surveillance System (hereafter EUROSUR) and the so-called 'smart borders package' including the Entry Exit System (hereafter EES). In other words, this chapter seeks to pose the following fundamentally important question: what do these proposals tell us about the development of the construction of illegal stay in EU? Ultimately, the legal instruments that regulate EU immigration databases have a role in shaping the legal regime of illegality. In doing so these legal documents contribute to the creation of a digital illegality that does not necessarily correspond to the regulation of illegality in EU legislation and contributes to the potential criminalisation of illegally-staying migrants and the creation of a two-tier regime of migration.

II. EU IMMIGRATION DATABASES UNDER CONSTRUCTION

The main elements of this argument can be summarised as follows. Borders are *per definitionem* a form of expression of a State's sovereignty. By determining who can gain access and who cannot borders are by their nature an instrument for exclusion. Borders have been gradually assigned new tasks after the implementation of the information exchange systems in the Area of Freedom, Security and Justice since the SIS in 1995. These new tasks are related primarily to the categorisation and access to the territory of migrants who want to enter the EU. Categorising people and, crucially, illegally-staying migrants, is intertwined with individual documentation and registration, as Broeders has stated:

> Border surveillance can be seen as a sorting machine designed to earmark, standardize and sometimes even privilege part of the migrant population whilst at the same time earmarking, denying access and attempting to exclude and expel another part.[5]

Furthermore, the introduction of information technology has also dictated the 'transformation of European borders to digital borders'[6] and the inclusion of

doppelgangers'. See also, JP Stumpf, 'Doing Time: Crimmigration Law and the Perils of Haste' (2011) 58 *UCLA Law Review* 1705, 1726, K Franko Aas, '"Crimmigrant" Bodies and Bona Fide Travelers: Surveillance, Citizenship and Global Governance' (2011) 15 *Theoretical Criminology* 331, 332.

[5] D Broeders, 'A European "Border" Surveillance System' in H Dijstelbloem and A Meijer (eds), *Migration and the New Tecnological Borders of Europe* (Basingstoke, Palgrave Macmillan, 2011) 47.

[6] M Besters and F WA Brom, 'Greedy Information Technology: The Digitalization of the European Migration Policy' (2010) 12 *European Journal of Migration and Law* 456.

biometric data the transformation to 'biometric borders'.[7] The enhancement of the borders leads to the weakening of the individual and allows the creation of phenomena such as the convergence of criminal law and immigration law that enables the state to use its powers to 'expel from society the deemed criminally alien'.[8] In the words of Stumpf, 'the merger of criminal and immigration law is both odd and oddly unremarkable. It is odd because criminal law seems a distant cousin to immigration law'.[9]

As part of Member States' border regimes EU databases play a crucial role in the categorisation of migrants in Europe. The registration of people in EU databases and the storing of their fingerprints or other types of personal data are attempts to catalogue those arriving in EU territory.[10] However the role of EU information systems is not limited to the collection of personal information on mobile third-country nationals. It also influences the way illegality is conceptualised in EU law. There is a lack of definition of the contours of the concept of illegality and a misappropriation of the concept of criminality in order to define it. The most recent modifications and proposals in the area of EU immigration databases have increased their functions, enlarged their purposes and increased the number of authorities with access to them (for instance as we will see in relation to the *accessibility clause* added to EURODAC analysed below).[11] However, such developments have also brought problems with regards to the accuracy in the use of biometrics,[12] the possibility of misleading interlinked alerts that are able to affect one's status, the erosion of the purpose limitation principle and in some cases unauthorised access to the databases.

Some commentators have already argued that the development of EU databases in the Area of Freedom, Justice and Security (hereafter AFJS) reveals an 'opportunist use of the competences in the area of migration and border management'[13] and others have questioned the lawfulness and proportionality of the further use of these databases.[14] Whilst these are very significant aspects of current EU law regulation of this area, the main focus of this chapter is not on either of these issues. What is central to this part of the book is a reflection on how the latest developments in the area of AFJS databases influence the concept of illegality in the EU and thus the categorisation of migrants under EU law. In sum,

[7] L Amoore, 'Biometric Borders: Governing Mobilities in the War on Terror' (2006) 25 *Political geography* 336.

[8] Stumpf, 'The Crimmigration Crisis' (n 4) 378.

[9] ibid, 379.

[10] Broeders (n 5) 43.

[11] See subsection IV.A of the present chapter.

[12] Approximately 5 per cent of the world population does not have fingerprints or their fingerprints are not readable by a machine, especially children and elderly people.

[13] J Rijpma, *Building Borders: The Regulatory Framework for the Management of the External Borders of the European Union* (Florence, European University Institute, 2009) 208.

[14] E Renate Brouwer, *Digital Borders and Real Rights: Effective Remedies for Third-country Nationals in the Schengen Information System*, vol 15 (Leiden, Brill, 2008) 144.

if European borders are 'being transformed into digital borders'[15] how does this digitalisation of borders affect irregular migrant statuses in the EU?

Three centralised, large-scale EU databases must be mentioned when analysing the exchange of personal information in relation to third-country nationals (and EU citizens in a lesser extent[16]): a) the SIS/SIS II; b) the VIS; and c) EURODAC. In recent years there has been a significant increase in the personal data stored by these information databases, relating increasingly to crime and law enforcement issues. The combination of the latter trends with broader access of law enforcement authorities to these information systems has contributed considerably to transforming their primary purposes. By carefully analysing how the change in their purpose has affected the European concept of illegality, it is argued in this chapter that the infamous 'digital explosion'[17] plays a momentous role. The following aspects must be taken into account throughout the chapter as guidelines for the analysis of the aforementioned Europe-wide information systems and as factors of the criminalisation of immigration:

(i) The erosion of the purpose limitation principle or the shift in purposes;
(ii) Enhanced accessibility *versus* proportionality concerns;
(iii) The shift from immigration to an instrumental use of databases.

A. Brief Overview of First Generation Immigration Databases

i. The Schengen Information System (SIS) and the Second Generation Schengen Information System (SIS II)[18]

Germany, France, Belgium, Luxembourg and the Netherlands signed the Schengen Agreement on 14 June 1985 marking the start of a brand new era for European migration and policy. The intergovernmental agreement was set up to gradually abolish restrictions on the movement of persons and goods at their internal borders.[19] The creation of a European database was a project proposed in 1987 and was the result of the negotiations for measures to compensate for the abolition of internal borders within the European Union. In the early stages the SIS mainly operated in the area of public policy and public security. The focal point

[15] Besters and Brom (n 6) 455: reference to the 'pixellisation of the border' in the same sense.

[16] These databases store data mainly on asylum seekers, irregular migrants, migrants with short-visas and criminals.

[17] H Abelson, K Ledeen and H R Lewis, *Blown to Bits: Your Life, Liberty, and Happiness after the Digital Explosion* (Boston, Addison-Wesley Professional, 2008).

[18] European Parliament and Council Regulation (EC) No 1987/2006 of the 28 December 2006 on the establishment operation and use of the second generation Schengen Information System (SIS II), [2006], OJ L 381/4.

[19] Arts 92 to 119 Schengen Agreement, signed on the 14 June 1985, [1985], OJ L 239/13. Later, in the Treaty of Amsterdam, the Schengen Agreement was added to the EU/EC legal framework.

of the SIS was registering persons and goods, including vehicles, that were to be refused entrance to the Schengen area or that were wanted by one of the Member States in a hit/no hit system.[20] From 1995 onwards the SIS was implemented and became the central system for information exchange between authorities in charge of border surveillance.[21] Facilitating free movement of people and goods while taking complementary measures to safeguard security and illegal immigration within the Schengen area were posited as the core principles of the SIS.[22]

Notwithstanding the fact that SIS serves immigration purposes as well as criminal law and policing purposes, it remains almost completely a third pillar measure, since the important provisions of the Schengen *acquis* were not included in the EC Treaty in 1999. While initially the SIS was a database with a purely a hit/no hit nature, in recent times it has been shifting towards becoming a more general intelligence database and a police investigation tool; a phenomenon which we will examine in this subsection.

The core purposes that the SIS II was meant to achieve were:[23] (i) increased capacity for the database in order to adjust to the increasing numbers of Schengen Member States; (ii) the use of new technology; (iii) fight against terrorism;[24] and (iv) the technology needed to accommodate the storage of biometrics.[25] Although intended to come into operation in 2007, SIS II only came into operation on 9 April 2013 due to a number of delays.

ii. EURODAC

On 11 December 2000 Council Regulation 2725/2000 (hereinafter the EURODAC Regulation)[26] established the EURODAC (European Dactylographic System). This database, which became operational in January 2003, was designed to assist in the determination of which Member State is responsible for examining an asylum claim lodged in a Member State, in accordance with the conditions set out in the

[20] The SIS II Regulation defines alert in Art 3 (1) a) as: 'a set of data entered in SIS II allowing the competent authorities to identify a person with a view to taking a specific action and in "hits" are define as a request made by the issuing State to the other Schengen countries take a certain action'.

[21] In 1990 was signed the Implementing Convention (Convention Implementing the Schengen Agreement CISA) and entered in force in 1995 at that time Italy, Portugal, Spain and Greece were already part of the Schengen area. Arts 92 to 119 of the CISA regulated the SIS.

[22] Art 17 of the Schengen Agreement.

[23] SIS II Regulation recital 12 and arts 1 and 2.

[24] Council Regulation (EC) No 871/2004 of 29 April 2004 concerning the introduction of some new functions for the Schengen Information System, including in the fight against terrorism [2004], OJ L 162/29; Council Decision 2005/211/JHA of 24 February 2005 concerning the introduction of some new function for the Schengen Information System, including in the fight against terrorism [2005], OJ L 68/44.

[25] For example photographs and fingerprints.

[26] Art 1 (1) of the Council Regulation (EC) No 2725/2000 concerning the establishment of 'Eurodac' for the comparison of fingerprints for the effective application of the Dublin Convention, [2000], OJ L 316/1, this Regulation became operational in 2003 (hereafter EURODAC Regulation).

Dublin Regulation.[27] The Dublin Regulation aims to prevent so-called 'asylum shopping'[28] and the EURODAC Regulation determines whether an individual has already sought sanctuary in another Member State. The UK and Ireland chose to be part of this Regulation that develops part of the Schengen *acquis*, similarly, Denmark and the Schengen Associated Countries are covered by the Dublin Regulation and EURODAC.[29] Both the EURODAC Regulation and the amended Dublin Regulation (hereinafter Dublin III Regulation) are closely intertwined due to the fact that EURODAC is necessary for the functioning of the Dublin regime.[30] As such, the two Regulations were amended together in June 2013.[31]

The EURODAC II Regulation entered into force on 19 July 2013 but would only apply from 20 July 2015 onwards. As such, the focus of this chapter will be on the most recent version of EURODAC for practical and logical reasons.[32] The EURODAC information system may collect and store fingerprints of three categories of migrants: asylum seekers, migrants who have crossed the borders of the EU irregularly and are arrested and migrants who have been found illegally staying within EU territory.[33]

The last two categories of migrants under the surveillance of EURODAC are the most relevant in terms of determining the influence that the database has in the contours of the concept of illegality, and it should be noted that the last one is optional in the sense that Member States have discretion as to whether or not to make use of it. Some scholars such as Brouwer have criticised the inclusion of illegally-staying migrants under the auspices of EURODAC, highlighting the fact that fingerprinting illegally-staying migrants is potentially problematic:

> [E]ven if the EURODAC Regulation only allows the use (or recording) of these fingerprints for the examination whether or not the person concerned has applied in another

[27] ibid, recitals 2 and 3, Council Regulation (EC) No 343/2003 of 18 February 2003 establishing the criteria and mechanisms for determining the Member State responsible for examining an asylum application lodged in one of the Member States by a third-country national, [2003] OJ L 50/1.

[28] Asylum shopping can be one of two situations. First, the abusive practice of claiming asylum in more than one Member State and second, the 'comparison and selection of one asylum rule among several'. For a more comprehensive note on the second meaning of 'asylum shopping': Ségolène Barbou Des Places, *Evolution of asylum legislation in the EU: Insights from regulatory competition theory*, RSCAS Working Paper, EUI RSC; 2003/16, (2003), 3–7.

[29] Rijpma (n 13) 201. However in the recast Ireland chose not to be part of EURODAC II Regulation.

[30] European Parliament and Council Regulation (EU) No 603/2013 of 26 June 2013 on the establishment of 'Eurodac' for the comparison of fingerprints for the effective application of Regulation (EU) No 604/2013 establishing the criteria and mechanisms for determining the Member State responsible for examining an application for international protection lodged in one of the Member States by a third-country national or a stateless person and on requests for the comparison with Eurodac data by Member States' law enforcement authorities and Europol for law enforcement purposes, and amending Regulation (EU) No 1077/2011 establishing a European Agency for the operational management of large-scale IT systems in the area of freedom, security and justice (recast), [2013], OJ 2013, L 180/1 (hereafter EURODAC Regulation II).

[31] European Parliament and Council Regulation (EU) No 604/2013 of the of 26 June 2013 establishing the criteria and mechanisms for determining the Member State responsible for examining an application for international protection lodged in one of the Member States by a third-country national or a stateless person (recast), [2013], OJ 2013, L 180/31.

[32] Art 46 of the EURODAC II Regulation.

[33] ibid, Arts 9 (1) and 14 (1).

> Member State for asylum, the group which is effected by the Regulation seems unacceptably large.[34]

The author argues that the inclusion of categories two and three of migrants is 'unacceptably large' due to the fact that since these persons have not applied for asylum it is difficult to justify how the Dublin Convention can justify such fingerprinting. Admittedly, under the revised EURODAC Regulation, which specifically lists law enforcement as one of the objectives of the regulation, this objection could in part be refuted.

iii. Visa Information System (VIS)

The events that took place on 9/11 were the catalyst for the creation of the VIS in the EU. The extraordinary Council meeting confirmed the influence of these terrorist attacks when the Home Affairs and Justice Ministers pointed out the need for a tightened procedure for issuing visas in the EU.[35] Additionally, the conclusions of the Presidency of the European Council in Seville 2002 stressed the need for the 'introduction, as soon as possible, of a joint identification system for visa data'.[36]

The VIS was established to control the legality of the stay of those migrants who enter the EU on a short-term visa. The Council Decision of 8 June 2004 established the VIS as an information system for the exchange of visa data between Member States.[37] A few years later in 2008 the VIS Regulation entered into force. This regulation aims to set out the conditions and data exchange procedure between Member States.

The VIS, like the SIS, is a centralised database which consists of a central information system (C-VIS), and an interface in each Member State; the national part (N-VIS) of the VIS. This structure creates the link between the national authorities (N-VIS) and the C-VIS. Like the SIS central database, VIS is located in Strasbourg, therefore there is a common technical platform that can be also extended to EURODAC, although their access remains separate at the moment. The deadline to make the VIS operational was 2009 but it was only in October 2011 that the VIS started operations in North Africa when all Schengen States connected their consular posts to the system in Algeria, Egypt, Libya, Mauritania, Morocco and Tunisia.[38] The European Commission was responsible for the management and

[34] ER Brouwer, 'Eurodac: Its Limitations and Temptations' (2002) 4 *European Journal of Migration and Law* 231, 236.

[35] Extraordinary Council meeting of 20 September 2001, Doc.1219/01 (Presse 327).

[36] European Council, Presidency Conclusions, Seville, 21–22 June 2002 (SN 200/02) see point 30.

[37] Council Decision 2004/512/EC establishing the Visa Information System (VIS), [2004] OJ L-213/5.

[38] Report from the Commission to the European Parliament and the Council COM(2013) 232 final on the development of the Visa Information System (VIS), [2013], 4.

the implementation process of the VIS until EU-LISA[39] took over the operational responsibility of the system on 1 December 2012.[40]

Three trends are identifiable in the SIS, VIS and EURODAC databases which play (or will play) a relevant role in the categorisation of migrants who happen to come to the EU and have their personal data collected either by SIS II, VIS or EURODAC. The inclusion of law enforcement purposes is examined as a core factor that has resulted in the conflation of illegality and criminality in this area. Along with this factor the widening of the access to these databases to law enforcement authorities and their gradual transformation into investigative tools is addressed. This exercise is crucial to assessing whether the concept of illegality is being stretched to include these purposes or is consequently reshaped by them and given a new significance.

III. THE EROSION OF THE PURPOSE LIMITATION PRINCIPLE

Purpose limitation is a fundamental principle of data protection law and applies to national and international rules concerning data. The principle of purpose limitation applies at two stages, first at the preliminary stage with regard to the objective of data processing and second at the subsequent stage when the data is being exchanged.

Article 5 of the Council Convention for the Protection of Individuals with regard to Automatic Processing of Personal Data helps us to understand the meaning of this principle by establishing that data automatically processed shall be:

> a) Obtained and processed fairly and lawfully, b) stored for specified and legitimate purposes and not used in a way incompatible with those purposes, c) adequate, relevant and not excessive in relation to the purposes for which they are stored, d) preserved in a form which permits identification of data subjects for no longer than is required for the purpose for which those data are stored.[41]

The purpose limitation principle was later included in Article 6(1)(b) of Directive 95/46[42] where it was restated that personal data must be acquired for specified, explicit and justified purposes and must not be subsequently processed in a manner which is incompatible with these purposes. In 2016, the General Data

[39] The Agency for large-scale IT systems is a regulatory agency in the area of freedom, security and justice with legal personality. The Agency was primarily created to manage SIS/SIS II, EURODAC and VIS. EU-LISA's main goal is to keep the IT systems under its responsibility functioning uninterruptedly ensuring the exchange of data between national authorities. See: http://ec.europa.eu/dgs/home-affairs/what-we-do/policies/borders-and-visas/agency/index_en.htm.

[40] Report from the Commission to the European Parliament and the Council, COM(2013) 232 final, 4.

[41] Art 5 of the Data Protection Convention.

[42] European Parliament and Council Directive 95/46/EC on the protection of individuals with regard to the processing of personal data and on the free movement of such data, [1995], OJ 1995, L 281.

Protection Regulation,[43] which repealed Directive 95/46, posited on Article 5 b) that personal data shall be 'collected for specified, explicit and legitimate purposes and not further processed in a manner that is incompatible with those purposes'. A 'ban on aimless data collection'[44] is imposed and the data must only be used for legitimate purposes.[45] Furthermore, these legitimate purposes must be specified previous to the collection and the use or disclosure of the data must be compatible with the specified prior purposes. Last, the principle of purpose limitation imposes that data may not be retained longer than the time need for the purposes for which the data was collected and stored.

From the year 2000 onwards, as we have seen above, new information technology has been developed, biometric data has started to be used, large-scale multi-purpose databases created and, simultaneously, data protection recognised as a human right in accordance with Article 8 of the Charter on Fundamental Rights of the EU and Article 8 of the European Convention on Human Rights (ECHR).[46] Brouwer argues that three objectives underlie the right to data protection. First, the protection of individual rights,[47] second, the protection of rule of law[48] and third, the protection of 'good governance' which combines the protection of the data subject and the data controller.[49]

The erosion of the purpose limitation principle, as demonstrated in the recent shift in the purposes of the immigration databases, is central to the argument that the illegality of a migrant's stay (an immigration law concept) and criminality (a criminal law concept) are increasingly intertwined in EU law and at the domestic level.[50] The following two subsections assess two equally important trends in the area of immigration information technology that contribute to the conflation of illegality and criminality. First, however, a word of clarification is needed. It is important to note that these trends, namely wider access to data granted to law enforcement authorities and the transformation of databases originally designed for immigration purposes into general intelligence databases, are corollaries of this loosening up of the databases' initial purposes. As such, there is a common relationship between the three arguments assessed in this chapter.

[43] European Parliament and Council Regulation (EU) No 679/2016 of the of 27 April 2016 on the protection of natural persons with regard to the processing of personal data and on the free movement of such data, and repealing Directive 95/46/EC (General Data Protection Regulation), [2016], OJ 2016, L 119/1.

[44] ER Brouwer, 'Legality and Data Protection Law: the Forgotten Purpose of Purpose Limitation' in L Besselink, F Pennings, S Prechal (eds), *The Eclipse of the Legality Principle in the European Union* (Alphen aan den Rijn, Kluwer Law, 2011) 275, designation used by Brouwer when referring to the prohibition of collecting and storing personal data for unknown or not specific purposes.

[45] See Art 5 (1) b) of the General Data Protection Regulation.

[46] See Art 8 of the ECHR and Art 8 of the Charter on Fundamental Rights of the EU.

[47] Brouwer (n 44) 275.

[48] See the Preamble of the Convention for the Protection of Individuals with regard to Automatic Processing of Personal Data, [1981], (hereafter Data Protection Convention).

[49] Brouwer (n 44) 275.

[50] For a US perspective on the phenomenon, see Stumpf, 'The Crimmigration Crisis' (n 4) 386.

In the light of the above, we can see that how one combines the creation of large-scale, multipurpose information systems (such as VIS and SIS II) and the respect of the principle of purpose limitation is not straightforward.[51] In addition, the shift in the original purposes of the SIS/SIS II, EURODAC and VIS is another difficult development to reconcile with the principle of purpose limitation. This latter trend can be illustrated by giving a taste of the meaning of recent legislative amendments. For instance, the primary purpose of SIS was to counterbalance the abolition of EU internal border checks by harmonising legislation, taking complementary measures and preventing illegal immigration. This purpose is very clearly formulated in Article 17 of the 1985 Schengen Agreement.[52] However, from the wording of Article 1 (2) of Regulation 1987/2006 of the SIS II Regulation, one can see that a considerably different general purpose has been developed by the second generation of SIS:[53]

> *[T]o ensure a high level of security* within the area of freedom, security and justice of the European Union, *including the maintenance of public security policy* and *safeguarding of security in the territories of the Member States*, and to apply the provisions of Title IV of Part Three of the Treaty relating to the movement of persons in their territories, using information communicated via this system.

The widening of this database's purposes is evident from a brief reading of the aforementioned provisions, as well as the security-focused nature of EU law in this area, which one may argue is the catalyst for this change.[54] Another relevant example of the departure from the initial purposes is the 2007 Council decision to include the Member States that acceded to the EU in 2004 in the SIS, crucially before they had removed their controls at internal borders.[55] The upgrade of the SIS has resulted in a significantly greater focus on security technologies, which currently come first in the EU's internal security agenda, and will directly affect those registered in the databases.[56] The inclusion of biometrical data and the interlinking of alerts are the key manifestations that illustrate the shift in purposes between the first and second generation SIS.

[51] ibid, 282.

[52] Art 17 of the Schengen Agreement: 'With regard to the movement of persons, the Parties shall endeavour to abolish checks at common borders and transfer them to their external borders. To that end they shall endeavour first to *harmonise*, where necessary, the laws, regulations and administrative provisions concerning the prohibitions and restrictions on which the checks are based and *to take complementary measures* to safeguard internal security and *prevent illegal immigration* by nationals of States that are not members of the European Communities'. (emphasis added)

[53] Art 1 (2) of the SIS II Regulation.

[54] For more on the dynamics between immigration control and security in EU law, see: V Mitsilegas, 'Immigration Control in an Era of Globalization: Deflecting Foreigners, Weakening Citizens, Strengthening the State' (2012) 19 *Indiana Journal of Global Legal Studies* 3, 17–24.

[55] Council Decision on the application of the provisions of the Schengen acquis relating to the Schengen Information System in the Czech Republic, the Republic of Estonia, the Republic of Latvia, the Republic of Lithuania, the Republic of Hungary, the Republic of Malta, the Republic of Poland, the Republic of Slovenia, and the Slovak Republic, [2007], OJ L 179/46.

[56] Joanna Parkin, 'The Schengen Information System and the EU rule of law', INEX Policy Brief No 13, 17 June 2011', 1.

Taking EURODAC as a further example, this database was not created to fight irregular migration nor to identify an illegal stay. Rather, EURODAC is an immigration database created to support the implementation of EU asylum policy. Yet, the fact that law enforcement authorities and Europol may have wide access to asylum seekers' fingerprints through EURODAC raises several concerns.[57] Concerns arise not only with regard to the protection of personal data but also with the discriminatory impact of these measures. Is it acceptable to impose a greater level of surveillance on anyone subjected to EURODAC than other migrants in the population? And a greater and different level of surveillance than originally planned on its purposes?

EURODAC's original purpose of facilitating the application of the Dublin Convention was set out in the first version of the EURODAC Regulation.[58] This formulation was retained in the amended EURODAC Regulation, although a more controversial point 2 was added to Article 1 EURODAC II Regulation.[59] This newly added provision raised significant concerns, not only with regards to changing the original core purpose of that information system, but also with the 'erosion of fundamental rights', as the European Data Protection Supervisor (hereinafter EDPS) stressed in 2012.[60] As such, Article 1(2) EURODAC II Regulation significantly affects the accessibility of EURODAC—expanding the number of bodies who have access to the database. Consequently, this amendment formalises the extension of the scope of EURODAC for law enforcement purposes, which is made clear from the wording of Recitals 7, 8 and 9.[61] Recital 7 states:

> It is essential in the fight against terrorist offences and other serious criminal offences for the law enforcement authorities to have the fullest and most up-to-date information if they are to perform their tasks. The information contained in Eurodac is necessary for the purposes of the prevention, detection or investigation of terrorist offences. ...

Once one understands the meaning of the aforementioned amendment to the EURODAC Regulation, one might ask whether the new regulation represents a form of 'function creep' as some have argued.[62] As one commentator has stated, function creep happens when 'the system is being stretched in order to fulfil an increasing number of different types of functions than those for which it was originally created'.[63] To take one example, personal data such as fingerprints stored for one specific objective might subsequently be made available for other purposes, such as for investigative police work.

[57] See Art 1 (2) of the EURODAC II Regulation.

[58] See Art 1 (1) of the EURODAC I Regulation.

[59] The accessibility clause as for the purposes of this chapter is analysed below in the next subsection.

[60] European Data Protection Supervisor, European Data Protection Supervisor Press Release, EDPS/12/12—EURODAC: erosion of fundamental rights creeps along, Brussels, 5 September (2012).

[61] Since 2007 the Commission alerted for the fact that the future developments of this database would probably focus on the use of the data for law enforcement purposes in the Report from the Commission to the European Parliament and the Council on the evaluation of the Dublin system, COM 299 final and SEC 742, [2007], 11.

[62] Besters and Brom (n 6) 465.

[63] Broeders (n 5) 55.

The situation with the VIS is slightly different due to the fact that there has not been a clear shift in the original purposes. Rather, the issue with the VIS is the vague formulation of its purposes from the beginning. The VIS's purposes can be found in Recital 5 and Article 2 of the VIS Regulation. The VIS has the purpose of 'improving the implementation of the common visa policy, consular cooperation and consultation between central visa authorities by facilitating the exchange of data between Member States' to achieve the following purposes:

(i) Facilitating the visa application procedure;
(ii) Preventing the bypassing of the criteria for the determination of the Member State responsible for examining the application;
(iii) Facilitating the fight against fraud;
(iv) Facilitating checks at external border crossing points and within the territory of the Member States;
(v) Assisting in the identification of any person who may not, or may no longer, fulfil the conditions for entry to, stay or residence on the territory of the Member States;
(vi) Facilitating the application of the Dublin II Regulation (Dublin task);
(vii) Contributing to the prevention of threats to the internal security of any of the Member State.[64]

A reading of the VIS purposes, and in particular Article 2 (e) of the VIS Regulation, reveals that this system of information has the purpose of identifying and re-identifying illegally-staying migrants (a purpose which is shared by SIS II and EURODAC). Similar to EURODAC which creates a link with an asylum file, VIS can inform the national immigration authorities of a visa application of an irregular migrant who has overstayed their visa.[65]

Nonetheless, unlike EURODAC, VIS collects more detailed information such as (i) basic information on the applicant; (ii) details on other visas; (iii) information on the company or person supporting the application (therefore, most likely information on EU citizens if they issued the invitation for the third-country national or in case they are sponsoring the applicant's stay); and, in addition, (iv) biometric data (such as 10 fingerprints and a photograph). This shared identification and re-identification is an example of individual identification, a topic which significantly contributes to the characterisation of the concept of illegality in the EU as one where border control and immigration databases may be used to identify a migrant in this position. The scope of Article 2 is broad given that it sets out seven purposes for the VIS and establishes a link between the 'improvement of the common visa policy' and national and European security interests. The purpose specified in Article 2 (g) of the VIS Regulation, namely to 'contribute

[64] Art 2 of the VIS Regulation and also for further reading on the analysis of the Regulation. See also S Peers, E Guild and J Tomkin, *EU Immigration and Asylum Law (Text and Commentary) Second Revised Edition*, vol 1 (Leiden, Martinus Nijoff Publishers, 2012) 339.

[65] Broeders (n 5) 56: 'The system also has an specific role of re-identifying illegal migrants'.

to the prevention of threats to the internal security of any of the Member States' is mainly responsible for broadening the initial goal of the VIS.[66]

The debate about the access granted to national law enforcement authorities to the personal data stored in the immigration databases gains added relevance when discussed together with the concept of interoperability. These two trends, providing access to law enforcement authorities to the data and enhancing interoperability are a result of the need to promote the fluidity of the exchange of personal data between the EU immigration databases, agencies and bodies for security reasons. The next subsection addresses the 'openness to the police' and 'the potential synergies' with other databases and use as evidence of the 'intertwining of criminal control and migration control'.[67]

IV. ENHANCED ACCESSIBILITY VERSUS PROPORTIONALITY AND NECESSITY CONCERNS

A. Law Enforcement Authorities and Europol Access to the Databases: EURODAC's *Accessibility Clause*

The present subsection focuses on the topic of the access to personal data stored in the immigration control information systems and in doing so analyses another trend which evidences the conflation of illegality and criminality. Both facets of the issue of access to the databases may potentially affect the purpose limitation of databases such as VIS and EURODAC and as such, corroborate the premise that criminality and illegality are increasingly intertwined. This is significant due to the fact that, as one commentator has remarked, 'the intertwinement of crime control and migration control' is the definition of crimmigration.[68]

The link with purpose limitation is not the only factor that the access granted to law enforcement authorities and the interoperability of databases have in common. Concerns with the proportionality and necessity of these measures have also been raised by the European Data Protection Supervisor (EDPS) and in the literature.[69] The expansion of the access to, for instance, EURODAC and VIS for law enforcement authorities is, on the one hand, the most relevant example of the extension of purpose of this database, and, on the other hand, supports this idea of instrumentalisation of the database for police purposes. A result of the growing 'surveillance society'[70] is the fact that the concept of illegality has been constructed from an unhappy marriage of criminal and immigration law and that the way that

[66] The initial purpose of the VIS was the improvement of the common visa policy.

[67] Aas (n 4) 337.

[68] J van der Leun, M van der Woude, 'A reflection on Crimmigration in the Netherlands' in Maria João Guia, Maartje van der Woude and Joanne van der Leun (eds), *Social Control and Justice—Crimmigration in the Age of Fear* (The Hague, Eleven International Publishing, 2013) 43.

[69] See for example: Brouwer (n 44).

[70] M Tzanou, *The Added Value of Data Protection as a Fundamental Right in the EU Legal Order in the Context of Law Enforcement* (Florence, European University Institute, 2012).

immigration databases have recently been updated is an example of that. The trust placed in recent technological developments affects the 'outline and development of the European migration' discourse.[71]

When first adopted, as we have seen above, the Regulation creating EURODAC did not contemplate police access or law enforcement purposes; the fingerprints that were collected for that database were for the sole purpose of determining which Member State was responsible for examining an asylum application. Despite the fact that EURODAC had more of a technical aim (namely facilitating the application of the Dublin Convention) since 2007 the Commission stated that the development of EURODAC would result in the 'use of data for law enforcement purposes'.[72] In 2009, a month after the Commission adopted a proposal for amendment of EURODAC, the EDPS Hustinx, pointed out the crucial point that granting law enforcement authorities access to EURODAC has potentially problematic consequences:

> The fight against terrorism can certainly be a legitimate ground to apply exceptions to the fundamental rights to privacy and data protection. However, to be valid, the necessity of the intrusion must be supported by clear and undeniable elements, and the proportionality of the processing of personal data must be demonstrated.[73]

In other words, using a database such as the EURODAC for a different purpose than it was originally designed to carry out may significantly assist in the fight against terrorism and crime as an investigative tool. However it may also violate not only the aforementioned principle of purpose limitation but also the legitimacy of the data processing. The EDPS has additionally questioned whether law enforcement access is necessary in the first place and has argued that the Commission has not shown any substantive reasons for it.[74] The Commission adopted a proposal on 30 March 2012 that concerned a recast of the EURODAC allowing access to EURODAC collected data by national law enforcement authorities and the Europol for law enforcement purposes.[75] This amendment to Article 1

[71] Besters and Brom (n 6) 457.

[72] Report from the Commission to the European Parliament and the Council on the evaluation of the Dublin system, COM 299 final and SEC 742, [2007].

[73] European Data Protection Supervisor Press Release, EDPS/09/11, Law enforcement access to EURODAC: EDPS expresses serious doubts about the legitimacy and necessity of proposed measures, Brussels, 8 October 2009.

[74] Opinion of the European Data Protection Supervisor on the amended proposal for a Regulation of the European Parliament and of the Council concerning the establishment of 'Eurodac' for the comparison of fingerprints for the effective application of Regulation (EC) No (…/…) (establishing the criteria and mechanisms for determining the Member State responsible for examining an application for international protection lodged in one of the Member States by a third-country national or a stateless person), and on the proposal for a Council Decision on requesting comparisons with Eurodac data by Member States' law enforcement authorities and Europol for law enforcement purposes, OJ C 92/1, 2010, 40.

[75] European Commission amended proposal for Regulation of the European Parliament and of the Council (COM (2012) 254 final), on the establishment of 'EURODAC' for the comparison of fingerprints for the effective application of Regulation (EU) No […/…] (establishing the criteria and mechanisms for determining the Member State responsible for examining an application for international

of the EURODAC Regulation is what for the purposes of this book is labelled as the *accessibility clause*. The *accessibility clause* states that under specific conditions 'Member State's designated authorities and the Europol may request the comparison of fingerprint data for law enforcement purposes'.[76] Before this amendment to EURODAC, as we have seen above, there were voices warning of the possible violation of the principle of purpose limitation and the principle of proportionality—an issue to which we shall return. However, before addressing that debate, a clarification of the relationship between the principle of purpose limitation and the EURODAC II Regulation's *accessibility clause* is required. In reality this relationship is straightforward since the amendment of the EURODAC Regulation. Concerns with the violation of the principle of purpose limitation were, at least in part (from a purely formal perspective), allayed when the Regulation expressly formalised the 'change of the original purpose of EURODAC'.[77] As such, it is now expressly recognised that EURODAC lays down the conditions under which Member States' designated authorities and the Europol may request the comparison of fingerprint data with those stored in EURODAC for law enforcement purposes.[78]

As such the requirements, which are imposed by the Council Convention for the Protection of Individuals with regard to Automatic Processing of Personal Data and by the General Data Protection Regulation, in relation to the principles of quality of the data, are formally respected by the *accessibility clause*. Nevertheless, one should keep in mind that there are still doubts with regard to whether EURODAC is a case of function creep with regard to its substance. The Court of Justice of the European Union (CJEU) has stated that, when interpreting a provision of EU law: 'it is necessary to consider not only its wording but also the context in which it occurs and the objectives pursued by the rules of which it is part'.[79]

As such, a substantive analysis is required.

B. Access to the VIS by Law Enforcement Authorities

With regard to the widening of access to the VIS, the Council Decision of June 2008 provided the authorisation for access of the VIS for designated authorities of Member States and to Europol for the purposes of the prevention, detection

protection lodged in one of the Member States by a third-country national or a stateless person) and to request comparisons with EURODAC data by Member States' law enforcement authorities and Europol for law enforcement purposes and amending Regulation (EU) No 1077/2011 establishing a European Agency for the operational management of large-scale IT systems in the area of freedom, security and justice, Brussels, 2012.

[76] Art 1(2) of the EURODAC II Regulation.

[77] Recital 13 of the EURODAC II Regulation.

[78] Recital 13 and Art 1 (2) of the EURODAC II Regulation.

[79] See Case C-84/12, *Koushkaki*, [2013], EU:C:2013:862, para 34.

and investigation of terrorist offences and other serious criminal offences.[80] Granting law enforcement authorities access to the personal data stored in information systems is not a decision to be taken lightly as the EDPS Opinion in 2006 on the VIS argues:

> As the purpose of the VIS is the improvement of the common visa policy, it should be noted that routine access by law enforcement authorities would not be in accordance with this purpose. While, according to Article 13 of Directive 95/46/EC, such an access could be granted on an ad hoc basis, in specific circumstances and subject to the appropriate safeguards, a systematic access cannot be allowed.[81]

What is distinctive in the case of the purpose of the VIS, compared to the other databases mentioned, is the inclusion of the broad and imprecisely defined purpose of fighting crime. Council Decision 2008/633 solved the issue of access for consultation of the VIS by national law enforcement authorities and Europol. However, the loose formulations granting access to the VIS to Europol 'for the performance' of its tasks,[82] as well as those granting access to designated authorities, are potentially a problematic issue, as a number of scholars have pointed out.[83] The fact that exceptional access to this personal data is not regulated in a more constrained way may feed doubts in relation to the lack of a guarantee of purpose limitation.

It is considered that access to the VIS, as the Council Decision stipulates, is to be granted on a case-by-case basis to avoid the risk of infringing not only the purpose limitation of the database but also an intrusion on the visa travellers' privacy. With regard to the construction of migrants' illegality, it is considered that the widespread accessibility to data stored in the VIS supports the previous arguments on the instrumentalisation of the databases for crime control purposes and individual identification of migrants as features of the concept of illegality. On the one hand, information that could lead to an illegal stay situation may not have the necessary access constraints, at the risk of being instrumentalised by national police authorities. On the other hand, at the level of individual identification and re-identification, there is the potential danger that, to give access to such vast and detailed information may allow the profiling of individuals by law enforcement authorities. A database that was apparently created as an administrative file,

[80] Council Decision 2008/633/JH concerning access for consultation of the Visa Information System (VIS) by designated authorities of Member States and by Europol for the purposes of the prevention, detection and investigation of terrorist offences and of other serious criminal offences, [2008], OJ L 218/129.

[81] Opinion of the European Data Protection Supervisor on the Proposal for a Council Decision concerning access for consultation of the Visa Information System (VIS) by the authorities of Member States responsible for internal security and by Europol for the purposes of the prevention, detection and investigation of terrorist offences and of other serious criminal offences (COM (2005) 600 final), OJ C 97, 2006.

[82] Art 7 (1) a) of the Council Decision 2008/633/JH.

[83] J Parkin, 'The Difficult Road to the Schengen Information System II: The Legacy of "Laboratories" and the Cost for Fundamental Rights and the Rule of Law', CEPS Liberty and Security in Europe, 4 April 2011', 29.

in practice seems to work as an intelligence tool,[84] which may raise concerns with regard to the proportionality and necessity of the means used to achieve the aim purposed.

C. Proportionality, Necessity and the Access to Immigration Databases by Law Enforcement Authorities

First, is important to note that the rights protected by the principle of purpose limitation in relation to the collection of biometric information, such as Article 8 ECHR, may allow some exceptions if the collection of that data is legitimate and proportionate and necessary in a democratic society.[85] The widespread access of law enforcement authorities to immigration databases may constitute an exception and in the case of EURODAC, for instance, should be in 'accordance with the law', 'formulated with precision', 'necessary in a democratic society to protect legitimate and proportionate aim and proportionate to the legitimate objective aims to achieve'.[86]

The ECtHR in the *S & Marper v United Kingdom*[87] judgment has taken a stance in relation to the limits of the collection and protection of biometrical data and considered that in that case the applicants were subject to a discriminatory treatment and a disproportionate restriction to their right to privacy. Mr S and Mr Marper, the applicants in this case, both had their fingerprints and DNA collected in 2001 and were suspected of having committed a criminal offence, but were never convicted for those purposes. The applicants both sought the destruction of these samples of data and both found their claim refused by the UK national authorities in charge. The Court, before analysing whether the interference with the right to privacy of the applicants was justified, made a crucial point in order to understand the significance of this type of data and its potential effects. Biometric data contain unique information about the individual and it is capable of affecting their private life:

> fingerprints objectively contain *unique information about the individual* concerned allowing his or her identification with precision in a wide range of circumstances. *They are thus capable of affecting his or her private life* and retention of this information without the consent of the individual concerned cannot be regarded as neutral or insignificant.[88]

The ECtHR then moved on to the assessment of whether the restriction to the applicants' right to privacy was a) in accordance with law, b) had a legitimate aim and c) was necessary in a democratic society. The decision stated that it was

[84] Boehm (n 1) 292.
[85] See Art 8 (2) ECHR.
[86] See Recital 13 of the EURODAC II Regulation.
[87] *S & Marper v United Kingdom*, ECHR (2009) App no 30562/04, 30566/04, judgment of 4 December 2008, para 127 and see also Arts 8 and 14 ECHR.
[88] ibid, para 84 (emphasis added).

not acceptable and that the nature of the powers of retention of the fingerprints, cellular samples and DNA of persons suspected but not convicted of offences was discriminatory.[89] Therefore the retention of Mr S and Mr Marper's personal data constituted an interference with their right to respect for private life.

Strikingly, if one makes a comparison between the reasoning in this decision and the recent enhancement of the access to EURODAC by law enforcement authorities, one is left with the feeling that standards were not taken into account. In short, an asylum seeker who has entered the EU and lodged a claim would have to allow the collection and retention of their biometric data independently of the fact of having or not being convicted for committing a crime.[90] This feature, in essence, brings together the asylum seeking, potential illegality (if the claim is refused or if they individual is an irregular migrant stopped at the border) and the criminality; this is a conflation that by itself raises questions of proportionality, necessity and non-discrimination.

Additionally, the debate on the restriction of purpose limitation has already been the topic of discussion in the CJEU, namely, in the *Rechnungshof v Österreichischer Rundfunk* and *Huber v Germany* cases.[91] The first case dealt with the interpretation of the Data Protection Directive 95/46 EC and the second with the relationship between the principle of purpose limitation and non-discrimination. These cases are important benchmarks of the jurisprudence of the CJEU in relation to the regulation of individuals' personal data, and are helpful counter examples with regard to what has been said about latest widening of the access to immigration databases.

Rechnungshof v Österreichischer Rundfunk addressed the issue of whether the rules on the data of the employees and pensioners of the Austrian Court of Auditors respected the Data Protection Directive and the principle of the protection of privacy. It is noteworthy that the CJEU declared that the scope of applicability of the Directive was to be interpreted in a broad manner and that the principle of purpose limitation has direct effect, thus allowing the individual to make use of it in a domestic court.[92] Another relevant aspect of this decision was the fact that the CJEU decided that the Data Protection Directive must be interpreted with respect to Article 8 ECHR, as such if the provision did not comply with that it could not be:

> [C]overed by any of the exceptions referred to in Article 13 of that directive, which likewise requires compliance with the requirement of proportionality with respect to the public interest objective being pursued.[93]

[89] ibid, paras 127–29.

[90] Opinion of the European Data Protection Supervisor on the amended proposal for a Regulation of the European Parliament and of the Council on the establishment of 'EURODAC' for the comparison of fingerprints for the effective application of Regulation (EU) No […/…] […] (Recast version), 2012, point 38.

[91] Case C-524/06, *Huber v Germany*, [2008], EU:C:2008:724 and Joint Affairs C-465/00, C-138/01, C-139/01, *Rechnungshof v Österreichischer Rundfunk and Others*, [2003], EU:C:2003:294.

[92] Para 100 of the *Rechnungshof v Österreichischer Rundfunk and Others* judgment, ibid.

[93] ibid, para 91.

Also relevant for the present analysis is the *Huber v Germany* case. This case concerned Mr Huber, an Austrian national who moved to Germany and was registered in the AZR (the centralised register of German national aliens administration). As an EU citizen exercising his right of free movement Mr Huber considered that such collection and retention of personal data was in violation of Article 18 TFEU (ex 12 EC) prohibiting the discrimination of EU citizens and the Citizens' Directive 2004/38 on the free movement of EU citizens and their family members. Three questions were referred to the CJEU by the German administrative court. The first query concerned the processing of personal data for the purposes of the application of the legislation relating to the right of residence, and the second for statistical purposes. Whereas the Court considered that the collection and retention of such data was necessary for the purposes of contributing to a more effective application of the legislation as regards the right to reside,[94] it decided the opposite and declared that in relation to the statistical purposes claim the necessity requirement was not met. The third question is the most relevant for this analysis as it concerned the storage of personal data relating to EU citizens for the purposes of fighting crime. The CJEU held that in this case there was a violation of the principle of non-discrimination posited in Article 18 TFEU (ex 12 EC). The Court stated that in a Member State 'the situation of its nationals cannot, as regards the objective of fighting crime, be different from that of Union citizens who are national of the Member State and who are resident in its territory'.[95]

The *Huber v Germany* decision plays an important role in understanding, even if by analogy, the potential discriminatory effects that processing data for different purposes may have on the individuals monitored.[96] If, in the words of the Court, there is discriminatory treatment of individuals if the 'difference of the treatment arises by virtue of the systemic processing of personal data relating only to Union citizens who are not nationals of the Member State concerned for the purposes of fighting crime,'[97] could we say that by analogy the same effect may occur with regard to third-country nationals? In other words, the 'unpleasant shadow' mentioned by Advocate-General Poiares Maduro in his Opinion, 'perpetuates the distinction between "us"—the natives—and "them"—the foreigners',[98] and the same thing could by analogy be said about the monitoring of third-country nationals for law enforcement purposes. In practical terms, if an information system that treats EU citizens differently in respect of their nationality for the purposes of fighting crime can potentially have stigmatising effects, then the fact that third-country nationals may be registered in different databases (with or without law enforcement depending on their origin or claim) can arguably also have the same effects.[99] For instance, one could give the example of EURODAC and

[94] Para 62 of the *Huber* judgment (n 91).
[95] ibid, para 79.
[96] Parkin (n 83) 29.
[97] Para 80 of the *Huber* judgment (n 91).
[98] Case C-524/06 *Huber v Germany* [2008], EU:C:2008:194, Opinion of AG Poiares Maduro, para 15.
[99] For example someone registered in EURODAC and someone not registered in that database.

question of whether there is an implicit differential treatment imposed on asylum seekers and irregular migrants registered on that database and other categories of migrants, or why would there be less strict criteria regulating these migrants than that imposed by the CJEU in *Huber v Germany*, in relation to EU citizens only. These are queries that raise concerns of the necessity of different treatment and the proportionality of these measures.

In sum, a database that was originally created with an administrative purpose in practice seems to work as an intelligence tool,[100] raising concerns with regard to the proportionality and necessity of the means used to achieve the aim purposed. This is demonstrated by the enhancement of the access of law enforcement authorities to these databases.

D. Interoperability

Accessibility within the databases or their interoperability also potentially impacts upon the principle of purpose limitation. The SIS II, VIS and EURODAC databases share some common features as we have seen throughout the chapter. All three databases are centralised, large-scale databases with the main purpose of registering third-country nationals including biometric data. The control of entrance of migrants is a shared goal of EU Member State governments and the development of centralised databases represents an extra tool to this end. The access to SIS II, VIS and EURODAC happens at external borders of Member States and also within the national territory and at the embassies and consulates of third countries. Interoperability and synergy between SIS II, EURODAC and VIS, given their similarities, is a crucial aspect for the development of the databases and the subject of heated debate in the literature and in the European political discourse in general. Before moving on to the heart of the debate to discuss whether interoperability contributes to a conflation of the concept of migrant illegality and migrant criminality, an introductory clarification of its meaning is required.

The Commission's 2005 Communication on this issue defined interoperability as the 'ability of IT systems and of the business processes they support to exchange data and to enable the sharing of information and knowledge'.[101] In the same document the Commission clarified that interoperability is a technical rather than a legal or political concept, therefore setting aside the issue of whether the data exchange is legally or politically possible or required.[102] Mitsilegas argues that despite the efforts of the Commission to label interoperability as a non-legal and non-political issue, it should be seen as an attempt to de-politicise a matter that

[100] Boehm (n 1) 292.

[101] Commission, Communication on Improved Effectiveness, Enhanced Interoperability and Synergies among European Databases in the Area of Justice and Home Affairs, COM (2005) 597 final and Brouwer (n 14) 144.

[102] COM (2005) 597 final and Besters and Brom (n 6) 462.

can potentially affect the protection of fundamental rights. This commentator states that it is striking that the Commission's communication treats interoperability as 'a merely technical concept, while at the same time using the concept to enable maximum access to databases containing a wide range of personal data'.[103]

Allowing access to data stored in immigration databases in order to explore their added value in the fight against terrorism is a transversal aspect of the three databases examined in the present chapter. The idea behind the move towards effectiveness and maximisation of police access to information lies in the premise that 'to combat terrorism and other serious crimes it is inevitable that police and security authorities have access to EU information systems'.[104] Yet the question arises as to whether combating terrorism and security concerns justifies mass surveillance. Whilst there is no easy answer to this question, the development of some of the immigration databases seems to suggest that such surveillance is justified. The VIS, for instance, is an example of an EU information system that has blurred its immigration control contours and provides access to police authorities in order to contribute to the prevention of threats to internal security of the Member States. Giving wider access to a wider range of authorities designated by the Member States as stated in the VIS Regulation can be seen a corollary of the attempt to enhance interoperability. As the EDPS has pointed out, interoperability is a 'powerful drive for de facto acceding or exchanging of these data'.[105]

Despite the fact that the Commission has an instrumental conception of technology, it is naïve to see information technology as merely means to achieve a defined purpose. Making information technology interoperable and available without precise boundaries and targets raises doubts with regard to compatibility with proportionality and non-discrimination. Consequently, in this context, one can argue that the interoperability of databases and the way this has been envisioned by the Commission leads to a clear distinction between: (i) those third-country nationals who need to be placed under greater supervision and control for security reasons, and; (ii) those who are also third-country nationals but are in possession of a long term visa or do not need to provide biometric data.

With regards to the construction of the concept of illegality it is argued that the 'pixellisation'[106] of borders' process intertwined with the development of interoperability consequently results in a depersonalisation of the law of migration. As such, the personal element loses its relevance: 'the migration machine by its nature tends to dehumanize the people it needs to process'.[107] This trend also

[103] Mitsilegas (n 1) 56.

[104] Council of the European Union, 'Draft Council Conclusions on access to Eurodac by Member State police and law enforcement authorities', Brussels, 20 April 2007, 1.

[105] Opinion of the European Data Protection Supervisor on the Communication from the Commission to the European Parliament and the Council entitled 'Strengthening law enforcement cooperation in the EU: the European Information Exchange Model (EIXM)', 2013, point 34.

[106] Baldaccini (n 1) 46.

[107] H Dijstelbloem and A Meijer, 'Reclaiming Control over Europe's Technological Borders' in H Dijstelbloem and A Meijer (eds), *Migration and the New Technological Borders of Europe* (Basingstoke, Palgrave MacMillan, 2011) 184.

consubstantiates on the one hand the risk of transforming these databases into investigative tools as addressed in the next subsection and also represents a danger to the respect of the principle of purpose limitation.

V. FROM IMMIGRATION TO GENERAL INTELLIGENCE DATABASES?

A. Biometrics

A clear trend can be identified with regard to the three immigration databases which are gradually becoming transformed into general intelligence databases. A number of factors can be seen as having contributed to or facilitated this trend including the erosion of the purpose limitation principle and the widening of the access to personal data by law enforcement authorities. In order to illustrate this shift from immigration to general intelligence databases two recently added functionalities are addressed: the use of biometrics and the interlinking of alerts. The following section aims to show that these are typically investigative tools as opposed to tools used solely for immigration purposes.

The inclusion of biometric information in immigration databases not only reflects a shift from their original purpose by making control and identification (and re-identification) of individuals a top priority, but also shows a recent preference for this type of information. The three databases analysed in this section all include some sort of biometric data, and as such the concerns and issues raised here thus apply to them all.[108] The significant role that biometric information plays in immigration control starts '*before* and *after* the entry of third country nationals in EU territory'.[109] Biometrics may have a strong impact in terms of granting access to EU territory and therefore they play a role even before the entry of a third-country national. In addition, biometric information also significantly influences the way these individuals are categorised within the European framework. The first generation SIS stored solely alphanumeric data, which provided a hit or a no hit result, whereas biometrics systems give a more detailed and effective result which is more amenable to being used in police investigations. Further, the fact that the biometric data will be available to national border control, police, customs, judicial and vehicle registration as well as Europol and Eurojust enhances the character of an investigative police tool as some commentators have already pointed out.[110]

Before turning to the possible shortcomings of the use of biometrics and how they may affect the position of a person whose biometric data is stored, a brief explanation of its *modus operandi* is required. For example, Article 22 of the SIS II Regulation establishes specific rules for photographs and fingerprints. At the first stage,

[108] SIS II and VIS store fingerprints and photographs and EURODAC only fingerprints.
[109] Mitsilegas (n 1) 53.
[110] ibid, 53 and Baldaccini (n 1) 37–39.

biometrics are designed to play a matching role, in accordance with Article 22(b), which states that biometrics: 'shall be only used *to confirm the identity* of a third-country national who has been located as a result of an alphanumeric search made in SIS II' (emphasis added).

In the future ('as soon as technically possible' in fact[111]) biometric data, as with fingerprints, will have more than the confirming or re-identification function it currently has and will serve to identify individuals on the basis of their biometric identifier. Thus, the use of biometric data will provide two different types of searches. First, a one to one search which compares biometric information with other biometric data and corresponds to the current searches provided by SIS II. Some authors seem to prefer this form of search, describing it as consistent and reliable.[112] Second, a one to many or one to more search which compares a given set of biometric data to all or almost all the biometrics in a database. This is what the new SIS II functionality will entail in the future. Identification of individuals is the main goal of this type of search, which may consequently transform the immigration control nature of the SIS into databases with an investigative purpose. Some authors see it as a possibility for 'fishing expeditions' (a tool to try and find a case within all the data collected) and a form of additional surveillance of all the people registered in the SIS II.[113] Allowing these speculative searches is an investigative tool functionality *par excellence*.

Interestingly the latter biometric search, one to many or one to more searches, contrasts with the individual identification of migrants, which is a trend that has been mentioned throughout this chapter in relation to the databases. The act of identifying and re-identifying migrants is an essential element of the EURODAC system, for instance. Therefore, whereas at first EURODAC had the main purpose of facilitating the application of the Dublin Regulation, the aim of this database now is not only the prevention of asylum shopping, but, and most importantly, to keep migrants' identities under close control. By this it is meant that the implementation of EURODAC and its most recent alterations have resulted in an instrumentalisation of the database itself in order to identify migrants mostly for the purposes of removal.[114] This can be seen in particular in relation to the third category of migrants covered by EURODAC, irregular migrants arrested within the EU.

Despite being an optional category, Member States have made widespread use of EURODAC in relation to this category, corroborating the view that EURODAC has features of an 'important tool in the domestic part of the European battle against illegal immigration'.[115] The same feature of individual identification of

[111] Art 22(c) of the SIS II.

[112] Rijpma (n 13) 205; Peers, Guild and Tomkin (n 64) 105 and Baldaccini (n 1) 37–38.

[113] Besters and Brom (n 6) 458, Tzanou (n 70) 200.

[114] D Broeders, *Breaking Down Anonymity: Digital Surveillance on Irregular Migrants in Germany and the Netherlands* (Amsterdam, Amsterdam University Press, 2009) 173.

[115] Broeders (n 5) 53.

migrants is a consequence of the new SIS II facility of interlinking of alerts, which is the next object of this analysis. It can then be said that the inclusion of investigative mechanisms in immigration databases creates a potent machinery of identification of migrants that works (or will work) in two different ways: an individual identification of individuals and larger group speculative searches, also known as 'fishing expeditions' or even possibly profiling.

Several concerns have been raised in the literature regarding the inclusion of biometric data in SIS II, which are also shared when one thinks of the application of VIS and EURODAC.[116] The EDPS pointed out in his Opinion on the draft SIS II legislation:

> [T]he tendency to use biometric data in EU wide information systems (VIS, EURODAC, Information System on driving licences etc) is growing steadfastly, but is not accompanied by a careful consideration of risks involved and required safeguards.[117]

The lack of consideration of the risks involved, as the EDPS put it, intrinsically relates to the risk of lack of accuracy that may result from a biometric search. Problems with accuracy are probably the greatest weakness of the use of biometrics.[118] Biometrics is a very advanced means of identification of people, although it can also negatively affect the legal position of those incorrectly identified. For instance, the misinterpretation of a US lawyer's fingertips by the FBI resulted in him being imprisoned for two weeks. This was the case of Brandon Mayfield, an attorney from Oregon whose fingerprints mistakenly matched those found in a parcel of detonators in the Madrid bombing attacks.[119] Mr Mayfield's case is an extreme example of the potentially serious effects of the misinterpretation of biometrics. On the one hand it is undeniable that this type of search represents a 'powerful tool for law enforcement authorities' but on the other hand it is also undeniable that it may have an impact on a migrant's legal status covered by these databases.[120]

In relation to biometrical data the CJEU stated in 2013 in the *Schwarz* decision that although the taking and storing of fingerprints by the national authorities 'constitutes a threat to the rights to respect for private life and the protection of personal data' it must nevertheless be assessed if that measure is justified.[121]

[116] ibid, 53; Tzanou (n 70) 199–203, Peers, Guild and Tomkin (n 64) 114; Besters and Brom (n 6) 458–59. In relation to VIS and the use of biometrics: Baldaccini (n 1) 38 and 49.

[117] Opinion of the European Data Protection Supervisor on the draft SIS II legislation, OJ 91/38, 2006, point 4.1, and Memorandum by the Meijers Committee, House of Lords European Union Commitee, Schengen Information System II (SIS II), 10 of July 2006, 4, (www.publications.parliament.uk/pa/ld200607/ldselect/ldeucom/49/6101107.htm).

[118] Y Liu, 'Scenario Study of Biometric Systems at Borders' (2011) 27 *Computer Law & Security Review* 36, 42.

[119] US Department of Justice, Office of the Inspector General, A Review of the FBI's Handling of the Brandon Mayfield case, March 2006 (www.justice.gov/oig/special/s0601/final.pdf).

[120] C Stacy Smith and LC Hung, *The Patriot Act: Issues and Controversies* (Springfield IL, Charles C Thomas Publisher, 2009) 174: 'Even if only one or a half per cent of the persons would be wrongly identified on the basis of biometrical data in SIS II or VIS, considering the millions of person to be recorded in these databases, still the number of persons affected by automatic negative decisions will be much too high'.

[121] Case C-291/12, *Michael Schwarz v Stadt Bochum*, [2013], EU:C:2013:670, para 23.

The unique nature of biometric data that allows more precise identification of individuals was already stressed above when discussing the *S & Marper* case—a point also made by the CJEU.[122] Whereas in some situations the use of biometrics may allow individuals listed in SIS, for example, to 'clear their names' and identify those who are duly the subject of an alert.[123]

However, three other critiques are also commonly put forward in relation to the use of biometrical data. First, there is the risk that criminal organisations may have easier access to biometrical data and misuse or manipulate it, as well as an increase in the risk of identity theft.[124] Second, one may also think of the possibility of transforming EU databases into systems used by law enforcement authorities as profiling tools. Third, it has been pointed out that the recourse to technology leads to the 'dehumanization of individuals via the instrumentalization of the human body,' providing the States with personal data can be accessed in different instances.[125]

In sum, as Aas has stated, 'the body becomes, in a sense, a passport or a password and an unambiguous token of truth',[126] a trend that makes immigration control databases resemble a police investigative tool.

B. Interlinking of Alerts

An additional investigative feature included in SIS II, namely the interlinking of alerts, also suggests a gradual transformation of immigration databases into general intelligence databases. As Baldaccinni has pointed out in relation to the SIS II, the purpose of this database has shifted from 'a border control tool to a reporting and investigation system for general crime detection purposes'.[127] The possibility of interlinking alerts is a new function included in the SIS II Regulation and may be interpreted as characteristic of an investigative database. Article 37 of the SIS II Regulation sets out the general power of Member States to 'create a link between alerts' within SIS II. Although the Regulation states that a link can only be created 'when there is clear operational need',[128] the definition of what a clear operational need is exactly is left to the Member States' discretion. With regard to access to

[122] ibid, para 27.

[123] Some scholars like De Hert and Sprokkereef argue that SIS II is 'privacy friendly': 'Despite these concerns about function creep and the use of a technology at such a large scale without substantial testing, SIS II is generally regarded as a privacy friendly system that fits in with the classical tradition of European criminal law', in AM Sprokkereef and P De Hert, 'Ethical Practice in the Use of Biometric Identifiers within the EU' (2007) 3 *Law Science and Policy* 177, 185.

[124] Peers, Guild and Tomkin (n 64) 116.

[125] Mitsilegas (n 54) 37 and for more in the same topic see H Dijstelbloem, 'Europe's New Technological Gatekeeper. Debating the Deployment of Technology in Migration Policy' (2009) 1 *Amsterdam Law Forum* (http://amsterdamlawforum.org/article/view/90/154).

[126] K Franko Aas, '"The Body does not Lie": Identity, Risk and Trust in Technoculture' (2006) 2 *Crime, media, culture* 143, 145.

[127] Baldaccini (n 1) 39.

[128] Art 37 (4) SIS II Regulation.

links by the authorities the Regulation established that 'authorities with no right of access to certain categories of alert shall not be able to see the link to an alert to which they do not have access'.[129] In other words, authorities have restricted access to the links, depending on whether or not they have access to that particular category of data. Nonetheless, the issue of whether these authorities with restricted access know about the existence of the link is not clear.[130]

The interlinking of alerts influences the legal position of the individual. The categorisation of migrants no longer depends on his or her personal actions but, if connected to the actions of other people, their immigration status could be affected. In practice what may occur, in extreme cases, is that an alert of an innocent individual may be linked to an alert of a criminal individual which would result in the legal status of the innocent individual being adversely affected. The creation of this new functionality of interlinking alerts within the SIS II reflects the ongoing transformation of this immigration database into an investigative tool with significant potential powers for profiling.

It goes without saying that the inclusion of biometrics and the interlinking of alerts affects the concept of illegality in its essence. By approximating the status of those illegally-staying migrants whose data is stored in the SIS II with the status of criminals and suspects, or at least by not providing the necessary differentiated treatment, illegality is shaped to resemble criminality or is someway conflated with it. The fact that SIS II has both immigration and criminal law purposes enhances the risk of making individuals registered for immigration purposes easier targets for criminal law enforcement measures.[131] Creating the possibility of interlinking alerts, in the words of Parkin, is a door that 'allows an "intelligence" logic to creep into the use of the system, further deepening associations between crime and migration and increasing the chances of negatively impacting on innocent person'.[132]

C. The Impact of the Current Regulation Immigration Databases on the Regulation of Migrant Illegality

The criminalisation of irregular migrants is not an isolated trend in the domestic immigration law of any one particular State. In fact, this phenomenon is a 'widespread trend all over the world'.[133] The analysis of a number of the most relevant immigration databases provided in the present chapter sought to draw conclusions about how the concept of illegality of a migrant's stay is affected by the way these databases are constructed and have been recently reconstructed.

[129] Art 37 (3) final part of the SIS II Regulation.
[130] Aas (n 4) 341 and the EDPS who states that those authorities who do not have access to that data should not be aware that the links were created.
[131] Mitsilegas (n 1) 59.
[132] Parkin (n 83) 29.
[133] Boehm (n 1) 280.

Three interrelated trends were observed: (i) the erosion of the purpose limitation principle; (ii) the enhancement of the access to the databases by law enforcement authorities; and (iii) the gradual transformation of immigration to general intelligence databases. These arguments support the claim that there is a transversal trend to SIS II, VIS and EURODAC, which amounts to the conflation of the concept of illegality and criminality. Whereas this conflation is the central element of this study, it seems important by way of conclusion of this first part of the chapter to draw some specific conclusions with regards to the three major effects that these information technology systems have or may have in with regards to the regulation illegality, in particular with regards stage I—Entry of the migrants' cycle of illegality, as explained in chapter one, subsection II.A.ii.

First, and common to the three databases, is the functionality of identification and re-identification of migrants, in particular, for the purposes of the removal of irregular migrants. This identification feature can be seen for example in the inclusion of biometrics and interlinking of alerts in SIS II, or in EURODAC's accessibility clause that promotes wider access to data by law enforcement authorities. For instance, law enforcement authorities with access to EURODAC may easily have a sample of a migrant's fingerprint and this makes the decision of entry into a Member State greatly dependent on the technology used and enables 'identification and denial of access at a distance'.[134]

Second, the new emphasis on the individual identification and re-identification and the availability of the data gives a rather instrumental role to the immigration databases. The instrumentalisation of the databases is shown by the fact that these information systems were originally designed to be immigration databases but today are being gradually transformed in investigative tools. For instance, the VIS, as we have seen, was originally designed for the purposes of immigration control but its purpose was later amended and expanded to include 'the prevention of threats to internal security'.[135] Another clear example of the instrumentalisation of immigration databases is the concept of 'latent development' included in the SIS.[136] 'Latent development' is a notion that implies that the technical requirements or pre-conditions needed for the development of new SIS functionalities are already part of the SIS since its origin. Thus, once the political and legal arrangements are in place they can be activated.[137] A border control information system with such flexible structure makes it difficult to provide a 'proper assessment of the potential implications' of, in this case, the SIS II and leaves the door open, on the one hand to a possible instrumentalisation of technology for political ends, and on the other, to a looser application of the principle of proportionality.[138]

[134] Aas (n 126) 155.
[135] See subsection II.A of this chapter.
[136] Council of the European Union, Doc. nr. 6387/03: Summary of discussions, 25 February 2003.
[137] Besters and Brom (n 6) 463.
[138] Commission, Communication to the Council and the European Parliament on the Development of the Schengen Information System II, COM (2001) 720 final, 11 and Joint Supervisory Authority Opinion on the development of the SIS II, 19.05.2004.

Last, the third consequence of the *modus operandi* of the immigration databases under analysis is a depersonalisation of the individuals whose data is stored. The difference between this consequence and the first point made in this subsection is that the fact that databases are identification tools for the purposes of removal has an individual identification effect on singular people. With regard to the depersonalisation of migrants, it can be said that this has a generalising effect (or profiling) of categorising people in a manner not regulated by law. The depersonalisation of mobile individuals is related to the creation of migrant profiles such as 'the suspected' or 'mala fide', the 'trusted' or 'bona fide traveller'[139] or the 'crimmigrant'.[140] This trend has a strong stigmatising effect on migrants, categorising them *ab initio* and socially excluding individuals who are not a perfect fit for these profiles.

Interestingly, these profiles are created for both third-country nationals with a visa, asylum seekers and mobile EU citizens as a consequence of the globalisation of surveillance.[141] An example of this phenomenon is the case of the definition of what can be considered 'extremely serious criminal' offences for the purposes of Article 99 of the Schengen Convention. Article 99 is one of the cases where an EU citizen can be put under surveillance and their mobility can be limited. In accordance with the previous Schengen Convention article an alert should be generated, for example: 'where there are real indications to suggest that the person concerned intends to commit or is committing numerous and extremely serious offences'.[142]

The implications of the broad terms used in the wording of Article 99 have been debated in the literature,[143] and doubts were raised about the inclusion of groups such as the 'violent troublemakers'.[144] In this particular case the Schengen Joint Supervisory Authority already clarified that 'violent troublemakers' is not a term used in any European or international agreement therefore it should not be considered included in the scope of Article 99.[145] However, other categories of migrants are a fit for this type of alert, the recent issue about the deportation of Roma from France and other Member States is an example of this stigmatisation that may occur even when migrants enjoy from a formal citizenship status. And one may say that the citizenship status of these migrants is 'irregular' or 'flawed' given that their freedom was restricted for reasons of their 'allegedly criminal status'.[146]

The next section moves on to assess whether the most recent initiatives in the area of border surveillance systems (such as the Smart Borders, in particular,

139 Opinion of the European Data Protection Supervisor on the Communication from the Commission to the European Parliament, the Council, the Economic and Social Committee and the Committee of the Regions on migration, 2011, point 34.

140 Aas (n 4) 336 and 338.

141 Mitsilegas (n 54) 3–5.

142 See Art 99 (2) a) of the Schengen Convention.

143 Aas (n 4) 338.

144 'Violent troublemakers' normally concern to mass gatherings in international sports or cultural events, G8 meetings, or other high profile events and other types of demonstrations.

145 Schengen Joint Supervisory Authority Activity Report—December 2005—December 2008, 33.

146 Aas (n 4) 338 and 339.

EUROSUR and the EES) are a step towards an era of potential digital criminalisation of illegally-staying migrants, which corroborate the thesis of the conflation of illegality and criminality that starts at the supranational level with the regulation of immigration databases.

VI. WHAT'S NEXT FOR IMMIGRATION INFORMATION SYSTEMS? A BRAND NEW WORLD OF TRANSNATIONAL SURVEILLANCE OF ILLEGALITY OR THE SAME OLD STORY?

The recent trend in EU regulation of information systems has demonstrated a distinct widening of access to immigration databases and the expansion of their content, as examined in detail earlier in the present chapter. Furthermore, in recent times we have seen the creation of new databases such as the database examined in this subsection. The first three databases examined (SIS II, EURODAC and VIS) cover most of the relevant categories of migrants who, after arriving in the EU, are most likely to become illegally-staying migrants. However, there remains one category of individuals, namely overstayers (individuals who remain after the expiration of their visa), who have not been, and continue not to be, completely covered by any of the previous immigration information systems.

This section addresses the most recent initiatives in the area of immigration systems of information, the so-called 'smart borders' and EUROSUR. Specifically, it will examine EUROSUR and the Entry-Exit System due to the fact these two initiatives can, potentially, significantly affect the concept of illegality. While the focus of EUROSUR is mainly humanitarian in aiming to protect the lives of migrants whilst preventing illegal migration and cross-border crime at external borders,[147] the purpose of EES is to identify those who can be classed as 'overstayers'.[148]

However, these initiatives have one clear common goal: closer control of the movements of travellers in and out of the territories of the Member States. Further, their development and effectiveness depend greatly on biometrics, and on interoperability with the other databases, such as the SIS II, EURODAC and the VIS.[149]

A. EUROSUR—An Obstacle to Asylum?

In 2008 the Commission started the development of the European Border Surveillance System, the EUROSUR, by issuing a Communication examining the

[147] Art 1 of the European Parliament and Council Regulation of the (EU) No 1052/2013 establishing the European Border Surveillance System (Eurosur), [2013], OJ L295/11.

[148] Art 1 and Art 5 (13) of the European Commission proposal (COM(2013) 95 final) for a Regulation of the European Parliament and of the Council establishing an Entry/Exit System (EES) to register entry and exit data of third country nationals crossing the external borders of the Member States of the European Union, Brussels, 2013.

[149] Hayes and Vermeulen (n 2) 28.

implications and challenges of its creation.[150] In December 2011 the EUROSUR[151] was proposed and, after much debate on the consequences of such a system,[152] the EUROSUR Regulation was approved by the Parliament in October 2013.[153] In accordance with Article 24 (2) of the EUROSUR Regulation it shall apply from 2 December 2013 in Bulgaria, Estonia, Greece, Spain, France, Croatia, Italy, Cyprus, Latvia, Lithuania, Hungary, Malta, Poland, Portugal, Romania, Slovenia, Slovakia and Finland. In the remaining Member States EUROSUR is applicable since from 1 December 2014.

Apropos of the purpose to be achieved by the EUROSUR, Article 1 of the Regulation establishes it as 'detecting, preventing and combating illegal immigration and cross-border crime and contributing to ensuring the protection and saving the lives of migrants'. EUROSUR is embedded in the function of identifying and re-identifying pointed out above in relation to other information systems, and this becomes clear from the reading of Article 2 (1) in connection with the first part of Article 1 of the EUROSUR Regulation:

> This Regulation shall apply to the surveillance of external land and sea borders, including the monitoring, *detection, identification, tracking*, prevention and interception of unauthorised border crossings for the purpose of *detecting*, preventing and combating illegal immigration and cross-border crime and contributing to ensuring the protection and saving the lives of migrants'. (emphasis added)

When one compares this with the wording of the articles dealing with the humanitarian purpose of the EUROSUR of protecting and saving migrants' lives[154] one can conclude that there are general references to compliance with fundamental rights and prioritising vulnerable groups, yet how this is to be achieved is not described in the Regulation:

> Member States and the Agency *shall comply with fundamental rights*, in particular the principles of non-refoulement and respect for human dignity and data protection requirements, when applying this Regulation. *They shall give priority to the special needs* of children, unaccompanied minors, victims of human trafficking, persons in need of

[150] Commission, Communication to the European Parliament, the Council, the Economic and Social Committee and the Committee of the Regions examining the creation of a European Border Surveillance System (EUROSUR), COM(2008) 68 final.

[151] European Commission proposal (COM(2011) 873 final, for a Regulation of the European Parliament and of the Council Establishing the European Border Surveillance System (EUROSUR).

[152] ibid. See also Communication from the Commission to the European Parliament, the Council, the Economic and Social Committee and the Committee of the Regions examining the creation of a European Border Surveillance System (EUROSUR), COM(2008) 68 final, Brussels, 2008; J Rijpma, 'Frontex: successful blame shifting of the Member States?' Análisis del Real Instituto Elcano (ARI, 13 April 2010).

[153] Only a week after the disastrous events in Lampedusa. (www.asylumlawdatabase.eu/en/content/council-european-union-adopts-regulation-establishing-eurosur-system); see also Julien Jeandesboz, 'An Analysis of the Commission Communications on Future Development of FRONTEX and the Creation of a European Border Surveillance System (EUROSUR)' Justice and Home Affairs, Challenge Liberty & Security, Research Paper No 11, August 2008.

[154] Stated both in Recital 1 and in Art 1 of the EUROSUR Regulation.

urgent medical assistance, persons in need of international protection, persons in distress at sea and other persons in a particularly vulnerable situation.[155]

With regard to the previous comparison of the purposes of the information system, no position is taken on the possible implications of the new EUROSUR Regulation. Rather, this subsection highlights the emphasis placed on the issue of surveillance in the regulation (Article 1 and Article 2 (1) of the EUROSUR Regulation).[156]

In light of the foregoing, it should be noted that the Commission's proposal in 2011 had included a reference to migrant profiling stating that the national situational picture: 'shall contain migrant profiles, routes, information on the impact levels attributed to the external land and sea border sections and facilitation analysis'.[157] However, this formulation was excluded from the final version of the EUROSUR Regulation, Article 5(3)(b) of which ensures 'the timely exchange of information with search and rescue, law enforcement, asylum and immigration authorities at national level'.

What can we glean from this brief analysis of the main purposes of the EUROSUR? With regards to the issue of the way EU immigration databases shape illegality, it is safe to argue that the prevalence of surveillance in its framework is enough to say that, once more, the status of illegality has not developed completely independently from security concerns. Mitsilegas argues that merging 'the logic of risk prevention with the logic of border security', in relation to these new models of surveillance may have implications for the protection of fundamental rights, in particular with regard to asylum seekers and for 'the relationship between the individual and the state'.[158]

This issue is particularly important when one examines EUROSUR and EURODAC. Asylum claims are harder to lodge if reaching the coast is made more difficult.[159] In addition, even in the case where an asylum claim is lodged, or if these migrants are stopped at the border, greater surveillance is imposed by their being registered in an immigration database that also has law enforcement purposes (EURODAC). Consequently, it can be argued, that it is not only those databases already established such as SIS II, VIS, and EURODAC that have the view of information technology systems as an identification tool with a particular focus on the removal of migrants or impeding their entrance but the new generation (EUROSUR and EES) are also being developed in this manner despite their humanitarian concerns and risk stigmatising certain categories of migrants.[160]

[155] Art 2 (4) of the EUROSUR Regulation (emphasis added).

[156] Hayes and Vermeulen (n 2) 18.

[157] Art 6 c) of the European Commission proposal for a Regulation establishing the European Border Surveillance System (COM (2011)0873) and Meijers Committee for a Regulation establishing the European Border Surveillance (COM (2011) 0873), CM1215, 12 September 2012, 1 and 4.

[158] Mitsilegas (n 1) 61.

[159] Mitsilegas (n 54) 60.

[160] Arts 1 and 2 of the EUROSUR Regulation.

B. The Entry/Exit System—A Presumption of Illegality?

In 2008 the Commission suggested the establishment of an Entry/Exit system (EES) in the Communication that focused on preparing the next steps in border management in the EU.[161] The role of the EES was to be to electronically register the dates and the places of entry and exit of each third-country national admitted to an EU Member State for a short stay (of up to three months).[162] The EES main purpose is the improvement of the management of the EU external borders and to reduce irregular migration by tackling the phenomenon of overstaying.[163] In those cases where a migrant was found to have overstayed an alert would be sent to the national immigration authorities. Three years later in 2011 the Commission issued a Communication on smart borders in which it stated that it intended to present proposals for an EES and a Registered Traveller Programme (RTP).[164] In February 2013 the Commission presented a proposal for a Regulation establishing the EES.

The structure of the system appears, in addition, to be inspired by the US-VIST System and the policies implemented under the George W Bush administration. The principle of the European and the US initiatives is analogous: the data on foreigners is collected before the entry in the territory at the arrival at the border and the retention of the same data allows checks after their entry.[165]

In 2016 the Commission presented a new Smart Borders Package[166] that is now being discussed by the co-legislators and withdrew the 2013 Proposal for an RTP.[167] The purpose and objectives were maintained in the revised proposals and the main

[161] Commission, Communication from to the European Parliament, the Council, the European and Social Commitee and the Committee of the Regions preparing the next steps in border management in the European Union, COM (2008) 69 final.

[162] Art 1 of the European Commission proposal for a Regulation of the European Parliament and of the Council (COM(2013) 95 final) establishing an Entry/Exit System (EES) to register entry and exit data of third country nationals crossing the external borders of the Member States of the European Union, Brussels, 2013 (hereinafter 2013 proposal for Regulation of the EES).

[163] See Art 4 of the 2013 proposal for Regulation of the EES and Art 5 of the European Commission proposal (COM(2016)194 final) for a Regulation of the European Parliament ando of the Council establishing an Entry/Exit System (EES) to register entry and exit data and refusal of entry data of third country nationals crossing the external borders of the Member States of the European Union and determining the conditions for access to the EES for law enforcement purposes and amending Regulation (EC) No 767/2008 and Regulation (EU) No 1077/2011 (hereinafter 2016 proposal for Regulation of the EES).

[164] Commission, Communication to the European Parliament and the Council on Smart borders—options and the way ahead, COM (2011) 680 final. And in 2009 the proposal to set up an EES was endorsed in the Stockholm Programme.

[165] Mitsilegas (n 1) 61.

[166] The 2016 proposal for Regulation of the EES.

[167] European Commission proposal (COM(2013) 97 final) for a Regulation of the European Parliament and of the Council establishing a Registered Traveller Programme, 2013. The RTP was part of the Regulation proposals adopted by the Commission on 28 February 2013 along with the EES Regulation. As set out in Art 3 (1) of the proposed RTP Regulation, the programme 'allows third-country nationals who have been pre-vetted and granted access to the RTP to benefit from facilitation of border checks at the Union external border'. The key purpose of this initiative was to benefit low-risk travellers wishing to enter the EU and grant them speedy access to the territory.

differences relate to the structure of the system (one system is proposed),[168] the interoperability between the EES and VIS,[169] the use of biometric identifiers rather than 10 fingerprints, the reduction in the personal data recorded (26 data items are recorded rather than 36), and data retention time is five years for all purposes.[170] In terms of law enforcement access, Member States' law enforcement authorities and Europol will have access to the EES from the beginning of the operations.[171]

Two particular matters result from the analysis of the recent proposals from EES and that may directly affect the way illegality is conceptualised: first the possibility of an automatic presumption of illegal residence of overstayers and second the prospect of access of law enforcement authorities to the EES.

In relation to the first issue, the automatic presumption of illegal residence, it is relevant to mention the information mechanism established in Article 11 of the proposal for the EES. This information mechanism intends to 'automatically identify which entry/exit records do not have exit data immediately following the data of expiry of authorised length of stay and identify records for which the maximum stay allowance has been exceeded'.[172] In other words, it is suggested that there should be a mechanism that automatically tracks the occurrence of an overstay and subsequently generates a list where the data on overstayers is made available to the 'designated competent authorities'.[173] Reading Article 11 of the 2016 proposed Regulation for the EES it is arguable that the information mechanism may lead to a situation of presumption or fiction of illegal residence.[174]

When linking the general understanding of legal presumption as a conclusion achieved from the existence or nonexistence of a fact that is proven to be true, one understands that the mechanism established in Article 12 of the 2016 proposed Regulation has that aim. Thus, the fact that overstayers are automatically identified and included on a list available for national authorities presupposes that these migrants included in the list are illegally staying within the territory of the EU and therefore should be issued an order of return.[175] In sum, the categorisation of an illegally-staying migrant is, if the Regulation is approved, based on a legal fiction that the migrant will have to refute. In other words the migrant has the onus of proving it wrong. This possibility highlights the importance of databases and registration of the categorisation of an irregular migrant and how they can be determinant to their legal status.

The prospect of allowing access to EES data for law enforcement purposes subject to strict conditions and safeguards may represent an important tool to identify

[168] Art 6 of the 2016 proposal for Regulation of the EES.

[169] Art 7 of the 2016 proposal for Regulation of the EES.

[170] Art 31 of the 2016 proposal for Regulation of the EES.

[171] Arts 26 to 30 of the 2016 proposal for Regulation of the EES.

[172] See Art 12 of the 2016 proposed Regulation for the EES.

[173] See Art 12 of the 2016 proposed Regulation for the EES.

[174] For a comprehensive view of the definition of legal fictions, see LL Fuller, *Legal Fictions* (Stanford CA, Stanford University Press, 1967).

[175] See the Return Directive.

the perpetrators of terrorist acts. This was suggested in the Impact Assessment[176] and from the wording of Recital 16 of the 2016 proposed EES Regulation: 'In the fight against terrorist offences and other serious criminal offences, it is imperative that law enforcement authorities have most up-to-date information if they are to perform their tasks.' The EDPS has raised some queries about the matter and most importantly recognised the existence of the general trend towards granting law enforcement authorities access to large-scale information and identification systems, for example the issue of access in EURODAC.[177] In addition, in relation to the 2013 proposal, the EDPS stressed the fact that, in principle, the people whose data is stored in EES are 'not suspected of any crime and should not be treated as such, since the system is in the first place designed mainly as a calculation tool for the duration of stay of third-country nationals'.[178]

It is relevant to raise this issue and point out some of the main concerns discussed on the prospect of the inclusion of law enforcement purposes, given that this supports the general argument of this chapter: the concept of a migrant's illegality in EU law is approximated with the concept of criminality. As we have seen throughout the chapter, the catalyst for this result is the general trend of granting law enforcement authorities access to data stored in information systems that originally were designed for immigration purposes. Nevertheless, as it is also important to recognise the role that information systems, such as the EES, may play in identifying unknown suspects, perpetrators and victims provided that there is an assessment of the necessity and proportionality of the access to that personal data. The fact that the EES included law enforcement purposes allows the conclusion to be drawn that, in the area of immigration databases, if there is no particular concern with proportionality and strict conditions for access are imposed then, the concept of migrant illegality may be conflated with the concept of criminality, although not necessarily. In effect, this means that migrants who overstay but have not committed any crime are surveilled in the same manner as an individual who had committed (or are suspected of committing) a crime would be. As a way of preventing this outcome the primary purpose of the EES must be border management and law enforcement a secondary one.[179]

[176] Commission Staff Working Document Impact Assessment accompanying the document Proposal for a Regulation of the European Parliament and of the Council establishing an entry/exit system to register entry and exit data of third-country nationals crossing the external borders of the Member States of the European Union COM (2013) 95, Brussels, 28 February 2013.

[177] Opinion of the European Data Protection Supervisor on the proposals for a Regulation establishing an Entry/Exit System (EES) and a Regulation establishing a Registered Traveller Programme (RTP), 2013.

[178] ibid, 68.

[179] See: Opinion of the European Data Protection Supervisor on the Second EU Smart Borders Package *Recommendations on the revised Proposal to establish an Entry/Exit System*, 2016 (https://edps.europa.eu/sites/edp/files/publication/16-09-21_smart_borders_en.pdf): 'the establishment of the described EES directly and primarily for law enforcement purposes would be unacceptable, and that the EES should remain a border management tool purely designed with this purpose in mind.' 19.

VII. THE ERA OF POTENTIAL DIGITAL CRIMINALISATION OF ILLEGALLY-STAYING THIRD-COUNTRY NATIONALS

What can be concluded from the most recent EU strategy for border control information systems? This question is not easy to answer, especially given the fact that the smart borders initiatives are still at the proposal stage and the EUROSUR is not fully operational. Several studies seem to indicate that not much will change and that there are still doubts about the necessity and effectiveness of these measures.[180] The fact that one can identify the trends previously addressed as factors of the conflation of illegality and criminality in recent proposals and Regulation, in respect of SIS II, VIS and EURODAC, paves the way for what has been a common premise of the present chapter: the potential digital criminalisation of illegally-staying migrants. There is a clear trend identified by the literature of criminalising immigration offences at a national level in the EU,[181] and the present chapter sought to show how at the level of the management supranational structures of surveillance in the area of justice and home affairs some practices can lead to the same result at the EU level.

In sum, the existence of the EU machinery of surveillance that puts some categories of mobile people under greater surveillance than others is clear for all to see. Even bona fide travellers, for example, despite their speedy entrance perks, do not escape the clutches of technology and border control. The story of mass surveillance and digital borders continues to be written under the premise that illegality and criminality can conflate.

VIII. CONCLUSION

Chapter four focused on the role of EU immigration databases with regard to the creation of a concept of illegality at the supranational level. At the heart of the chapter was the premise that EU instruments in charge of regulating EU immigration databases influence the legal regime of illegality to a significant extent. This is so not only because they may generate a sort of 'digital illegality' considering their impact on the categorisation of migrants, but also for allowing for a conflation of illegality with criminality. The first part of the chapter argued that in the

[180] Opinion of the European Data Protection Supervisor on the proposals for a Regulation establishing an Entry/Exit System (EES) and a Regulation establishing a Registered Traveller Programme (RTP), 2013, point 83, 20 and 25, in 2010 these scholars after having provided a comparison between the EES and the US-VISIT, stated that 'the effectiveness of an entry-exit system can only be insured if an entry record can be matched against an exit', which was a feature that was not part of the EES proposal in 2013.

[181] P Dumas, *L'accès des ressortissants des pays tiers au territoire des États membres de l'Union européenne* (Brussels, Bruylant, 2013) 310.

SIS/SIS II, VIS and EURODAC there is a conflation between illegality and criminality. This argument was evidenced by three main trends common to these databases: the erosion of the principle of purpose limitation, the widening of access to data by law enforcement authorities and the metamorphosis of immigration databases into potential general intelligence databases. The final section of the fourth chapter debated whether these trends could be found in the EU's new surveillance initiatives, such as the EUROSUR and the EES.

A potential digital criminalisation of illegally-staying third-country nationals was the common premise that brought together the debate about the first generation immigration databases and the most recent initiatives, given that the trends identified in the beginning of this chapter were also identifiable in the most recent immigration databases initiatives or proposals. In relation to the definition of a supranational concept of illegality, this chapter proved that at the level of surveillance of the categories of migrants that may cross the borders of the EU, there is the risk that the distinction between illegally-staying irregular migrants and criminals with regards the treatment of their personal data is insufficiently clear in practice.

5

Access to Legality in the EU: An Instrumental or Corrective Mechanism?

I. INTRODUCTION

THE FINAL CHAPTER aims to provide a conclusion to the cycle of the phenomenon of illegality. The role played by EU law in this matter in conjunction with national legislation regulating the topic is particularly important for understanding the main questions posed in this part of the study, namely: what potential role could EU law have in shaping and reshaping the routes to legality (routes which are primarily created by Member States at the domestic level)? And further, how can EU law address the issues that arise from the regulation of illegality? EU law creates situations of illegality (voluntarily or otherwise), deals with certain aspects of the regulation of illegality (as shown in the preceding chapters) and logically also has a say in how to provide a way out of illegality.

Access to legality both at the supranational and national level can have an instrumental or a corrective use. As such this chapter addresses these two types of use of the access to legality, first, instrumental to Member States's domestic interests and, second, corrective of the issues that arise from the regulation of illegality in EU law. Even though both uses of the mechanisms that allow access to legality are lawful, the latter addresses issues that arise from the regulation of illegality. The chapter analyses the instrumentalisation of the access to legality at the national level and looks into practices such as naturalisation, investor citizenship and investor residency programmes. The Portuguese case of golden visas is used as an example to illustrate the instrumental paths to legality that may be created at the national level and that reveal a clear preference from the Member States for the protection of values such as investment stability and the recovery of the real estate market in a bailout country.[1]

Second, Part II of chapter five focuses on the analysis of the potential corrective role of the access to legality. This part of the study starts by looking at legal

[1] B Queiroz, 'Vistos Gold: nem tudo o que reluz é ouro!' *Público* (2014), (http://p3.publico.pt/actualidade/sociedade/14611/vistos-gold-nem-tudo-o-que-reluz-e-ouro?fb_action_ids=10204452019558441&fb_action_types=og.likes).

mechanisms that may have a corrective function, such as the regularisation of migrants. The chapter provides an examination of EU law's intervention and impact on the creation of the corrective mechanisms that place the focus on the regulation of the access to legality, rather than on the 'illegalisation of migrants'.

Third, the final part of the chapter provides suggestions based on the corrective access to legality rationale, which finds its normative claim in the need for a 'reset' in the context of regulation of illegality at the EU level: the creation of a corrective temporary protection status, making the purposes of immigration databases expressly define and exhaustive and creating limits to the commodification of access to legality and guaranteeing the respect for the principle of sincere cooperation at the EU level.

II. ACCESS TO LEGALITY IN EU MIGRATION LAW: THE DEFINITION, INSTRUMENTAL USE AND CORRECTIVE POTENTIAL

A. Definition of Access to Legality

The concept of illegality of a migrant's stay, a temporary phenomenon, at least *per definitionem*, is mainly characterised by the absence of a lawful stay or the breach of immigration law, as explained in chapter one.[2] Consequently, in theory, the illegality of a migrant's stay is a transitory situation (although, for some, such as non-removable migrants, it may be prolonged for an indeterminate amount of time)[3] of those who are either waiting to be removed or to be able to access a regular immigration status. Interestingly, one may discern patterns in relation to the degree of difficulty that a migrant may face with regard to accessing legality and the degree of difficulty that the same migrant may have in falling back into illegality. A clear example of these dynamics can be shown by comparing EU citizens and third-country nationals accessing legality. EU citizens move more swiftly from illegality to legality, given that 'union citizens decide autonomously whether they relocate their home across national borders. It's the preference of the individual, not public policy objectives, which primarily guides the mobility of Union citizens within the single market'.[4]

As such, it goes without saying that legality and, in particular, access to legality is an easier process for EU citizens (in comparison to third-country nationals). Not only do they always have a legal status (nationality) from their Member State of origin (which is also usually a safe country to return to) but the requirements to legalise their stay in the host Member State are also less strict to

[2] See chapter one for the view adopted on illegality.

[3] See chapter three for more on this issue and also look at the Case C-34/09, *Gerardo Ruiz Zambrano*, [2011], EU:C:2011:124 for an example.

[4] D Thym, 'EU Migration Policy and its Constitutional Rationale: A Cosmopolitan Outlook' (2013) 50 *Common Market Law Review* 711.

comply with.[5] In addition, the degree of difficulty in terms of accessing legality is inversely proportionate to the degree of difficulty to fall out of it. Consequently, and in broad terms, for EU citizens it is easier to access legality and harder to be unlawfully staying in the territory of the host Member State; whereas for third-country nationals it is more difficult to have access to legality but easier to be illegally staying.

In the abstract, accessing legality depends on several variables, although in relation to third-country nationals one thing is certain: to be legally staying in the territory of a Member State a migrant must be granted a residence permit or some other type of authorisation or documentation. With regard to residence permits EU law has clarified the meaning of this document in the wording of the Council Regulation (EC) No 1030/2002: '(a) "residence permit" shall mean any authorisation issued by the authorities of a Member State allowing a third-country national to stay legally on its territory'.[6]

This Regulation does not cover (a) visas, (b) permits issued pending examination of an application for a residence permit or for asylum or (c) authorisations issued for a stay of a duration not exceeding six months by Member States not applying the provisions of Article 21 of the Convention implementing the Schengen Agreement.[7] As stated elsewhere, the policy of access to the territory of Member States is based on two types of rules: one that aims to limit the migration of 'ordinary' third-country nationals and the other that tends to benefit the mobility of 'privileged' third-country nationals.[8] The conditions imposed by the Regulation imposing a uniform format for residence permits is a clear example of the implicit categorisation of people created by the supranational regulation of certain, in this case formal, parts of the access to legality of third-country nationals living within EU Member States' territories.

Theoretically, when one thinks of the different moments which are part of the process of accessing legality there are three fundamental moments. First, the element of mobility: a migrant trying to access legality has to have moved or be willing to move to the territory of one of the Member States and thus has to be mobile. Second, the substantive element, the third-country national has to substantially fulfil the requirements imposed by the legislation (either national or European) to be granted legal access to the territory or to have their access legalised. Third, the formal element, the access to a regular or legal immigration status depends on the possession of documentation, authorisation or a permit providing prove of it.

Supranational and national levels of regulation are closely intertwined in relation to access to legality by third-country nationals trying to enter the EU and

[5] See for example Citizens' Directive 2004/38 Arts 7 and 8.

[6] Art 1 (2) a) of the Council Regulation (EC) No 1030/2002 laying down a uniform format for residence permits for third-country nationals, [2002], OJ L 157/1.

[7] Art 1(2) a), ibid.

[8] P Dumas, *L'accès des ressortissants des pays tiers au territoire des États membres de l'Union européenne* (Brussels, Bruylant, 2013).

impact on the three fundamental moments of the access to legality. It is important to remember that in accordance with Article 79(5) of the Treaty on the Functioning of the European Union (TFEU) Member States have the final say in relation to the numbers of economic third-country nationals wanting to reside within their territory. Although, as Dumas has stated, Member States are no longer the only entity responsible for the categorisation of third-country nationals who wish to access their territory: EU law plays an increasingly significant role in this area.[9] Since it is impossible to focus solely on one of the modes of governance of immigration (EU law or national law) as they regulate different parts of the last stage of the cycle of illegality (the access to legality), at the heart of the next sections is the peculiar dynamics established between EU law and national immigration law. Whereas the first may be gradually constraining some aspects of the latter; the latter creatively designs ways in the EU that 'tend to be more interested in the own "office journeys" than responding to increasing human mobility, migrant labour has been used to fill gaps in labour markets without attention to long-term horizons and the welfare of human beings'.[10]

The analysis of the interaction of levels of regulation of the access to legality aims to reveal the functions that this mechanism may serve, both at a European and national level, an analysis that focuses, respectively, on the instrumental use and the corrective potential of the mechanisms that provide access to legality within the EU.

B. Access to Legality: Instrumental Use and Potential Corrective Role

Having access to legality means one of two things. First, it can mean that a migrant's immigration status shifts from being irregular to regular through being regularised by the host Member State while already living unlawfully in the host Member State's territory (for example if the migrant is granted the citizenship of the Member State of residence through naturalisation). Second, a migrant may enter the host Member State in possession of a legal immigration status if they fulfil the relevant conditions in relation to one of the legal channels of migration created by Member States or by the EU. In both situations the final outcome is that a third-country national may legally stay within the territory of the host Member State.

As described above, having access to legality in EU migration law means *sensu stricto* entering and staying legally within the territory of a Member State of the EU. Therefore the mechanisms that do not provide access to legality in the EU, such as toleration statuses (de facto or de iure), are excluded. Toleration statuses

[9] ibid, 780.

[10] D Acosta Arcarazo, D Kostakopoulou and Tine Munk, 'EU Migration Law: the Opportunities and Challenges Ahead' in D Acosta Arcarazo and Cian C Murphy (eds), *EU Security and Justice Law—After Lisbon and Stockholm* (Oxford, Hart Publishing, 2014) 129.

do not result in the attribution of a residence permit to the illegally-staying migrant and simply prolong (formally or otherwise) the uncertain situation of non-removable migrants as explained in more detail in chapter three.[11] In the broad sense, the meaning and the outcomes of the regulation of access to legality goes beyond the attribution of a residence permit producing impacts both at EU and national level, as follows. In previous chapters the EU's regulation of illegality was criticised, whereas this chapter focuses on access to legality as a final phase of the overreaching phenomenon of illegality that can be used as an instrumental tool or as a corrective mechanism.

The complexity of the issue of access to legality by third-country nationals is due to a large extent to the multi-level character of the system that regulates it. Its regulation includes both supranational and national legal sources that are not only intertwined and interdependent (for example, the long-term resident status is granted at the European level, but the integration requirements are assessed at the national level),[12] but may also be mutually exclusive (for example, long-term resident status is not granted if the requirements to be granted a temporary residence permit at the national level do not match the Directive).[13] Whereas Member States have greater discretion to naturalise and regularise third-country nationals who have migrated to the territory of a Member State, EU law may influence or facilitate the creation of paths that allow legalisation, naturalisation or any other type of authorisation to stay either permanently or temporarily. The dynamic between these two sources of legality (supranational and national) is at the heart of the present subsection, especially with regard to how EU law may intervene or impact upon national legislation creating legal channels of migration.

The regulation of illegality does not sufficiently provide for all eventualities which may arise, leaving entire categories of migrants with uncertain or atypical (as seen in chapter three) migration statuses. As a result of the loopholes left in the regulation of illegality other problematic cases surface such as the categorisation of unlawfully staying EU citizens (as seen in chapter two). Finally, the fact that the legislation which regulates immigration information systems does not include sufficient safeguards to prevent the potential criminalisation of illegally-staying third-country nationals (as seen in chapter four) can also be highlighted.

As such, the following analysis focuses on the different mechanisms that facilitate the transformation of an illegal stay into a legal stay at a national level and is divided into two parts. Part I addresses the instrumentalisation of legality by Member States, examining (i) naturalisation; and (ii) investor citizenship and residence programmes. Part II assesses the corrective potential of legality, including (iii) regularisation. This overview takes into account the fact that these are interactions resulting from the combination of both levels of regulation as well as the instrumental or corrective use of these mechanisms. Shaw and Miller argue

[11] See chapter three.
[12] Arts 4, 5 and 19 of the 2003/109 Directive.
[13] Art 3 (1) b) of the 2003/109 Directive.

that there is a paradox in the EU's multi-level legal order, which 'demands that the EU and national legal orders be simultaneously both proximate and interlinked, and also in some respects separate'.[14]

III. PART I: THE INSTRUMENTALISATION OF THE ACCESS TO LEGALITY

A. Member State Discretion and the Functions of Access to Legality

Member States make use of their discretion to grant national citizenship or a residence permit to stay within its territory and in doing so also provide access to EU citizenship. The essence of the regulation of nationality and EU citizenship in the EU is a complex 'interdependency of national laws of citizenship and EU law'.[15] EU law has tools to intervene (either directly or indirectly) in the way national legislators shape their channels for accessing legality and to restrict access to supranational rights. The other side of this dynamic between both levels of the regulation is the instrumental use by Member States of their wider margin of discretion with regards to the control of immigration.

In order to demonstrate the instrumentalisation of the regulation of the access to legality by Member States there are three examples of functions: (i) economic stability, (ii) migration management and (iii) a symbolic function. It must be noted that these practices become more relevant when Member States, in using their competence to define the admission of third-country nationals to their territories, grant access or facilitate access to rights and legal statuses that belong to the realm of EU law.

For example, national legislation that creates 'investor citizenship or residence programmes' allow the 'world's moneyed elite'[16] to have swift access to enjoy supranational citizenship and the rights and freedoms attached to it. The functions protected by this type of national legislative initiative that creates investor citizenship programmes as in Malta or Cyprus protect both economic stability and migration management. This is the case due to the fact that this particular national legislation not only imposes a financial investment threshold, but also because the status granted to the investors includes the right to move freely within the Schengen Area, as citizens of the Union. Within the context of the 'Eurocrisis' the function of economic stability became a particularly relevant tool for some of the 'bailout countries' that implemented investor residency

[14] J Shaw and N Miller, 'When Legal Worlds Collide: An Exploration of What Happens When EU Free Movement Law Meets UK Immigration Law', (2013) 38 *European Law Review* 1.

[15] N Shuibhne and J Shaw, 'General Report', in Ulla Neergaard, Catherine Jacqueson and Nina Holst-Christensen (eds), *Union Citizenship: Development, Impact and Challenges,The XXVI FIDE Congress in Copenhagen, 2014, Congress Publications* Vol 2 (2014), 151.

[16] A Shachar, 'Dangerous Liaisons: Money and Citizenship' in Ayelet Shachar and Rainer Bauböck (eds), *Should Citizenship be for Sale?*, EUI Working Papers, RSCAS 2014/01 Robert Schuman Centre for Advanced Studies EUDO Citizenship Observatory, 2014, 3.

programmes in an attempt to attract investment and create employment. This is, for instance, the case with regard to Portugal, which will be examined later in this study. However, economic stability is not the only function that may motivate the instrumentalisation of access to legality. In particular, the need to manage legal migration is another pressing consideration.

One further function that deserves to be mentioned has a symbolic character. One can point out several examples of cases where Member States have used their discretion to grant national citizenship to third-country nationals in a symbolic manner. To be more concrete, Italy posthumously granted citizenship to migrants that died trying to reach its shores in 2014, a gesture that 'is not so much empty as restorative of statist order'.[17] Furthermore, still symbolic but with a rather different aim is the example of Portuguese and Spanish national legislation granting the nationality of these two Member States to descendants of Jews persecuted 500 years ago.[18] Or for instance, when Matteo Renzi threatened to put in practice his 'plan B' of granting temporary residence permits to illegally-staying third-country nationals as way of negotiating more solidarity from the EU in the context of the asylum crisis.[19]

These three examples show how Member States, when exercising their discretion to confer citizenship or temporary residence permits, do not always do so in a strategic way to encourage investment or manage the number of migrants within national territory, in fact they also determine who may access legality (at national and supranational levels) through gestures designed to reaffirm their own sovereignty or to serve diplomatic purposes.

B. Mechanisms at the National Level Allowing the Instrumentalisation of the Access to Legality

The present section focuses on the analysis of mechanisms of transformation of migrant statuses (naturalisation and investor citizenship and residence programmes), which are created and regulated by the domestic laws of Member States. The aim of this analysis is twofold: first, to clarify what is meant by the practice of instrumentalisation of the access to legality by Member States, and

[17] C Costello, 'Reflections on an Anniversary: EU Citizenship at 20' in Bridget Anderson and Michael Keith (eds), *Migration: The COMPAS Anthology* (Oxford, COMPAS, 2014) 19.

[18] See on this issue: *The Guardian*, 'Portugal to grant citizenship to descendants of persecuted Jews' (www.theguardian.com/world/2015/jan/29/portugal-citizenship-descendants-persecuted-sephardic-jews).

[19] EU Parliamentary question for written answer to the Commission, 16 June 2015, (www.europarl.europa.eu/sides/getDoc.do?pubRef=-//EP//TEXT+WQ+E-2015-009804+0+DOC+XML+V0//EN&language=en). See also, for the declarations of Matteo Renzi on the 16 June in Rome about these proposal, *Ansa*, 'Renzi says Italy will do what EU can't', 16 June 2015, (www.ansa.it/english/news/politics/2015/06/16/renzi-says-italy-will-do-what-eu-cant_88eee2cc-b19d-4a8b-ab37-145b91128a47.html): 'temporary residence permits as a reserve weapon'.

second to use the specific example of national legislation which regulates one of the mechanisms that selectively grants access to a legal immigration status to certain categories and then juxtapose it with EU law rules to explore the dynamics between the two levels of regulation.

i. Naturalisation

In relation to the naturalisation of third-country nationals, this mechanism results in the granting of citizenship of the host Member State to the migrant. Naturalisation has been defined in the literature as 'a transformative process whereby an immigrant, or more generally someone outside of the national political community, "becomes natural" by becoming a full member of that community through citizenship acquisition'.[20] Goodman additionally stresses that there is very little to the natural character of this process of acquisition of citizenship, as the focus lies on the application for naturalisation of the person to the responsible national authorities.[21] The type of status granted to a migrant through naturalisation (namely citizenship) is the strongest protection that they could apply for, thus being the 'most debated and most densely regulated form of access to citizenship'.[22]

Conventionally, the requirements for ordinary naturalisation at the domestic level range from a minimum length of residence[23] to language and civic knowledge tests, and can include a clean criminal record requirement and, in some cases such as Bulgaria, Croatia and Slovenia, renunciation of prior citizenship.[24] Facilitated naturalisation, or in other words, a naturalisation procedure that has simpler or fewer requirements, is usually acquired on the grounds of a family link with a citizen of the Member State granting citizenship, historic and cultural connection and special achievements, contribution or public interest to the Member State where the migrant applied to be naturalised.[25] The instrumental use of this naturalisation can be seen in particular on the way Member States shape their discretionary prerogative to facilitate the naturalisation of certain groups of foreigners.

As such, the latter set of reasons for granting citizenship of a Member State is of special relevance to the development of this study. This is due to the fact that

[20] S Goodman Wallace, 'Naturalisation Policies in Europe: Exploring Patterns of Inclusion and Exclusion', Comparative Report, RSCAS/EUDO-CIT-Comp. 2010/7, Robert Schuman Centre for Advanced Studies, EUDO Citizenship Observatory, 2010, 3.

[21] ibid, 3.

[22] R Baubock and S Goodman Wallace, 'EUDO Citizenship Policy Brief No. 2—Naturalisation', Robert Schuman Centre, European Union Democracy Observatory on Citizenship, (http://eudo-citizenship.eu/docs/policy-brief-naturalisation_revised.pdf)', 1.

[23] The minimum period of residence within the EU to fulfil this requirement is three years in Belgium.

[24] Baubock and Goodman Wallace (n 22) 2–6.

[25] A contribution in the areas for example of: science, sport, economy and culture.

it is illustrative of the way Member States may make instrumental use of their discretionary powers to ignore or lower some of the requirements to naturalise people with the justification of national interest. Džankić concludes that one cannot argue that there is any uniformity within Member States' legislation regarding the requirements for the acquisition of naturalisation through this facilitated channel.[26] This author has also pointed out the fact that not all Member States waive their residence requirement and that some, such as France and Belgium, in fact lower it without excluding it completely.[27]

It is within national discretion to define this 'special service' or 'exceptional achievement,' thus some Member States make express reference to economic interest, like Bulgaria, and others (in fact the majority) leave it as an open reference to be specified by the Member State.[28] Consequently, Member States may interpret these provisions as fitting their own agendas, for instance the French 'exceptional service'[29] or the Italian 'distinguished service'[30] can be in the form of an investment with conditions defined by the Member State.

While EU law may not, at least directly, affect the regulation of the naturalisation of third-country nationals at the national level (as it does not possess competence to do so), the acquisition of national citizenship through the process of naturalisation results in the additional attribution of EU citizenship[31] and the consequent enjoyment of the residence rights and freedom of movement.[32] The definition of who can enjoy the supranational form of citizenship (EU citizenship) happens through the regulation of national citizenship as is mentioned in chapter two.

As such, we can see that national measures, which grant access to legality at the national level, can also have an impact at EU level—this can be termed *bottom-up* interaction. This idea of bottom-up interaction can be seen in particular when Member States instrumentalise their discretion to naturalise an individual on the grounds of an exceptional economic contribution to society. Notwithstanding the fact that there is an exceptional contribution on the migrant's part to the country of naturalisation and that it may be in the shape of investment (resulting in economic prosperity and the creation of jobs, for example); having a pecuniary contribution enabling access to a supranational personal status (such as EU citizenship) necessarily shapes the regulation of the acquisition, in this case by attaching a price tag to it.

[26] J Džankić, 'Investment-based citizenship and residence programmes in the EU', EUI Working Paper RSCAS 2015/08, Robert Schuman Centre for Advanced Studies Research Paper No RSCAS, 2015, 7.

[27] ibid, 8.

[28] ibid, 9.

[29] ibid, 14–15.

[30] ibid, 15.

[31] See Art 20 TFEU: 'Citizenship of the Union shall be additional to and not replace national citizenship'.

[32] Baubock and Goodman Wallace (n 22) 1.

ii. Investor Citizenship Programmes

We now turn to investor citizenship programmes, yet another means of acquiring a legal immigration status that has been described by some as the act of *selling* permits to stay or visas in a Member State.[33] In recent years this practice has been advocated by a growing number of Member States and is a topic fiercely debated by academics.[34] The issue of 'citizenship for sale', which is a national practice that instead of a residence permit grants citizenship of the host Member State, has featured in numerous newspaper headlines,[35] in particular with regard the recent Maltese legislation,[36] and has raised questions that touch upon the nature of EU citizenship itself and the necessity of regulation by EU law.[37]

In short, investor citizenship programmes are mechanisms that have a pecuniary contribution as their main condition in exchange for the nationality of a Member State (and within the EU this also of course entails EU citizenship). Cyprus is the sole EU Member State that has 'pure investor' programmes, which means that the only conditions imposed on individuals seeking citizenship in addition to investment are due diligence, clean criminal record and one visit to the country.[38] Whenever an investor citizenship programme imposes other conditions, the scheme is hybrid in nature and commonly the migrants are required to have complied with a period of residence in the Member State before naturalisation, as is the case with Malta, Bulgaria and Romania. As Džankić points out, even when the investor citizenship programme is hybrid in nature and prior residence is a condition, the conditions for obtaining citizenship are often significantly lower compared to ordinary naturalisation.[39] This in itself is illustrative of the way in which Member States can manipulate access to nationality at the domestic level.

In addition to the challenge that these programmes represent in terms of global justice and the original premise of EU citizenship, investor citizenship programmes work as a tool to attract 'the rich, the beautiful and the smart'.[40] Similar to the naturalisation facilitated on the grounds of national interest, as discussed above, investor citizenship programmes are a clear example of the instrumentalisation of the access to legality that this book has sought to examine.

It is important to clarify that the purpose of this part of the chapter is not to judge the merits of these citizenship programmes, but rather to highlight and

[33] The act of selling the access to citizenship for example in the case of Malta.

[34] M Baldwin-Edwards and A Kraler, *REGINE-Regularisations in Europe* (Amsterdam, Pallas Publications, 2009) 7, S Carrera, 'How Much does EU Citizenship Cost? The Maltese Citizenship-for-sale Affair: A Breakthrough for Sincere Cooperation in Citizenship of the Union?' CEPS Liberty and Security in Europe, no 64, April/2014.

[35] Kim Gittleson, 'Where is the cheapest place to buy citizenship? BBC New York, June 2014 (www.bbc.com/news/business-27674135).

[36] Shuibhne and Shaw (n 15) 157.

[37] Shachar and Bauböck (n 16).

[38] J Džankić, (n 26) 9.

[39] ibid, 14.

[40] D Kochenov, 'Citizenship for Real: Its Hypocrisy, Its Randomness, Its Price' in Shachar and Bauböck (n 16) 28.

illustrate their instrumental character and show how Member States may craft access to legality according to their own needs, for instance in order to address pressing problems they are faced with at the national level, such as economic instability and unemployment in this particular case. In short, it is argued that access to legality is capable of being manipulated and used as a normative tool as a result of the sovereign prerogatives of the Member States.

iii. Investor Residency Programmes

So far two types of national mechanisms to access legality have been mentioned: (i) naturalisation and (ii) investor citizenship programmes. Both of these mechanisms were argued to be instrumental legal tools that Member States may make use of within the limits of the law (both supranational and national) to privilege their internal interests and to facilitate access to legality for certain categories of migrants. The last mechanism which deserves attention in this part of the study is investor residency programmes which grant third-country nationals access to a legal immigration status through investment (a residence permit eventually being granted at the national level). Commonly known as 'golden residence programmes' or simply 'golden visas', these mechanisms are another domestic means of allowing privileged access to legality to certain groups of people who fulfil requirements deemed important by the host Member State.

Within this type of programme the promise of EU citizenship is not express, as the migrants are granted a residence permit rather than full citizenship, however it is clear that such permits can help to facilitate the fulfilment of the conditions for naturalisation. For instance, generally in Portugal to be naturalised one must have lived within the Portuguese territory for six years, however for those who are granted a golden visa the requirement of living in country is relaxed to merely spending a few weeks in the country per year. The analysis of this type of mechanism specifically in relation to Portuguese legislation is an illustration of the domestic instrumentalisation of the routes to legality by Member States.

C. Portugal—An Example of the National Instrumentalisation of a Route to Legality

Access to a legal immigration status within the Member States of the Union may be acquired via national legislation which creates alternative routes to legality favouring certain categories of third-country nationals. To illustrate this practice, Portuguese legislation which grants residence permits to third-country nationals prioritises the values of investment and creation of jobs.[41] Understanding the

[41] These mechanisms are called immigrant investor or golden visa/residence programmes. Bulgaria, Cyprus, Greece, Hungary, Ireland, Latvia, Spain, the UK and Portugal are examples of Member States that have adopted this practice.

dynamics between this route to legality, which is created at the national level and which does not run up against any impediments in EU law, is particularly revealing with regard to the autonomy of Member States to give preference in terms of entry to certain categories of migrants. The dynamics between supranational and domestic legislation in the area that regulates the creation of illegality, or *a contrario* such as in the case of Portuguese legislation the creation of ways out of it, is an essential feature to understand the phenomenon as a whole.

In 2012 Portuguese Immigration Law Act no 23/2007 was amended by Act no 29/2012.[42] The amendment served, among other purposes, to transpose into the domestic legal order the Return Directive. The Portuguese legislator established hereafter a legal mechanism that allows foreign investors access to a fast track procedure to obtain a legal immigration status within the EU. The residence permit not only allows the third-country national to reside within the territory of the host Member State (Portugal), but also grants the right to visa-free travel in Schengen countries.

In relation to the legal requirements that an investor is obliged to comply with in order to be granted a golden visa (or a 'autorização de resedência para o investimento' (ARI)) in Portugal, there are three types: (i) minimum quantitative requirements related to an investment activity;[43] (ii) a minimum investment time requirement; and (iii) a minimum permanence period. The minimum quantitative requirements state that the third-country national has to facilitate within the national territory at least one of the following investments: a capital transfer of one million euros or more, the creation of 10 jobs,[44] or the purchase of a real estate property worth at least 500,000 euros.[45] The investment is required to last for a minimum of five years and only after will the residence permit be granted.[46] With regards the minimum permanence period for the purposes of renewal of the residence permit, the third-country national has to provide proof of their permanence in the territory: in the first year of seven days, consecutive or otherwise and in subsequent years 14 days.[47] In June 2015 another amendment to the regulation of golden visas was adopted in Portugal.[48] This amendment focused mainly on adding new areas of investment activities to be considered for a residence permit (such as sponsoring artistic production) and clarifying the scope of the ones which were already included in the previous version.[49]

[42] Lei no 29/2012 of August 9, amends Lei no 23/2007 of July 4, laying down the legal framework for the entry, permanence and exit of foreigners from national territory, see also Order no 11820-A/2012 and Order no 1661-A/2013 (www.sef.pt/documentos/35/11820-A-2012.pdf and www.sef.pt/documentos/35/ORDER_11820_A_2012.pdf).

[43] Art 3 of the Order no 11820-A/2012 and Order no 1661/2013 for other amendments.

[44] The first version of this mechanism (Order no 11820-A/2012) imposed that at least 30 jobs had to be created, one year later the requirement was lowered.

[45] Art 3 (1) a) b) and c) of Regulation no 1661/2013.

[46] ibid, Art 4.

[47] ibid, Art 5. This requirement was also lowered in the most recent version of the legislation.

[48] Lei no da Assembleia República no 63/2015 de 30 de Junho, terceira alteração à Lei no 23/2007, de 4 de julho, que aprova o regime jurídico de entrada, permanência, saída e afastamento de estrangeiros do território nacional, Diário República, 1.a série—No 125 (hereafter Lei no 63/2015).

[49] See for example, Art 3 (1) d) v) vi) and vii) of Lei no 63/2015.

This programme is not just 'attractive'[50] because of the gradual lowering of the requirements that has happened in the most recent version of the Portuguese legislation setting out the conditions to acquire a golden visa, the attractiveness of the programme lies also in the range of rights that are granted to the investor. Not only does it allow for a five-year permanent residence authorisation (that may eventually lead to the granting of Portuguese citizenship and consequently EU citizenship), but it also facilitates movement within Schengen countries and includes family reunification rights.[51] Ayelet Shachar points out that an investor citizenship programme such as the Portuguese one would clash with the International Court of Justice's decision in *Nottebohm* which posits that '"real and effective ties" between the individual and the state are expected to undergird the grant of citizenship'.[52] Mutatis mutandis the question posed here is that of whether this type of legislation is in conformity with EU law, especially with regard to the 2003/109 Directive, addressed in the previous section.

D. What is EU Law's Position with Regard to the Portuguese Instrumentalisation of the Investor Residency Programme?

The EU has not taken a strong position in relation to this type of national legislative initiative that privileges certain categories of migrants by securing their right to reside in a Member State territory on the grounds of financial investment. It is not straightforward to argue that these practices are a violation of EU law, as Shaw has argued (in relation to citizenship-granting investor programmes): 'it may be a mercantilist practice, but it is not arbitrary according to the norms of EU law'.[53] However, what one can say is that EU law creates conditions that must be complied with in order to enjoy more than a national legal residence status. For instance, in order to enjoy long-term residence, the third-country national (even when granted a golden visa) at the national level would have to comply with the conditions imposed by 2003/109 Directive.

In line with the arguments made by Carrera, it is fair to say that it is not in the spirit of the 2003/109 Directive that Member States could 'sell long-term resident status to rich non-nationals'.[54] This commentator also highlights that the ways in which Member States may benefit specific categories of third-country nationals, in this case wealthy investors, have been overlooked. Recital 6 of the 2003/109 Directive states that:

> 'The main criterion for acquiring the status of long-term resident *should be the duration of residence in the territory of a Member State*. Residence should be both *legal* and *continuous* in order to show that the person has put down roots in the country. Provision should be

[50] Carrera (n 34) 13.

[51] Shachar (n 16) 3.

[52] ibid, 4.

[53] J Shaw, 'Citizenship for Sale: Could and Should the EU Intervene?' in Shachar and Bauböck (n 16) 33.

[54] Carrera (n 34) 19.

made for a degree of *flexibility* so that account can be taken of circumstances in which a person might have to leave the territory on a temporary basis'. (emphasis added)

In accordance with Recital 6, Article 4 of the Directive imposes a five-year continuous and legal residence in the national territory period to be eligible for a long-term resident status. As previously explained, in relation to the Portuguese golden visa programme, Member States may reduce the requirement of a minimum residence period for the purposes of renewal of the residence permit to the third-country national on those grounds. As such, in this particular scenario, to have their national residence authorisation, a foreign investor in the first year would not have to spend more than seven days residing in Portuguese territory. The question which arises at this stage is: how does this national legislation fit with the conditions imposed by 2003/109 Directive? Is it within national discretion to control the conditions for the attribution of a golden visa in a way that allows the third-country national to apply *a posteriori* (after five years of residence) for a long-term residence permit under the scope of the 2003/109 Directive?

The answer to this question can be found in the combination of Recital 17 and Articles 4 (3) and 13 of the 2003/109 Directive which set out, respectively, the regime for exceptions to the minimum duration of the residence requirement and the possibility of more favourable national provisions. While Member States are free to 'issue permits with a permanent or unlimited validity on conditions that are more favourable than those'[55] provided by the Directive, the residence permits granted under more favourable conditions 'shall not confer the right of residence in the other Member States'.[56] The continuity of the five-year residence allows for some exceptions, in accordance with Article 4(3). Exceptional periods that are not taken into account for the purposes of the acquisition of the long-term resident status must be less than six consecutive months and not more than 10 months within the overall five-year period.[57]

What can one make of the combination of the two levels (supranational and national) of regulation of residence status? It seems fair to argue that in cases such as the Portuguese investor residency programme (used as an illustrative scenario) EU law plays a restrictive role, even if the restriction relates mainly to the mobility of the migrant and not to the access to the right to stay. It is within a Member State's own discretion to create a more favourable residence status that for instance may facilitate the acquisition of a residence permit in exchange for investment and reduced periods of continuous de facto residence within the national territory. Nevertheless, these are conditions that serve the purpose of that national legislation and do not imply any flexibility at supranational level with regards the permanency of the residency of those third-country nationals, unless they have complied with the requirements imposed by the 2003/109 Directive 'the status cannot be EU permanent residence in light of EU law'.[58]

[55] Recital 17 of the 2009/103 Directive.
[56] ibid, Art 13.
[57] ibid, Art 4(3).
[58] Carrera (n 34) 19.

In practical terms this means, for instance, that a Chinese investor who holds a Portuguese golden visa is not entitled to move and live in any other Member State other than Portugal. This situation may only change after this third-country national completes a five-year continuous and legal residence period in accordance with the 2003/109 Directive. Notwithstanding, the restrictive role played by EU law in relation to the third-country national's right to move and reside in other Member States; with regards to the acquisition of national citizenship and additionally EU citizenship, it is not straightforward to restrict Member States' discretion with supranational arguments.

It is important to point out that the Portuguese investor residency programme is a clear example of the instrumental use of routes to legality created at a national level as it is a piece of legislation crafted to fulfil the function of economic stability and the creation of jobs. Ostensibly, tailoring migrants' access to legality in accordance to the needs of the Member State it is not in violation of the law. Nonetheless, given that the core of this study is the phenomenon of illegality, this type of instrumentalisation of access to legality is not the most satisfactory way to make use of legality as a tool to answer to the consequences of the supranational regulation of illegality. Instead, these practices emphasise the two-tier regime of access to legality within the EU which favours the wealth of the migrants wanting to legally stay within the territory of the Member States. Therefore, a closer look has to be taken into the corrective potential of legality, as an alternative to the aforementioned instrumental role.

IV. PART II: THE POTENTIAL CORRECTIVE ROLE OF ACCESS TO LEGALITY AT THE SUPRANATIONAL LEVEL

A. Why is Regularisation not Enough to Address Illegality in the EU?

Considering access to legality (or access to a legal immigration status) from a solely instrumental perspective is not sufficient as it does not take into consideration the full potential of the mechanisms that provide illegally-staying migrants with a legal status. This part of the chapter challenges that view and moves on to prove that the mechanisms that grant access to legality have the power to correct the consequences of the current regulation of illegality.

The regularisation of migrants is examined for two main reasons: first, because regularisation of migrants is the procedure *par excellence* associated with the transformation of migrant statuses. Second, despite the fact that the argument of expanding the EU's regularising powers has been debated thoroughly by scholars,[59] thus far the arguments made in support of regularisation as the solution for tackling all issues related to illegality are not entirely convincing.

[59] For example see: J Apap, P De Bruycker and C Schmitter, 'Regularisation of Illegal Aliens in the European Union-Summary Report of a Comparative Study' (2000) 2 *European Journal of Migration & Law* 263.

Regularisation can be defined as the procedure through which any Member State grants third-country nationals who are illegally staying in the host Member State a legal status.[60] Regularisation presupposes that the migrant has previously been living irregularly or in breach of national immigration rules in the host Member State and 'it is precisely this that establishes the illegality of the *de facto* situation to be regularised'.[61] Desmond argues there are two myths concerning regularisation that have to be debunked. The first myth is that this is a measure which is seldom used. In fact, from 1996 to 2008 around six million migrants were regularised in the EU.[62] The second myth relates to the fact that the majority of migrants are returned to the country of origin, when actually no more than 40 per cent return home.[63]

The regularisation of third-country nationals is still part of the Member State's discretion; therefore it is not included as part of the EU *acquis* on irregular migration.[64] To be more precise, the EU (and in particular the Commission) have not encouraged the regularisation of illegally staying third-country nationals as it is seen as a pull factor for irregular migration.[65] Mass regularisation of third-country nationals was hereafter considered harmful for other Member States. Consequently, a mutual information exchange system was created which obliges Member States to notify other Member States of measures that may affect them, and the European Council made sure that Member States only regularise migrants on a case-by-case basis according to the European Pact on Immigration and Asylum.[66]

Scholars have also already contributed significantly to the development of the topic of the regularisation of irregular migrants in EU law, especially in relation to human rights. Thym, for instance, thoroughly discussed the possibility of a human right to regularisation of illegal stays,[67] and Desmond has taken a more comparative approach and compared EU law tools to regularise illegal stays with the US immigration regime.[68] The present contribution aims to go further and develop research that has been done in the area of the transformation of migration status from irregular to legal not by addressing the direct ways in which EU law regularises the status of migrants, but rather by focusing on the ways in

[60] A Kraler, *Regularisation: Misguided Option or Part and Parcel of a Comprehensive Policy Response to Irregular Migration?* IMICOE Working Paper No 24, February 2009, 7.

[61] Apap, De Bruycker and Schmitter (n 59) 263.

[62] A Desmond, 'Regularization in the European Union and the United States—The Frequent Use of an Exceptional Measure' in A Wiesbrock, and D Acosta Arcarazo, *Global Migration: Old Assumptions, New Dynamics. Santa Barbara, California. eBook Collection* (Westport, Praeger, 2015) 70.

[63] Council of the European Union, 7007/14, An Effective EU Return Policy (Brussels: Council of Europe).

[64] R Cholewinski, 'EU Acquis on Irregular Migration: Reinforcing Security at the Expense of Rights' (2000) 2 *European Journal of Migration & Law* 170.

[65] Desmond (n 62) 73.

[66] ibid, 73 and Council of the European Union, 13440/08, European Pact on Immigration and Asylum [2008].

[67] D Thym, 'Residence as de facto Citizenship? Protection of Long-Term Residence under Article 8 ECHR' in Ruth Rubio-Marín (ed), *Human Rights and Immigration* (Oxford, Oxford University Press, 2014).

[68] Desmond (n 62) 83–91.

which EU law intervenes and impacts upon national legislation that creates legal immigration statuses in a corrective way. In addition, regularisation is most often seen as a solution in the case of non-removable migrants. However, and crucially, non-removability is not the only concern that arises with regard to the regulation of illegality as shown earlier.

B. Measuring the Corrective Potential Role of the Mechanism of Regularisation

To measure the corrective potential of the regularisation of illegally-staying third-country nationals, one has to highlight its effects to then juxtapose them with the consequences of the current regulation of illegality from a EU law perspective set out in previous chapters. Illegality is analysed as justified in the first chapter,[69] from a holistic perspective. Consequently, the tools used to address this phenomenon are also designed to have an overreaching effect. This section claims that whereas there is no panacea in terms of tackling the problems that result from the current illegality regime, a focus on expanding the EU's regularisation powers of illegally-staying migrants is not satisfactory for the following reasons.

First, the procedure of regularisation is intrinsically linked to the discretion of Member States, something that immediately highlights a problem of lack of competence of the EU. Additionally, regularisation underlines the imminent legislative focus on the return of illegally-staying migrants that drives secondary EU legislation,[70] in particular the Return Directive. Article 6 (4) of this piece of legislation, which creates the opportunity for Member States to regularise migrants at any moment for compassionate, humanitarian or other reasons is an exception to the obligation to return illegally-staying migrants.[71] This mechanism was analysed within the scope of chapter three of this study, however it is important to recall the fact that while it could be argued that it is implicit that 'return should give way to regularization where certain factors as family life and children are sufficiently strong',[72] this possibility is not included as a duty within the text of the Directive. As such, it could be argued that this tool suggests somewhat wishful thinking rather than a positive obligation to regularise when return is not possible for certain reasons. In addition the Court of Justice of the European Union (CJEU) has not (yet) addressed the meaning of the mechanism of Article 6 (4) in its jurisprudence on the Return Directive despite the fact that some of these cases would fall within the scope of this regularising provision, such as the case of Mr Kadzoev.[73] The crucial point which ought to be stressed is that from an EU

[69] See chapter 1 subsection II.A.i.

[70] Desmond (n 62) 73.

[71] P De Bruycker, 'L'Émergence d'une Politique Européenne d'Immigration' in Jean-Yves Carlier (ed), *L' étranger face au droit, XXes Journées d'études juridiques Jean Dabin* (Brussels, Bruylant, 2010) 361.

[72] Desmond (n 62) 74.

[73] See Case C-357/09 PPU *Said Shamilovich Kadzoev*, [2009], EU:C:2009:741.

law perspective, expanding the regularising powers of the EU seems to be a limited argument, due to lack of competence, first of all.

Second, the next feature which has to be examined is the scope of regularisation. It can be said that this mechanism has a particular focus on remedying the issues posed by the way illegality is regulated mostly with a specific focus on solving non-removability situations. However, even though a the case of non-removable illegally-staying third-country nationals is a very pressing matter, as shown in chapter three, it is not the only problematic issue which arises in terms of migration statuses under the current regime of regulation.

For instance, the aforementioned scenario of unlawfully-staying EU citizens within the EU stressed the creation of a new category of migrants that are 'simply present' within the territory of the Member States, that have no access to social assistance but who can re-enter the day after they are expelled from the host Member State. The problems posed by this category of migrants go beyond the regularisation of these people, as they shift from legality to illegality easily and may live more or less securely within illegality depending on the host Member State they chose to migrate to. The regularisation procedure is suited to third-country nationals and has a particular focus on non-removable third-country nationals, leaving those EU citizens outside the scope of the measure without the possibility of normalising their situation or addressing their lack of access to social benefits.

Third, and finally, the impact of the regularisation of illegally-staying third-country nationals must also be examined. As it is presented, regularisation is limited in terms of competence and scope; logically its effects are going to be directed to the groups of migrants affected by the measure. Throughout the previous chapters of this book there are two rationales which have been found to influence not only the policy-making in the area, but also the legislative initiatives at both the national and the EU level: the criminalisation of migrants and the existence of an implicit two-tier regime of regulation of illegality and access to legality based on the wealth, knowledge and even origin of the migrants. With regards the criminalisation of migrants, chapter four showed us that EU law does not actively prevent such criminalisation and that the current immigration databases created at this level in fact facilitate it. The existence of this so called two-tier regime is clear not only from the regulation of the situation of unlawfully-staying EU citizens, but also from what was demonstrated earlier in this chapter with regard to the instrumentalisation of the access to legality by Member States. The effect of the individual regularisation of third-country nationals does not have a strong impact on these side effects of the legislation.

The problems identified within the regulation of illegality are transversal to both sides of the most traditional binaries: 'legal and illegal', 'us and them', 'EU citizens and third-country nationals', 'internal market and Area of Freedom Security and Justice'. Consequently, the normative remedy to be presented to this set up has to be more comprehensive in order to accommodate the array of complex issues involved.

V. THE CORRECTIVE FUNCTION OF REGULATING LEGALITY FROM AN EU LAW PERSPECTIVE

A. EU Law's Corrective Role in the Regulation of Legality

EU law has great potential to intervene in a corrective manner in the legal mechanisms that grant access to legality. The binaries that are formed within the debates on irregular migration in some cases are not illustrative of the consequences that arise from the regulation of the phenomenon of illegality in the EU.[74] Rather than thinking in such terms what is needed is a shift in the focus in terms of how the regulation of irregular migration is thought of in EU law.

Bosniak develops, among other models, an amnesty model of 'administrative reset',[75] which is an administrative and political mechanism focused on administrative failure:

> [T]here is a pragmatic need to bring the law and actual behavior into closer alignment for purposes of effective governance and systemic legitimacy. The amnesty mechanism serves, therefore, as account clearing and slate-wiping; the transgression is to be institutionally forgotten in favor of systemic functionality.[76]

The rationale of the corrective function of access to legality finds its normative claim in the need for a 'reset' in the context of regulation of illegality at the EU level. In other words, if EU law is responsible for some of the problematic consequences that arise from the conceptualisation and regulation of illegality, then it should be also through EU law that, at least in part, this situation is remedied.

It is important to stress that this book does not argue for an expansion of the regularising powers of the EU as considered and eschewed in subsection IV.B given how limited and contingent on the Member States they are. Instead it advocates more effective use of the tools that already exist within EU law in a way which accords with the rationale of utilising legality in a corrective manner. This can be seen in a number of examples which taken together suggest a more viable approach to the regulation of irregular migration, such as the creation of corrective protection statuses for illegally-staying migrants.

Ultimately, within the area of migration it is Member States who are both responsible for formalising the legality of the stay of third-country nationals and, crucially, who are also in charge of determining the 'volumes of admission of third-country nationals coming from third countries to their territory in order to seek work, whether employed or self-employed'.[77] Therefore, the impact of EU law is constrained to this extent. However, EU law can affect the substance of legality

74 Thym (n 4) 735.

75 L Bosniak, 'Amnesty in Immigration: Forgetting, Forgiving, Freedom' (2013) 16 *Critical Review of International Social and Political Philosophy* 344, 348.

76 ibid.

77 Art 79(5) TFEU.

or the enjoyment of a legal migration status in other ways. For instance, it can create legal statuses that protect mobile people and attach rights to it. In addition, despite the constraints on the EU, certain room for manoeuvre nevertheless exists in which EU law can play a corrective role with the aim of normalising unwanted consequences of the regulation of illegality.

EU migration law, when regulating parts of the phenomenon of illegality, focuses to a large extent on combatting illegal migration, the removal and return of illegally-staying third-country nationals and ensuring security within the borders of the EU.[78] EU law's action within the area of irregular migration has been motivated by concerns of terrorism, combatting illegal migration and trafficking of human beings in accordance with the objectives established in Article 79 (1) of the TFEU.[79] These objectives are part of the common policy on asylum, immigration and external border control framed by the EU within the Area of Freedom, Security and Justice, as posited in Article 67(2) TFEU. Importantly, the same provision states that this common policy is 'based on solidarity between Member States, which is fair towards third-country nationals'. This solidarity among Member States is also at the origin of the corrective argument that is made in this section to which we will return presently.

Despite the concerns that have motivated EU acts in line with the common policy on asylum, immigration and external border control to date, in order to address some of the issues that arise from the management of irregular migration set out earlier in this book, there should be counterbalancing corrective action on the part of the EU. The ultimate goal of this intervention (EU law's corrective role, in other words) is to produce harmonising measures that through the access to legality could give a solution, for example, to the atypical status of non-removable migrants and also provide equal access to some of the existing avenues to a legal migration status which currently exist at the national level.

Next, in order to unpack this abstract argument the three consequences identified throughout the book as a result of the way illegality is managed in EU law will be juxtaposed to the corrective rationale as an illustration of possible responses to these issues.

B. Corrective Measures for the Consequences of the EU Regulation of Illegality

The corrective intervention of EU law in access to legality would be put in practice by the CJEU, the Commission and the Parliament. It can be anticipated that objections may be raised regarding certain organs acting ultra vires if they were to act in this way. In practical terms the actors would exercise this role by developing: (i) a corrective temporary and effective protection status; (ii) exhaustive grounds

[78] Thym (n 4) 735 and D Acosta Arcarazo, 'Civic Citizenship Reintroduced? The Long-Term Residence Directive as a Post-National Form of Membership' (2015) *European Law Journal* 19.

[79] C Barnard and S Peers, *European Union Law* (Oxford, Oxford University Press, 2014) 784–85.

of visa admission and the enforcement; and (iii) control of the principle of sincere cooperation between Member States in relation to the domestic creation of paths to legality that may have an impact on other Member States by the EU institutions, namely the Parliament and the Commission. This could remedy some of the existing weaknesses in EU migration law, as we will see in the following sections.

Just as a referee officiates a football match, EU law can officiate and intervene in the process of access to legality and in doing so could play a corrective role (whilst perhaps not solving every outstanding issue) in improving the current legal situation.

i. *Legal Uncertainty and Ill-fitting Categorisation of Migrants*

If EU law is indeed to play the role of the referee, previous chapters have shown that a number of red cards deserve to be shown. The first problematic consequence of the current regulation of migrant legality in the EU relates to legal uncertainty and the ill-fitting categorisation of migrants which results from the combination of issues discussed in chapters two and three of this study. For instance, the case of non-removable illegally-staying third-country nationals (even when tolerated by the national authorities), there exists no clear definition of what is covered by this atypical status that keeps these migrants designated as irregular, with no order to return to their home countries.[80]

A potential solution to this problematic legal situation is the creation of a temporary protection status for these migrants. This path would produce corrective effects at the level of the ill-fitting categorisation of irregular migrants and with regard to the resulting legal uncertainty in which some migrants live for the time they are not granted access to a legal status.

This argument is based on a literal interpretation of provisions of the Return Directive in combination with recent CJEU decisions on the matter that appear to have opened the Pandora's box of strengthening the protection of those living between illegality and legality by granting them an effective status while they wait for a decision on the legality of their stay. One may look at this as an embryonic corrective protective status[81] enshrined in the Return Directive for migrants who are left in limbo.

There is the potential to develop a corrective and temporary type of protection for migrants with the purpose of correcting a problem that was created by the regulation of illegality both at the national and the supranational level. This corrective protective migrant status could provide a temporary safety net for the

[80] For more on non-removability of illegally staying third-country nationals see chapter three of this book.

[81] See Peers for a similar position on the creation of an alternative protective status: S Peers, 'Could EU law save Paddington Bear? The CJEU develops a new type of protection', EU Law Analysis—Expert insight into EU law developments, (2014), http://eulawanalysis.blogspot.it/2014/12/could-eu-law-save-paddington-bear-cjeu.html.

third-country nationals in possession of this atypical status.[82] Furthermore, the creation of a corrective protection status could potentially strengthen the status of those within the process (waiting for a decision) of return and correct some of the unwanted consequences that arise from it.

This corrective protection status can be read into Article 14 of the Return Directive (which was analysed in great detail in chapter three) in the same manner as the CJEU did in the recent *Abdida* case. Whilst it is not the purpose of this subsection to re-examine the status of non-removable migrants, it is suggested that there is the potential (should those decision-makers with the power to do so be inclined to take such a course of action) to improve the situation of these migrants by granting them a more effective protective status during the process that leads to a decision on their authorisation to stay or otherwise.

In *Abdida* the Court decided that where an illegally-staying third-country national suffering from a serious illness had their return decision postponed they were entitled to the protection of their basic needs.[83] As such, the Court inferred a type of protection for those affected by legal uncertainty and an ill-fitting legal categorisation. Such protection is necessarily limited and underdeveloped due to the fact that the scope of this type of protection seems to extend only to those who have the decision on their return postponed. Nevertheless, it should be noted that a legal instrument such as the Return Directive that once was known as the 'Directive de la honte'[84] has only a few years later been accepted by the Court as having protective potential. How this potential will be managed by the CJEU will necessarily have an impact on the central issues addressed in this book.

In the 1990s Weiler stressed the importance of the role played by the Court in these matters:

> Of course, the European Court has to operate within a binding normative framework of rules and principles. But, like similar high jurisdictions, it also plays a role in shaping and developing the binding normative framework within which it operates. Likewise, its pronouncements not only resolve specific disputes but also constitute an important voice in the overall rhetoric which is constitutive of the political culture of the polity.[85]

In accordance with this idea a shift in the rationale behind the regulation of irregular migration away from the general rule of returning migrants towards accessing legality in atypical limbo cases involving migrants with an illegal stay

[82] This proposal is distinct from the proposal presented by Collier of creating a 'guest worker' migrant category permeable enough in order to allow States to instrumentalise this status and make it impossible to accede to legality or possible to be deported with no appeal when the migrant's criminal record is not clear, see P Collier, *Exodus: How Migration is Changing our World* (Oxford, Oxford University Press, 2013) 266.

[83] Case C-562/13 *Abdida* [2014], para 62.

[84] JY Carlier, 'La "directive retour" et le respect des droits fondamentaux' *L'Europe des Libertés, Revue d'actualité juridique*, N°26, 2008 (http://leuropedeslibertes.u-strasbg.fr/IMG/EdL_26_doctrine_2_bis_v1-0.pdf) 13.

[85] JHH Weiler, 'Thou Shalt Not Oppress a Stranger: on the Judicial Protection of the Human Rights of Non-EC Nationals-a Critique'(1992) 3 *European Journal of International Law* 65, 69.

and no enforceable return decision is advocated. The Court has already made tentative moves in this direction but the question remains as to whether EU law could go any further and provide a path for these migrants to access legality.

But how would this work in practical terms? The CJEU has the tools to make this protection effective in cases where a third-country national is left in a legal vacuum. It could be concluded from the protection granted in *Abdida* (health care) that, at least in these cases of migrants who cannot be removed, there is a more comprehensive protection of the basic needs of those migrants. This is so because it would not be logical to grant health care to a non-removable illegally-staying migrant if there was not a more general protection of for example food and shelter, as seen in chapter three.[86]

This idea of an corrective temporary protection status can also be justified by the fact that, for example, the Employers Sanctions Directive allows for the possibility of Member States authorising illegally-staying third-country nationals whose removal has been delayed 'to work in accordance with national law'.[87] Additionally, Advocate General Bot has recently argued for the existence of a form of protection akin to that suggested above based on 'the respect for human dignity and the right to life, integrity and health' and 'the prohibition of inhuman or degrading treatment contained in Article 4 of that Charter'.[88] Advocate General Bot clarified that although the definition of 'basic needs' is left to the discretion of Member States by Article 14 of the Return Directive, it necessarily includes 'a decent standard of living' with 'secure accommodation' and any special needs.[89] In the same sense Floris De Witte argues that:

> While European Union (EU) law can be understood as an instrument for the incorporation of the demands of justice and the articulation of 'the good' beyond the nation state, it also potentially skews the distributive criteria and assumptions of justice that underlie the national welfare state.[90]

Overall, this position fits within the initial text of the Commission's Proposal for the Return Directive, and by accepting at least in part (with regards health care) the existence of this need for the protection of the basic needs of non-removable people, the CJEU in its decision has recognised the existence of a type of protection that could be a potential avenue to correct the legal uncertainty and ill-fitting categorisation of migrants that arise from the regulation of illegality.[91]

If such a corrective temporary protection status were to be considered an effective and enforceable protection it would necessarily need to be complemented

[86] Peers (n 81).

[87] Art 3 (3) of the Employers Sanctions Directive.

[88] Case C-562/13 *Abdida* [2014], Opinion of AG Bot, para 155.

[89] ibid, para 157.

[90] F De Witte, 'Transnational Solidarity and the Mediation of Conflicts of Justice in Europe' (2012) 18 *European Law Journal* 694.

[91] European Commission proposal (COM(2005) 391 final) for a Directive of the European Parliament and of the Council on common standards and procedures in Member States for returning illegally staying third country nationals, 2005.

by an element of temporality. This status would only be of value if it was temporary and if there was a possibility of accessing legality once a certain amount of time has passed the person has not been returned and was integrated in the host society. In this case the exceptional measure of Member States granting at any moment an 'autonomous residence permit' or 'authorisation to stay'[92] would become a right attached to this temporary protection that cannot be protracted in time indefinitely at risk of weakening the *effet utile* of the Return Directive, namely that 'the removal of any illegally staying third-country nationals is a matter of priority for the Member States' in accordance with the scheme of the Return Directive and the *Achughbabian* judgment.[93]

ii. The Potential Digital Criminalisation of Illegally-staying Migrants in the EU

The second implication that results from the regime of illegality is the lack of safeguards to avoid the conflation of illegality with criminality that consequently allows for a marginalisation of illegally-staying third-country nationals in the EU. This issue was thoroughly analysed in chapter four. The following section seeks to show how the corrective function of EU law could also contribute towards addressing this problematic issue.

Again the CJEU is the most pertinent EU actor in relation to this particular issue. Recent judgments delivered by the CJEU show that EU law has already played a corrective function through the lens of the access to legality by explicitly ruling that the grounds to annul and revoke a visa in accordance with the Visa Code and the Schengen Borders Code are exhaustive. In doing so the Court has made the right to cross the external borders of the EU independent of the discretion of the national authorities.

The two cases that are responsible for this harmonisation of access to a visa are *Koushkaki*[94] and *Air Baltic*.[95] In the first judgment the Court stated that the national authorities of a Member State are under the obligation to issue a uniform visa if the requirements imposed by the visa code are verified and if there is 'no reasonable doubt' that the applicant plans to leave the host Member State after the visa expiration.[96] The Court went further and determined 'that the competent authorities cannot refuse to issue a uniform visa to an applicant unless one of the grounds for refusal of a visa provided for in those articles can be applied to the applicant'.[97] In the second decision, *Air Baltic*, the Court confirmed this interpretation and established the independent existence of two separate documents: the passport and the visa. Consequently, the Court clarified that the

92 Art 6(4) of the Return Directive.

93 P De Bruycker and S Mananashvili, 'Audi Alteram Partem in Immigration Detention Procedures, between the ECJ, the ECtHR and Member States: G & R' (2015) 52 *Common Market Law Review* 575.

94 Case C-84/12, *Koushkaki*, [2013], EU:C:2013:862.

95 Case C- 575/12, *Air Baltic*, [2014], EU:C:2014:2155.

96 Para 66 of the *Air Baltic* judgment, ibid.

97 ibid, para 77.

entry of third-country nationals does not require that 'at the border check, the valid visa presented must necessarily be affixed to a valid travel document'.[98] In sum, the CJEU has expressly restricted the discretion of the Member States in determining that they cannot refuse 'a third-country national entry to its territory by applying a condition that is not laid down in the Schengen Borders Code'.[99] This is undoubtedly an important move by the Court since in making these grounds of admission exhaustive it has guaranteed a right to enter the EU and redefined the external borders.

As we have seen earlier in chapter four, those who are granted entrance to the EU on a visa have the legality of their stay controlled through the data registered in information technology systems. For instance, the Visa Information System (VIS) must be consulted for the purposes of verification of entry conditions and risk assessment in the course of any application for a visa in accordance with Article 21(2) of the Visa Code. Information technology systems or immigration databases are, as such, responsible for the preliminary categorisation of those migrants. As was also shown in previous parts of this book, the erosion of the purpose limitation principle as a consequence of the enhanced accessibility of law enforcement authorities to the data stored in these databases has led to a facilitation of a digital criminalisation of illegally-staying migrants and to the transformation of what were once immigration databases to general intelligence databases capable of being used for other undetermined purposes.[100]

But how can the corrective role of EU law practically contribute towards the resolution of this problematic legal situation? The practical remedy for this consequence of the regulation of illegality at a supranational level would be to further develop the reasoning behind *Koushkaki* and *Air Baltic* to not only restrict the discretion of Member States with regards to admission to the EU on a visa, but also to ensure that the data that results from this procedure can only be used in accordance with uniform rules imposed by EU law which respect the principle of purpose limitation. The idea behind this practical suggestion is simple: to make expressly defined purposes of the immigration databases exhaustive and consequently to ensure that the right to have personal data included (or not) in these systems could be enforced.

This corrective rationale would undoubtedly complement the objective of the recent CJEU jurisprudence to facilitate legitimate travel and to tackle irregular migration through further harmonisation of national legislation.[101] However, and crucially, it would also impact positively and work to provide some safeguards against the potential criminalisation of illegally-staying migrants through proportional processing and rightful access granted to their personal data.

[98] ibid, para 50.
[99] ibid, para 69.
[100] See chapter four.
[101] Recital 3 of the Visa Code.

iii. Two-tier Rationale based on Wealth and the Instrumentalisation of the Access to Legality by Member States

The third consequence of the regulation of illegality within the EU arises simultaneously from the instrumentalisation of the access to a legal status (addressed earlier in the first part of this chapter), the aforementioned potential digital criminalisation of illegally-staying third-country nationals and, in addition, from free movement rules in relation to EU citizens as discussed within the scope of chapter two. Interestingly, this last consequence can be found in different areas of the regulation of immigration in the EU.[102] A clear trend can be seen with regard to the prioritisation of wealth as a factor to grant fast track access to a legal status both at the EU and national level.

The previous two subsections suggested potential avenues to rectify the unwanted effects that result from the problematic regulation of illegality within the EU. Likewise, this last subsection looks at how EU law's intervention could move towards a democratisation of the grounds to access legality and respect for the principle of sincere cooperation between Member States.[103] Looking at the concrete example of instrumentalisation of the avenues to legality analysed in earlier sections of this chapter, the citizenship investor programmes and golden visas, some have stressed that from a 'purely legal'[104] point of view it is difficult to use EU law to counterbalance this 'mercantilist practice' as it is not, in principle, 'arbitrary according to the norms of EU law'.[105] However, a number of others (including EU institutions in January 2014 in relation to the Maltese case) consider such practices to be a threat to the respect for the principle of sincere cooperation in accordance with Article 4 (3) of the TEU.[106]

The *modus operandi* for the intervention of the EU in this particular case was a joint reaction from the Commission and the Parliament condemning national measures that could result in the commodification of citizenship. This statement warned Member States 'to be careful when exercising their competences in this area and to take possible side-effects into account', and insisted on the creation of a 'genuine link' with the host country.[107] Among the side effects to which the Parliament makes reference is the contribution to the management of migration through a two-tier regime logic based on wealth and as well the risk

[102] A Balch and A Geddes, 'The Development of the EU Migration and Asylum Regime', in Huub Dijstelbloem and Albert Meijer (eds), *Migration and the New Technological Borders of Europe* (Basingstoke, Palgrave Macmillan, 2011) 36.

[103] Carrera (n 34).

[104] Kochenov (n 40) 29: 'From a purely legal perspective, Malta's case is solid: EU law is unquestionably on its side'.

[105] Shaw (n 53) 33.

[106] Carrera (n 34) 6. See also Viviane Reding Speech at the European Parliament Strasbourg Plenary Session of 15 January 2014—'Citizenship must not be for sale' (http://europa.eu/rapid/press-release_SPEECH-14-18_it.htm).

[107] Point 6 of the European Parliament resolution on EU citizenship for sale, 2013/29995 (RSP), 16 January 2014.

of undermining the essence of EU citizenship. The Parliament, within the scope of this joint reaction, produced a resolution that called upon the need for the Commission's assessment of:

> [V]arious citizenship schemes in the light of European values and the letter and spirit of EU legislation and practice, and to issue recommendations *in order to prevent such schemes from undermining the values that the EU* has been built upon, as well as guidelines for access to EU citizenship via national schemes.[108]

Even though this joint reaction was created in the context of the Maltese citizenship investor programme (and only produced direct consequences in relation to this particular domestic legislative initiative), this action has broader implications for golden visas more generally, such as the Portuguese case described above at section III.C. This is the case since Member States are responsible for informing the Commission and other Member States of measures that they intend to take in the area of asylum and immigration that may affect other Member States or the EU as a whole.[109]

In practical terms the impact of the instrumentalisation of access to legality goes far beyond the literal violation of the law, as suggested by some authors.[110] Since the effects of the instrumentalisation of these avenues without a supranational 'referee' affect the whole definition of what the EU citizenry is, the last problematic trend of the regulation of illegality deserves a more holistic solution that takes into account its effects within the broader picture of EU law. In short, the unregulated instrumentalisation of access to legality not only defines those who can more easily access the EU but also defines those who will find it more difficult to achieve legality.

For that reason, as Carrera has argued, through clearer EU guidelines on the type of restrictions imposed on Member States that aim to enforce the duty of the principle of sincere cooperation in accordance with the EU Treaties, the definition of who may have access to EU citizenship should go far beyond 'the size of someone's wallet or bank account'.[111] As such, stronger oversight of the citizenship schemes and the establishment of guidelines for access to EU citizenship via national schemes by the Commission and EU Parliament would create supranational boundaries to the commodification of access to legality and the respect of the principle of sincere cooperation (Article 4 (3) TEU).

In short, what is advocated is a better policing of national legislation that may instrumentalise the access to legality in a corrective way. This means that the Commission and EU Parliament within their competences and for example

[108] Point 11 of the European Parliament Resolution on EU citizenship for sale, 2013/29995 (RSP), 16 January 2014.

[109] Council Decision 2006/688/EC on the establishment of a mutual information mechanism concerning Member States' measures in the areas of asylum and immigration, [2006] OJ L 283/40 and Carrera (n 34) 29.

[110] For example: Kochenov (n 40).

[111] Viviane Reding Speech (n 106).

in the shape of joint reactions (similar to what happened with the Maltese case) could proceed to a more in-depth oversight of certain paths to legality created domestically by Member States that may represent a challenge for European values and EU legislation.[112]

Of course this suggestion has the potential to interfere with Member States' discretion (and for that reason could meet some opposition), the balance between Member States' interests and the original idea of EU citizenship would have to be maintained in order for this measure to be truly corrective rather than an imposition on Member States. For instance, when national legislation, such as the Portuguese legislation examined above, establishes more favourable criteria for foreign investors to be granted residence permits at a national level, the Commission and the Parliament should ensure careful oversight with regard to the subsequent application for supranational statuses such as the long-term resident status in accordance with 2003/109 Directive or even naturalisation.

Mutatis mutandis former Advocate General Maduro has stated in his Opinion on the *Rottman* case that the 'miracle of Union citizenship'[113] lies in the ties that are strengthened 'between us and our States' and in the simultaneous emancipation of 'us from them (in so far we are now citizens beyond our States)'.[114] This emancipation from the State is on the basis of the supranational prerogative to control the compatibility of the rules that allow access to a legal status (nationality or even temporary residence permit that may eventually lead to nationality) with EU law and in particular with the duty of sincere cooperation.

VI. CONCLUSION

Chapter five combined the analysis of the role played by EU law in dealing with alternative forms of access to a legal immigration status (an area that is strongly associated with the sovereign powers of Member States) with national legislation with the same purpose that privileges certain categories of mobile people to others. The structure of the chapter was organised taking into consideration two possible functions played by the access to legality: instrumental and corrective. As such the analysis focused in the reasoning behind the mechanisms that grant access to legality.

The first part of the chapter was devoted to the instrumental role of access to legality. Member States are an example of actors that may make instrumental use of the mechanisms that grant legal immigration statuses at the national level

[112] Point 11 of the European Parliament Resolution on EU citizenship for sale, 2013/29995 (RSP), 16 January 2014.

[113] Para 23 of the Case C-135/08 *Janko Rottmann v Freistaat Bayern* [2009], EU:C:2009:588, Opinion of AG Poiares Maduro.

[114] ibid.

and in certain cases at the supranational level in accordance with their interests. For instance, an example of a potential instrumentalisation practice of access to legality happened when the former Italian Prime Minister threatened to put into practice his 'plan B' of granting temporary residence permits to illegally staying third-country nationals as a way of negotiating more solidarity from the EU by reaffirming national discretion in this area.[115]

The second part of the chapter advocated a corrective intervention of EU law in access to legality as a way to remedy the consequences that arose from the supranational regulation of illegality. First, the legal uncertainty and ill-fitting categorisation of migrants it is suggested can be remedied by the creation of an corrective temporary protection status. Second, the potential digital criminalisation of illegally-staying migrants in the EU can be addressed by making the purposes of immigration databases expressly defined and exhaustive. Third, the two-tier regime rationale based on wealth would benefit from the creation of supranational limits to the commodification of access to legality and a more widespread respect for the principle of sincere cooperation (Article 4 (3) TEU) in this context.

[115] EU Parliamentary question for written answer to the Commission, 16 June 2015, (www.europarl.europa.eu/sides/getDoc.do?pubRef=-//EP//TEXT+WQ+E-2015-009804+0+DOC+XML+V0//EN&language=en). See also, to see the declarations of Matteo Renzi on the 16 June in Rome about these proposal, *Ansa* (n 19): 'temporary residence permits as a reserve weapon'.

Conclusions

> There is no simple, nor single, answer to the challenges posed by migration. And nor can any Member State effectively address migration alone. It is clear that we need a new, more European approach.[1]

THIS BOOK HAS not attempted to give an all-encompassing, theoretical solution to the present EU migration crisis. To do so would be akin to trying to empty the sea with a bucket. Rather, it looked at the supranational regulation of a type of migration that impacts broadly on the general conceptualisation of the mobility of people both within and from outside the EU: the illegality of stay of third-country nationals. Whilst '[t]he current EU fascination with illegal migration expresses itself most clearly as an abstract idea',[2] a political argument or a newspaper headline, illegality in relation to a migrant's status is first and foremost a legal phenomenon. On top of this, this legal phenomenon is extremely complex, being the result of a combination of laws and from an EU law perspective as well as the intersection of national and supranational regulation.

EU law's regulation of people's movements has increased gradually and today regulates such movement in relation to a number of different (and not always entirely complementary) reasons such as movement within the internal market 'abolishing internal borders and constructing a new external border' and the creation of a common immigration and asylum regime.[3] The dynamics of this complex interaction characterises EU migration and has 'led to a structuration of the field which is very much organized around the distinction between legal and illegal migration'.[4]

The aim of the book was to question the contours of the overarching concept of illegality at the EU level. Due to the fact that EU law does not comprehensively regulate nor adequately address the complex phenomenon of the illegality of a migrant's stay, EU Member States have been left to fill the gaps left unregulated

[1] Brussels, 6 August 2015, Statement by First Vice-President Frans Timmermans, High-Representative/Vice-President Federica Mogherini and Migration and Home Affairs Commissioner Dimitris Avramopoulos on the recent incident in the Mediterranean, Statement /15/5480, (http://europa.eu/rapid/press-release_STATEMENT-15-5480_en.htm).

[2] E Guild, 'Who is an Irregular Migrant' in C Cholewinski, B Bogusz, A Szyszcak (ed), *Irregular Migration and Human Rights: Theorectical, European and International Perspectives, Immigration and Asylum and Policy in Europe* (Leiden, Martinus Nijhoff Publishers, 2004) 16.

[3] J Chia, 'Immigration and its Imperatives' in D Thym and F Snyder (eds), *Europe—A Continent of Immigration? Legal Challenges in the Construction of European Migration Policy* (Brussels, Bruylant, 2011) 13.

[4] Loïc Azoulai and Karin de Vries, *EU Migration Law: Legal Complexities and Political Rationales* (Oxford, Oxford University Press, 2014) 4.

at the supranational level. The incomplete regulation of illegality at the supranational level has potentially problematic consequences, including: (i) increased fragmentation of legal statuses for migrants resulting in legal uncertainty and ill-fitting categorisation of migrants; (ii) potential digital criminalisation of migrants; and (iii) creation of a two-tier regulation of migration which privileges wealth and allows the instrumentalisation of the access to legality by Member States. These consequences were examined and subsequently a potential normative route to address these problematic issues was advocated, namely the corrective intervention of EU law in the last stage of access to legality. In order to support this argument the legal analysis took place over the course of five chapters.

Chapter one focused on the conceptual perspective of illegality and presented a holistic conceptualisation of the phenomenon. The starting point of the book was intended not only to provide clarity about the perspective adopted to address illegality (EU law), but also to highlight the intersection between supranational and national sources of illegality. The intrinsic dynamic character of this phenomenon is the result of the influence of multiple actors at various stages and also of a combination of levels of governance and sources of law. The combination of these variables, the conceptual construction of the phenomenon and the combination of sources and the EU institutional framework are the background and basis for the creation of a supranational concept of illegality of a migrant's stay.

Having set the scene in conceptual terms, chapter two is the first of two chapters which demonstrate that the concept and the reasoning behind the construction of illegality in EU law are not only inadequate but also result in gaps being left unregulated at the supranational level. The case of unlawfully-staying EU citizens illustrates the fragmentation of migrant statuses and the resulting possibility of heterogeneous interpretation and application of EU law. One example discussed at length was the enforceability and efficacy of the expulsion of EU citizens from the territory of a host Member State. This is illustrative of how intertwined these two levels of regulation are and also of the impact that it may have in the definition of the citizenry of the EU.

Chapter three examined in detail situations of non-removability of illegally-staying third-country nationals. The case of non-removable migrants represents yet another example of how obsolete the categorisation of migrants based on the traditional binary of legal and illegal has become. EU law was shown to play a role in the creation of legal grey areas in two distinct ways. First of all the Return Directive's provision of both compulsory and optional reasons for the postponement of removal of third-country nationals actively contributes to the creation of situations of legal limbo. Furthermore, EU law (as a result of factors such as the Commission's original proposal on the provisions dealing with non-removable migrants and the non-committal way the Return Directive addresses the issue) leaves considerable discretion to Member States. However, Member States often address this situation in very different ways (if they address them at all) resulting in a lack of uniformity and potentially problematic legal regulation of the issue as a whole.

Chapter four departed from conceptual analysis and moved on to then examine the potential side effects or consequences of the EU's framing of illegality of a migrant's stay as a legal phenomenon. In short, the way the EU constructs the contours of illegality in effect may conflate illegality with criminality. EU databases were utilised as an illustrative example of this issue in this chapter. These databases develop the legal regime of illegality of a migrant's stay to the point that they are responsible for the creation of a digital illegality. This digital illegality at times fails to respect the proper categorisation of mobile people in the EU and results in differential treatment of illegally-staying migrants whose unlawful immigration status may be conflated with criminality. By setting far-reaching goals for border control whilst designing the aforementioned surveillance instruments the EU has attempted to address existing concerns regarding the prevention of irregular migration and cross-border criminality. Nonetheless, the means designed to achieve this purpose are controversial; not only because they endanger the right to privacy but also because they risk putting mobile third-country nationals and criminal suspects under the same surveillance methods, therefore treating different types of illegality and criminality alike.

Finally, chapter five outlined two functions that the access to legality may serve: instrumental and corrective. Member States are the main actors with significant discretion to shape and reshape routes to legality. This chapter showed that the purposes and aims behind those decisions is what determines whether they serve a purely instrumental function, as in the case of the Maltese investor citizenship programmes or the Portuguese case of golden visas.

The question of who is granted a legal migration status, when and on what legal basis, is at the top of the political agenda at the EU level but also at the global level. In Europe, Dimitris Avramopoulos, the Commissioner for Migration, Home Affairs and Citizenship, stressed the need to improve the legal routes for entry into the EU as '*[o]ne* of the reasons for so many lost lives is that *it is too difficult* for people seeking protection to enter the EU *legally*'.[5] The current tense social atmosphere and intense political debate make the intervention with regards the paths that grant access to legality for illegally-staying third-country nationals top of the agenda.[6]

[5] Dimitris Avramapoulos, 'Fundamental Rights: the Pillar for EU Migration Policy'- European Commission Speech, 10 November 2014, (http://europa.eu/rapid/press-release_SPEECH-14-1601_en.htm).

[6] In relation to migrants within the EU freedom of movement has recently been called into question by certain Member States. The UK Government for instance, among other immigration-related proposals, has threatened to restrict free movement rules by inserting an annual quota or a so-called 'emergency brake' on EU migration. These proposals have prompted strong opposing reactions from several EU leaders. Such proposals to restrict free movement have not, thus far, entered into force as they would result, in Angela Merkel's words, in an interference with the fundamental principles of free movement in Europe (see, Stephen Brown and Gareth Jones, 'Germany Warns "No Going Back" if Britain Curbs EU Immigration—Report' *Reuters* 2 November 2014 (http://uk.reuters.com/article/2014/11/02/uk-germany-britain-eu-idUKKBN0IM0J120141102).

In relation to the corrective function of the access to legality, at the EU level this type of intervention could remedy the consequences that result from the regulation of illegality as exposed in the first four chapters. The proposal of regulating illegality through access to legality and providing normative answers based on that paradigm is what brings the entire book together. In this regard, the President of the Commission Jean-Claude Juncker published his five pillars for reform of EU migration policy, the fourth of which is the need for 'more political determination when it comes to legal migration'.[7] Juncker proposed the establishment of an organisation to deal with legal migration based on 'sound policy that allows migrants to come to Europe legally and in a controlled manner'.[8] Whether this plan will take into account the categories of migrants that are left in limbo or Member States' practices of 'selling' access to legality, for example, is yet to be seen.

Clarity and legal certainty about the construction of illegality in Europe, in particular, requires more than heated debates which most of the time are based on questionable facts and numbers. The main aim of this book was to produce a legal analysis of a phenomenon that is a top priority of every Member States' negotiating team. Having argued that the concept of illegality that is behind the supranational and national regulation of this phenomenon is not sufficiently inclusive and in certain cases is even obsolete (and pointing out the side effects that arise from it) it is important to emphasise that the normative proposals made in this book are routed in the competences that the EU already has. The corrective intervention of the EU is crucial, whether it be in the form of a corrective protection status or ensuring respect for the principle of sincere cooperation. If no such corrective intervention is made, the EU risks more fragmentation with regards migrant statuses in particular at a domestic level and the proliferation of more discriminatory routes to legality based on a commodification logic rather than belonging to an ever-closer Union.

[7] Jean-Claude Juncker, 'My Five Point-Plan on Immigration', European's People Party, 23 April 2014, (http://juncker.epp.eu/sites/default/files/attachments/nodes/en_02_immigration.pdf).

[8] ibid.

Bibliography

BOOKS, CHAPTERS AND ARTICLES

Aas, KF, '"Crimmigrant" Bodies And Bona Fide Travelers: Surveillance, Citizenship And Global Governance' (2011) 15 *Theoretical Criminology* 331.

—— '"The Body Does Not Lie": Identity, Risk And Trust In Technoculture' (2006) 2 *Crime, media, culture* 143.

Abelson, H, Ledeen, K and Lewis, HR, *Blown To Bits: Your Life, Liberty, And Happiness After The Digital Explosion* (Boston, Addison-Wesley Professional, 2008).

Ackerman, E, '"What Part Of Illegal Don't You Understand?": Bureaucracy And Civil Society In The Shaping Of Illegality' (2014) 37 *Ethnic and Racial Studies* 181.

Acosta, AD, Kostakopoulou, D and Munk, T, 'EU Migration Law: the Opportunities and Challenges Ahead' in D Acosta A and C Murphy C (eds), *EU Security and Justice Law—After Lisbon and Stockholm* (Oxford, Hart Publishing, 2014).

Acosta Arcarazo, D, 'The Charter, Detention And Possible Regularization Of Migrants In An Irregular Situation Under The Returns Directive: *Mahdi*', (2015) 52 *Common Market Law Review*.

—— 'Civic Citizenship Reintroduced? The Long-Term Residence Directive as a Post-National Form of Membership' (2015) *European Law Journal* 21.

—— 'Returns Directive: Possible Limits and Interpretation' in Karin Z (ed), The Returns Directive: Central Themes, Problem Issues, and Implementation in Selected Member States (Nijmegen, Wolf Legal Publishers, 2011).

—— 'The Good, The Bad And The Ugly In EU Migration Law: Is The European Parliament Becoming Bad And Ugly? (The Adoption Of Directive 2008/15: The Returns Directive)' 11 *European Journal of Migration and Law* 19.

Amaya-Castro, JM, 'Illegality Regimes And The Ongoing Transformation Of Contemporary Citizenship' (2011) 4(2) *European Journal of Legal Studies*.

Amoore, L, 'Biometric Borders: Governing Mobilities In The War On Terror' (2006) 25 *Political geography* 336.

Anderson, B and Ruhs, M, 'Researching Illegality And Labour Migration' (2010) 16 *Population, Space and Place* 175.

—— 'Semi-Compliance And Illegality In Migrant Labour Markets: An Analysis Of Migrants, Employers And The State in the UK' (2010) 16 *Population, space and place* 195.

Anderson, B, *Us And Them?: The Dangerous Politics Of Immigration Control* (Oxford, Oxford University Press, 2013).

Andersson, R, 'Illegal, Clandestine, Irregular: On Ways of Labelling People,' (2014), (http://bordercriminologieslawoxacuk/illegal-clandestine-irregular/).

—— Illegality, Inc.: Clandestine Migration and the Business of Bordering Europe, vol 28 (Univ of California Press, 2014).

Àngel, G, Chueca, S, *Derechos Humanos, Inmigrantes en situación Irregular y Unión Europea* (Madrid, Lex Nova, 2010).

Apap, J, De Bruycker, P and Schmitter, C, 'Regularisation of Illegal Aliens in the European Union-Summary Report of a Comparative Study' (2000) 2 *European Journal Migration and Law* 263.

Azoulai, L and Coutts, S, 'Restricting Union Citizens' Residence Rights on Grounds of Public Security. Where Union Citizenship and AFSJ meet' (2013) 50 *Common Market Law Review*.

Azoulai, L and de Vries, K, *EU Migration Law: Legal Complexities And Political Rationales* (Oxford, Oxford University Press, 2014).

Azoulai, L, 'A Comment On Ruiz Zambrano Judgement: A Genuine European Integration', European Union Democracy Observatory on Citizenship, (2012).

—— 'The (Mis)Construction Of The European Individual Two Essays On Union Citizenship Law' (2014) EUI Law.

Balch, A and Geddes, A, 'The Development of the EU Migration and Asylum Regime', in Huub Dijstelbloem and Albert Meijer (eds), *Migration and the New Technological Borders of Europe* (Basingstoke, Palgrave Macmillan, 2011).

Baldaccini, A, 'Counter-Terrorism And The EU Strategy For Border Security: Framing Suspects With Biometric Documents And Databases' (2008) 10 *European Journal of Migration and Law* 31.

—— 'The Return And Removal Of Irregular Migrants Under EU Law: An Analysis Of The Returns Directive' (2009) 11 *European Journal of Migration and Law* 1.

Baldwin-Edwards, M and Kraler, A, 'Study on practices in the area of regularisation of illegally staying third-country nationals in the Member States of the EU' in Baldwin-Edwards M and Kraler A (eds), *REGINE Regularisations in Europe*, (Amsterdam, Pallas Publications, 2009).

Balibar, E, *We, the People of Europe?: Reflections on Transnational Citizenship* (Princeton, Princeton University Press, 2003).

Barbou Des Places, S, Evolution of asylum legislation in the EU: Insights from regulatory competition theory, RSCAS Working Paper, EUI RSC; 2003/16, (2003).

Barnard, C and Peers, S, *European Union Law* (Oxford, Oxford University Press, 2014).

Basaran, T, 'Saving Lives at Sea: Security, Law and Adverse Effects' (2014) *European Journal of Migration and Law* 16.

Basilien-Gainche, ML, 'Immigration Detention under the Return Directive: The Shadowed Lights' (2015) *European Journal of Migration and Law* 17 104.

Baubock, R and Goodman Wallace, S, 'EUDO Citizenship Policy Brief No. 2—Naturalisation, Robert Schuman Centre, European Union Democracy Observatory on Citizenship, (http://eudo-citizenship.eu/docs/policy-brief-naturalisation_revised.pdf).

Baubock, R, 'Reinventing Urban Citizenship' (2003) 7 *Citizenship studies* 139.

Bauder, H, 'Why We Should Use the Term "Illegalized" Refugee or Immigrant: A Commentary' (2014) 26 *International Journal of Refugee Law*.

Beduschi, A, 'Detention of Undocumented Immigrants and the Judicial Impact of the CJEU's Decisions in France' (2014) 26 *International Journal of Refugee Law*.

Bell, M, 'Irregular Migrants: Beyond the Limits of Solidarity' in Malcom Ross and Y Borgmann-Prebil (ed), *Promoting Solidarity in the European Union* (Oxford, Oxford University Press, 2010).

Besters, M and Brom, FW, 'Greedy Information Technology: The Digitalization of the European Migration Policy' (2010) 12 *European Journal of Migration and Law*.

Betts, A, 'Towards a "Soft Law" Framework for the Protection of Vulnerable Irregular Migrants' (2010) 22 *International Journal of Refugee Law*.

Bigo, D, 'Criminalisation of "Migrants": The Side Effect Of The Will To Control The Frontiers And The Sovereign Illusion' in B Bogusz and others (eds), *Irregular Migration and Human Rights: Theorectical, European and International Perspectives* (Leiden, Martinus Nijhoff Publishers, 2004).

Błuś, A, 'Beyond the Walls of Paper. Undocumented Migrants, the Border and Human Rights' (2013) 15 *European Journal of Migration and Law.*

Boehm, F, *Information Sharing and Data Protection in the Area of Freedom, Security and Justice: Towards Harmonised Data Protection Principles for Information Exchange at EU-level* (Berlin Heidelberg, Springerverlag, 2012).

Boeles, P and others, *European Migration Law* 2nd edn (Antwerp, Intersentia, 2014).

Bosniak, L, 'Amnesty In Immigration: Forgetting, Forgiving, Freedom' (2013) 16 *Critical Review of International Social and Political Philosophy* 344.

—— *The Citizen And The Alien: Dilemmas Of Contemporary Membership* (Princeton, Princeton University Press, 2008).

—— 'Membership, Equality, And The Difference That Alienage Makes' (1994) 69 *New York University Law Review* 1047.

Broeders, D, 'A European "Border" Surveillance System' in H Dijstelbloem and M Albert (eds), *Migration and the New Tecnological Borders of Europe* (Basingstoke, Palgrave Macmillan, 2011).

—— *Breaking Down Anonymity: Digital Surveillance On Irregular Migrants In Germany And The Netherlands* (Amsterdam, Amsterdam University Press, 2009).

Brouwer, E, 'Eurodac: Its Limitations and Temptations' (2002) 4 *European Journal of Migration and Law.*

—— 'Legality And Data Protection Law: The Forgotten Purpose Of Purpose Limitation' in L Besselink, F Pennings, S Prechal (eds), *The Eclipse of the Legality Principle in the European Union* (Alphen aan den Rijn, Kluwer Law 2011).

—— *Digital Borders And Real Rights: Effective Remedies For Third-Country Nationals In The Schengen Information System* (Leiden, Brill, 2008).

Carens, J, *The Ethics of Immigration* (Oxford, Oxford University Press, 2013).

Carlier, JY, 'La "directive retour" et le respect des droits fondamentaux' *L'Europe des Libertés, Revue d'actualité juridique*, N°26, 2008.

Carrera, S and Faure Atger, A, 'Implementation of Directive 2004/38 in the context of EU Enlargement' A proliferation of different forms of citizenship, CEPS Special Report, 9 April 2009.

Carrera, S and Parkin, J, 'Protecting and Delivering Fundamental Rights of Irregular Migrants at Local and Regional Levels in the European Union' Centre for European Policy Studies, 2011.

Carrera, S, 'How much does EU citizenship cost? The Maltese citizenship-for-sale affair: A breakthrough for sincere cooperation in citizenship of the union?' CEPS Liberty and Security in Europe, no 64, April/2014.

—— 'The Framing of the Roma as Abnormal EU Citizens—Assessing European Politics on Roma Evictions and Expulsions in France' in G Elspeth, CJ Gortázar Rotaeche and D Kostakopoulou D (eds), *The Reconceptualization of European Union Citizenship* (Leiden, Brill Nijhoff, 2014).

Carrera, S, Hernanz, N and Parkin, J, 'The "Lisbonisation" of the European Parliament: Assessing progress, shortcomings and challenges for democratic accountability in the area of freedom, security and justice' CEPS Liberty and Security in Europe, no 58, 2013.

Castles, S and Miller, M, *The Age of Migration: International Population Movements in the Modern World* (London, Macmillan, 1993).

Chavez L, *Shadowed Lives: Undocumented Immigrants in American Society* (Andover, Cengage Learning, 2012).

—— 'The Condition of Illegality' (2007) 45 *International Migration.*

Chia, J, 'Immigration and its imperatives' in Thym D and Snyder F (eds), *Europe—A Continent of Immigration? Legal Challenges in the Construction of European Migration Policy* (Brussels, Bruylant, 2011).

Cholewinski, R, 'EU Acquis on Irregular Migration: Reinforcing Security at the Expense of Rights' (2000) 2 *European Journal of Migration & Law.*

—— Study on obstacles to effective access of irregular migrants to minimum social rights (Council of Europe 2005).

Collier P, *Exodus: How Migration is Changing our World* (Oxford, Oxford University Press, 2013).

Costello, C, *The Human Rights of Migrants and Refugees in European Law* (Oxford, Oxford University Press, 2015).

—— 'Reflections on an Anniversary: EU Citizenship at 20' in Bridget Anderson and Michael Keith (eds), *Migration: The COMPAS Anthology* (Oxford, COMPAS, 2014).

—— 'Human Rights and the Elusive Universal Subject: Immigration Detention under International Human Rights and EU Law' (2012) 19 *Indiana Journal of Global Legal Studies.*

—— 'Citizenship of the Union: Above Abuse? in Rita de la Feria and Stefan Vogenauer (eds) *Prohibition of Abuse of Law: A New General Principle of EU Law* (Oxford, Hart Publishing, 2011).

Craig, P and De Búrca, G, *EU Law: Text, Cases, and Materials* (Oxford, Oxford University, Press, 2011).

Crosby, A, 'The Boundaries of Belonging: Reflections on Migration Policies in the Twenty-First Century' in S Pratim Basu (ed), *The Fleeing People of South Asia: Selections from Refugee Watch* (London, Anthem Press, 2009).

Dashwood, A and others, *Wyatt and Dashwood's European Union Law* (Oxford, Hart Publishing, 2011).

Dauvergne, C, *Making People Illegal: What Globalization means for Migration and Law* (Cambridge, Cambridge University Press, 2008).

De Bruycker, P and Mananashvili, S, 'Audi alteram partem in immigration detention procedures, between the ECJ, the ECtHR and Member States: G & R' (2015) 52 *Common Market Law Review.*

De Bruycker, P, 'L'Émergence d'une Politique Européenne d'Immigration' in JY Carlier (ed), *L' étranger face au droit, XXes Journées d'études juridiques Jean Dabin* (Brussels, Bruylant, 2010).

De Hart, B, 'Introduction: The Marriage of Convenience in European Immigration Law' (2006) 8 *European Journal of Migration & Law.*

Dembour, MB, *When Humans Become Migrants: Study Of The European Court Of Human Rights With An Inter-American Counterpoint* (Oxford, Oxford University Press, 2015).

Desmond, A 'Regularization in the European Union and the United States—The Frequent Use of an Exceptional Measure' in A Wiesbrock and D Acosta Arcarazo, *Global Migration: Old Assumptions, New Dynamics. Santa Barbara, California. eBook Collection* (Westport, Praeger, 2015).

De Witte, F, 'Transnational Solidarity and the Mediation of Conflicts of Justice in Europe' (2012) 18 *European Law Journal* 694.

Dijstelbloem, H and Meijer, A, 'Reclaiming Control over Europe's Technological Borders' in H Dijstelbloem and A Meijer (eds), *Migration and the New Technological Borders of Europe* (Basingstoke, Palgrave Macmillan, 2011).

Dijstelbloem, H, 'Europe's New Technological Gatekeeper. Debating the Deployment of Technology in Migration Policy', (2009) 1 *Amsterdam Law Forum* (http://amsterdamlaw-forum.org/article/view/90/154).

Dollat, P, *La citoyenneté européenne: théorie et statuts* (Brussels, Bruylant, 2008).

Dumas, P, *L'accès des ressortissants des pays tiers au territoire des États membres de l'Union européenne* (Brussels, Bruylant, 2013).

Duvell, F, 'Framing and Reframing Irregular Migration' in Bridget Anderson and Michael Keith (eds), *Migration: The COMPAS Anthology* (Oxford, COMPAS 2014).

—— 'Paths into Irregularity: The Legal and Political Construction of Irregular Migration' (2011) 13 *European Journal of Migration and Law* 275.

—— 'The Pathways in and out of Irregular Migration in the EU: A Comparative Analysis' (2011) 13 *European Journal of Migration and Law* 245.

Dzankic, J, 'Investment-based citizenship and residence programmes in the EU', EUI Working Paper RSCAS 2015/08, Robert Schuman Centre for Advanced Studies Research Paper No RSCAS, 2015.

Editorial Comments, 'The Free Movement Of Persons In The European Union: Salvaging The Dream While Explaning The Nightmare' (2014) 51 *Common Market Law Review.*

Foblets, MC, 'Diversité et Catégories de Personnes dans les Sociétés Contemporaines' in C JY (ed), *L' étranger face au droit, XXes Journées d'études juridiques Jean Dabin* (Brussels, Bruylant, 2010).

Fuller, LL, *Legal Fictions* (Redwood, Stanford University Press, 1967).

Garth, B, 'Migrant Workers and Rights of Mobility in EC and USA' in M Cappelletti, M Seccombe and J Weiler (eds), *Integration Through Law Europe and the American Federal Experience*, vol Volume 1 Methods, Tools and Institutions, Book 3 Forces and Potential for a European Identity (Berlin, Walter de Gruyter, 1986).

Gehring, J, 'Roma and the Limits of Free Movement in the European Union' in W Maas (ed), *Democratic Citizenship and the Free Movement of People* (Leiden, Martinus Nijhoff Publishers, 2013).

Gicquel, H, 'Citoyenneté européenne, qualité d'étranger et éventualité d'une discrimination à rebours' (2013) *AJDA—L'actualité juridique Droit administrative.*

González-Enríquez, C, 'Spain: Irregularity as a Rule', in A Traindafyllidou (ed), *Irregular Migration in Europe. Myths and Realities* (Surrey, Ashgate, 2020).

Goodman Wallace, S, 'Naturalisation Policies in Europe: Exploring Patterns of Inclusion and Exclusion', Comparative Report, RSCAS/EUDO-CIT-Comp. 2010/7, Robert Schuman Centre for Advanced Studies, EUDO Citizenship Observatory, 2010.

Goodwin-Gill, GS, 'Article 31 of the 1951 Convention Relating to the Status of Refugees: Non-Penalization, Detention, and Protection', June 2003.

Grant, S, 'The Recognition Of Migrants' Rights Within The UN Human Rights System, The First 60 Years' in MB Dembour and Tobias Kelly (eds), *Are Human Rights For Migrants? Critical Reflections on the Status of Irregular Migrants in Europe and the United States* (Abingdon, Routledge, 2011).

Groenendijk, K, 'Differential Treatment or Discrimination' in E Guild and JY Carlier (eds), *L'avenir de la libre circulation des personnes dans l'UE* (Brussels, Bruylant, 2006).

—— 'Introduction: Migration and Law in Europe' in E Guild and P Minderhoud (eds), *The First Decade of EU Migration and Asylum Law* (Leiden, Martinus Nijhoff Publishers, 2012).

Guia, MJ, 'Crimmigration, Securitisation and the Criminal Law of the Crimmigrant' in Guia MJ, van der Woude M and van der Leun J (eds), *Social Control And Justice : Crimmigration In The Age Of Fear* (The Hague, Eleven International Publishing, 2013).
Guild, E and Niessen, J, *The Developing Immigration and Asylum Policies of the European Union: Adopted Conventions, Resolutions, Recommendations, Decisions and Conclusions* (Alphen aan den Rijn, Kluwer, 1996).
Guild, E, 'Who is an Irregular Migrant' in B Bogusz, A Szyszcak (ed), *Irregular Migration and Human Rights: Theorectical, European and International Perspectives, Immigration and Asylum and Policy in Europe* (Leiden, Martinus Nijhoff Publishers, 2004).
—— *The Legal Elements of European Identity: EU Citizenship and Migration Law* (The Hague, Kluwer Law International, 2004).
Guild, E, Peers, S and Tomkin, J, *The EU Citizenship Directive: A Commentary* (Oxford, Oxford University Press, 2014).
Handmaker, J and Mora, C, '"Experts": The Mantra Of Irregular Migration And The Reproduction Of Hierarchies' in M Ambrus and others (eds), *The Role of 'Experts' in International and European Decision-Making Processes* (Cambridge, Cambridge University Press, 2014).
Hathaway, JC and Foster, M, *The Law of Refugee Status* (Cambridge, Cambridge University Press, 2014).
Hayes, B and Vermeulen, M, 'Borderline—The EU's New Border Surveillance Initiatives—Assessing the Costs and the Fundamental Rights of EUROSUR and the "Smart Borders" Proposals', A Study by the Heinrich Böll Foundation, June 2012.
Holston, J, *Cities and citizenship* (Durham NC, Duke University Press, 1999).
Horsley, T and Reynolds, S, 'The United Kingdom Citizenship within Directive 2004/38 EC—Stability of Residence for Union Citizens and their Family Members' in Ulla Neergaard, Catherine Jacqueson and Nina Holst-Christensen (eds), *Union Citizenship: Development, Impact and Challenges, The XXVI FIDE Congress in Copenhagen*, 2014, Congress Publications Vol. 2 (2014).
IOM, *Glosario sobre Migración*, Series de Derecho International sobre Migration (ed. IOM, 2006) http://publications.iom.int/system/files/pdf/iml_7_sp.pdf.
Isin, E, *Being Political: Genealogies of Citizenship* (Minneapolis, University of Minnesota Press, 2002).
Izquierdo Sans, C, 'Artículo 13.1—Los Derechos Fundamentales de los Extranjeros', in Maria Emilia Casas Baamonde, Rodríguez-Piñero y Bravo-Ferrer (eds), *Comentarios a la Constitución Española XXX Aniversario* (London, Wolters Kluwer, 2009).
Jandl, M, 'The Estimation of Illegal Migration in Europe' (2004) *Studi Emigrazione* 141.
Jandl, M, Vogel, D and Iglicka, K, 'Report on methodological issues' Research Paper, CLANDESTINO Undocumented Migration: Counting the Uncountable, 2008.
Jeandesboz, J, 'An Analysis of the Commission Communications on Future Development of FRONTEX and the Creation of a European Border Surveillance System (EUROSUR)' Justice and Home Affairs Challenge Liberty & Security, Research Paper No 11, August 2008.
Karakayali, S and Rigo, E, 'Mapping the European Space of Circulation' in N De Genova and N Peutz (eds) *The Deportation Regime* (Durham NC, Duke University Press, 2010).
Kochenov, D and Pirker, B, 'Deporting the Citizens within the European Union: A Counter-Intuitive Trend in Case C-348/09, PI V Oberburgermeisterin der Stadt Remscheid' (2013) 19 *The Columbia Journal of European Law* 369.

Kochenov, D, 'Citizenship for Real: Its Hypocrisy, Its Randomness, Its Price' in A Shachar and R Bauböck (eds), *Should Citizenship be for Sale?* EUI Working Papers, RSCAS 2014/01Robert Schuman Centre for Advanced Studies EUDO Citizenship Observatory, 2014.

Koser, K, 'Dimensions and Dynamics of Irregular Migration' (2010) 16 *Population, Space and Place* 181.

—— 'Why Migration Matters' (2009) 108 *Current History* 147.

D Kostakapoulou, 'Irregular Migration and Migration Theory: Making State Authority Less Relevant' in B Bogusz and others (eds), *Irregular Migration and Human Rights: Theorectical, European and International Perspectives* (Leiden, Martinus Nijhoff Publishers, 2004).

—— 'The Evolution of European Union Citizenship' (2008) 7 *European Political Science* 285.

—— 'When EU Citizens Become Foreigners' (2014) 20 *European Law Journal.*

Kraler, A and Reichel, D, 'Measuring Irregular Migration and Population Flows–What Available Data Can Tell' (2011) 49 *International Migration* 97.

Kraler, A, 'Regularisation: misguided option or part and parcel of a comprehensive policy response to irregular migration?' IMICOE Working Paper No 24, February 2009.

Kubal, A, 'Conceptualizing Semi-Legality in Migration Research' (2013) 47 *Law & Society Review* 555.

Łazowski, A, 'Children of the Lesser Law: Comment on Ziolkowski and Szeja' (2013) 38 *European Law Review* 404.

Le Bot, F, 'La Directive "Retour": Directive de la Honte ou Progrès dans la construction d'une politique européenne en matière d'immigration?' in D Thym and F Snyder (eds), *Europe: Un continent d'immigration? Défis juridiques dans la construction de la Politque européenne de migration* (Brussels, Bruylant, 2011).

LeMay, MC, *Illegal Immigration: a Reference Handbook* (Santa Barbara, Abc-clio 2007).

Lindahl, H, 'A-Legality: Postnationalism and the Question of Legal Boundaries' (2010) 73 *The Modern Law Review* 30.

Liu, Y, 'Scenario Study of Biometric Systems at Borders' (2011) 27 *Computer Law & Security Review* 36.

Longo, E, 'Seeking a Better Life: Human Welfare of Migrants in Irregular Situations in the United States and Europe' Working Paper Series #5, (2013) The Program on Law & Human Development, University of Notre Dame.

Lutz, F, *The Negotiations on the Return Directive* (Nijmegen, Wolf Legal Publishers, 2010).

Marleen, M, 'The Implementation of the Return Directive in Belgium: Focus on Suspension of Removal' in Karin Zwaan (ed) *The Returns Directive: Central Themes, Problem Issues, and Implementation in Selected Member States* (Nijmegen, Wolf Legal Publishers, 2011).

McDonald, J, 'Migrant Illegality, Nation Building, and the Politics of Regularization in Canada' (2009) 26 *Refuge: Canada's Journal on Refugees.*

McNevin, A, *Contesting Citizenship: Irregular Migrants and New Frontiers of the Political* (New York, Columbia University Press, 2011).

—— 'Political Belonging in a Neoliberal Era: The Struggle of the Sans-Papiers' (2006) 10 *Citizenship Studies* 135.

Melis, B, *Negotiating Europe's Immigration Frontiers* (The Hague, Kluwer Law, 2001).

Menjívar, C and Kanstroom, D (eds), *Constructing Immigrant "Illegality"—Critiques, Experiences and Responses* (Cambridge, Cambridge University Press, 2014).

Menjívar, C, 'Liminal Legality: Salvadoran and Guatemalan Immigrants' Lives in the United States1' (2006) 111 *American Journal of Sociology* 999.

Mincheva, E, 'Case Report on Kadzoev, 30 November 2009' (2010) 12 *European Journal of Migration and Law* 361.

Mitsilegas, V, 'Immigration Control in an Era of Globalization: Deflecting Foreigners, Weakening Citizens, Strengthening the State' (2012) 19 *Indiana Journal of Global Legal Studies* 3.

—— 'The Borders Paradox: The Surveillance of Movement in a Union without Internal Frontiers' in H Lindahl (ed), *A Right to Inclusion and Exclusion: Normative Fault-lines of the EU is Area of Freedom, Security and Justice* (Oxford, Hart Publishing, 2009).

—— 'The Changing Landscape of the Criminalisation of Migration in Europe: The Protective Function of European Union Law' in Maria João Guia, Maartje van der Woude and Joanne van der Leun (eds), *Social Control and Justice—Crimmigration in the Age of Fear* (The Hague, Eleven International Publishing, 2013).

Morehouse, C and Blomfield, M, 'Irregular Migration in Europe' (Washington DC, Migration Policy Institute, 2011).

Neergaard, U, Jacqueson, C and Holst-Christensen, N, *Union Citizenship: Development, Impact and Challenges, The XXVI FIDE Congress in Copenhagen, 2014*, Congress Publications Vol 2 (2014).

Nic Shuibhne, N and Shaw, J, 'General Report' in Ulla Neergaard, Catherine Jacqueson and Nina Holst-Christensen (eds), *Union Citizenship: Development, Impact and Challenges, The XXVI FIDE Congress in Copenhagen, 2014, Congress Publications* Vol 2 (2014).

Nic Shuibhne, N, 'Limits Rising, Duties Ascending: The Changing Legal Shape of Union Citizenship' (2015) 52 *Common Market Law Review*.

—— 'Derrogating from the Free Movement of Persons: When can EU Citizens be Deported? (2005–06) 8 *CYELS* 187.

Nicholas, P and Genova, D, 'Migrant "Illegality" and Deportability in Everyday Life' (2002) 31 *Annual Review of Anthropology* 419.

Noll, G, 'Article 31 (Refugees Unlawfully in the Country of Refuge)' in A Zimmermann (ed), *The 1951 Convention Relating to the Status of Refugees and its 1967 Protocol: A Commentary* (Oxford, Oxford University Press, 2011).

Nyers, P, 'No One is Illegal between City and Nation' (2010) 4 *Studies in social justice* 127.

O'Brien, C, 'Civis Capitalist Sum: Class as the New Guiding Principle of EU Movement Rights' (2016) 53 *Common Market Law Review*.

—— 'I trade, therefore I am: personhood in the European Union' (2013) 50 *Common Market Law Review*.

Olivas, M and Kochenov, D, 'Case C-34/09 Ruiz Zambrano: A Respectful Rejoinder' (2012) *University of Houston Public Law and Legal Theory Series*.

O'Nions, H, 'Roma Expulsions and Discrimination: The Elephant in Brussels' (2011)13 *European Journal of Migration and Law* 361.

Olsen, E, 'European Citizenship: Toward Renationalization or Cosmopolitan Europe?' in E Guild, CJ Gortázar Rotaeche and D Kostakopoulou (eds), *The Reconceptualization of European Union Citizenship* (Leiden, Brill Nijhoff, 2014).

Parkin, J, 'The Difficult Road To The Schengen Information System II: The Legacy Of "Laboratories" And The Cost For Fundamental Rights And The Rule Of Law' CEPS Liberty and Security in Europe, 4 April 2011'

—— 'The Schengen Information System and the EU rule of law', INEX Policy Brief No 13, 2011.

—— 'The Criminalisation of Migration in Europe: A State-of-the-Art of the Academic Literature and Research' CEPS Liberty and Security in Europe, no 61, October 2013.

Peers, S and others (eds), *EU Immigration and Asylum Law (Text and Commentary)*, Second Revised Edition, vol 2 (Leiden, Martinus Nijoff Publishers, 2012).

Peers, S, 'Can Unemployed EU Citizens be Expelled and Banned from Re-entry?', EU Law Analysis—Expert insight into EU law developments (2014).

—— 'Could EU law save Paddington Bear? The CJEU develops a new type of protection', EU Law Analysis—Expert insight into EU law developments, (2014).

—— 'Irregular Migrants and EU Employment Law', EU Law Analysis—Expert insight into EU law developments, (2014).

—— *EU Justice and Home Affairs Law* (Oxford, Oxford University Press, 2011).

Plender, R, *International Migration law*, vol 2 (Leiden, Martinus Nijhoff Publishers, 1988).

Portes, A, 'Introduction: Toward a Structural Analysis of Illegal (Undocumented) Immigration' (1978) *International Migration Review* 469.

Prak, M, 'Burghers into Citizens: Urban and National Citizenship in the Netherlands during the Revolutionary Era (c 1800)' (1997) 26 *Theory and Society* 403.

Provera, M, 'The Criminalisation of Irregular Migration in the European Union', CEPS Liberty and Security in Europe, no. 80/February, 2015.

Ramos, AG, 'Inmigrantes en situación irregular y la Organización Internacional para las Migraciones' in Àngel G, Chueca Sancho, *Derechos Humanos, inmigrantes en situación irregular y Unión Europea* (Madrid, Lex Nova, 2010).

Rijpma, J, *Building Borders: The Regulatory Framework for the Management of the External Borders of the European Union* (Florence, European University Institute, 2009).

—— 'Frontex: Successful Blame Shifting of the Member States?' Análisis del Real Instituto Elcano (ARI, 13 April 2010).

Rodríguez, C, and Rubio-Marín, R, 'The Constitutional Status Of Irregular Migrants, Testing The Boundaries Of Human Rights Protection In Spain And The United States' in MB Dembour and T Kelly (eds), *Are Human Rights For Migrants? Critical Reflections on the Status of Irregular Migrants in Europe and the United States* (Abingdon, Routledge, 2011).

Rubio-Marin, R, *Immigration as a Democratic Challenge Citizenship and Inclusion in Germany and the United States* (Cambridge, Cambridge University Press, 2000).

Sandru, DM, Banu, CM and Calin, D, 'The Preliminary Reference in the Jipa Case and the Case Law of Romanian Courts on the Restriction on the Free Movement of Persons' (2012) 18 *European Public Law.*

Schotel, B, *On the Right of Exclusion: Law, Ethics and Immigration Policy* (Abingdon, Routledge, 2011).

Sciortino, G and Bommes, M, *Foggy Social Structures: Irregular Migration, European Labour Markets and the Welfare State* (Amsterdam, Amsterdam University Press, 2012).

Shachar, A and Bauböck, R (eds), Should Citizenship be for Sale? EUI Working Papers, RSCAS 2014/01Robert Schuman Centre for Advanced Studies EUDO Citizenship Observatory, 2014.

Shachar, A, 'Dangerous Liaisons: Money and Citizenship' in Ayelet Shachar and Rainer Bauböck (eds), *Should Citizenship be for Sale?*, EUI Working Papers, RSCAS 2014/01 Robert Schuman Centre for Advanced Studies EUDO Citizenship Observatory, 2014.

Shaw, J and Miller, N, 'When Legal Worlds Collide: An Exploration of What Happens When EU Free Movement Law Meets UK Immigration Law' (2013) 38 *European Law Review.*

Shaw, J, 'Citizenship for Sale: Could and Should the EU Intervene?' in Ayelet Shachar and Rainer Bauböck (eds), *Should Citizenship be for Sale?*, EUI Working Papers, RSCAS 2014/01, Robert Schuman Centre for Advanced Studies EUDO Citizenship Observatory, 2014.

Sigona N, 'EU Citizenship, Roma Mobility and Anti-Gypsyism: Time for Reframing the Debate?' in B Anderson and M Keith (eds), *Migration: The COMPAS Anthology* (Oxford, COMPAS 2014).

Smith, CS and Hung, LC, *The Patriot Act: Issues and Controversies* (Springfield, Charles C Thomas Publisher 2009).

Sprokkereef, A and De Hert, P, 'Ethical Practice in the Use of Biometric Identifiers within the EU' (2007) 3 *Law Science and Policy* 177.

Strumia, F, 'Looking for Substance at the Boundaries: European Citizenship and Mutual Recognition of Belonging' (2013) 32 *Yearbook of European Law* 432.

Stumpf, JP, 'Doing Time: Crimmigration Law And The Perils Of Haste' (2011) 58 *UCLA Law Review* 1705.

—— 'The Crimmigration Crisis: Immigrants, Crime, and Sovereign power' (2006) Bepress Legal Series, Working Paper 1635.

Thym, D, 'The Elusive Limits Of Solidarity: Residence Rights Of And Social Benefits For Economically Inactive Union Citizens' (2015) 52 *Common Market Law Review*.

—— 'Residence as de facto Citizenship? Protection of Long-Term Residence under Article 8 ECHR', in Ruth Rubio-Marín (ed), *Human Rights and Immigration* (Oxford, Oxford University Press, 2014).

—— 'EU Migration Policy And Its Constitutional Rationale: A Cosmopolitan Outlook' (2013) 50 *Common Market Law Review*.

—— 'Respect for Private And Family Life Under Article 8 ECHR In Immigration Cases: A Human Right To Regularize Illegal Stay?' (2008) 57 *International and Comparative Law Quarterly* 87.

Toner, H, Boeles, P, den Heijer, M, Lodder, G and Wouters, K, *European Migration Law* (Antwerp, Intersentia, 2010).

Triandafyllidou, A, *Irregular Migration in Europe: Myths and Realities* (Farnham, Ashgate Publishing Company, 2010).

Tzanou, M, *The Added Value of Data Protection as a Fundamental Right in the EU Legal Order in the Context of Law Enforcement* (Florence, European University Institute, 2012).

van der Leun, J and van der Woude, M, 'A Reflection on Crimmigration in the Netherlands' in MJ Guia, M van der Woude and J van der Leun (eds), *Social Control and Justice—Crimmigration in the Age of Fear* (The Hague, Eleven International Publishing, 2013).

Verschueren, H, 'Free Movement or Benefit Tourism: The Unreasonable Burden of Brey' (2014) 16 *European Journal of Migration and Law* 147.

Vogel, D and Cyrus, N, 'Irregular migration in Europe–Doubts about the effectiveness of control strategies' Policy Brief No 9, Focus Migration, 2008.

Vollmer, B and McNeil, R, 'Briefing: "Irregular Migration in the UK: Definitions, Pathways and Scale"', The Migration Observatory at the Oxford University 2011.

Vollmer, BA, *Policy Discourses on Irregular Migration in Germany and the United Kingdom* (Basingstoke, Palgrave Macmillan, 2014).

Walters, W and others, *The Deportation Regime: Sovereignty, Space, And The Freedom Of Movement* (Durham NC, Duke University Press, 2010).

Weiler, JHH, 'Thou Shalt Not Oppress A Stranger: On The Judicial Protection Of The Human Rights Of Non-EC Nationals-A Critique' (1992) 3 *European Journal of International Law* 65.

Wray, H, 'An Ideal Husband? Marriages of Convenience, Moral Gate-keeping and Immigration to the UK' (2006) 8 *European Journal of Migration and Law* 303.

—— *Regulating Marriage Migration into the UK: a Stranger in the Home* (Farnham, Ashgate Publishing, 2011).

NEWSPAPER ARTICLES

Brown, S and Jones, G, 'Germany warns 'no going back' if Britain curbs EU immigration—report' *Reuters* (2nd November 2014).

Downes, L and Steinbrenner, G, 'What Part of "Illegal" Don't You Understand?' *The New York Times* (28 October 2007).

Gittleson, K, 'Where is the cheapest place to buy citizenship? *BBC New York* (June 2014).

González, M and Fariza, I, 'Rajoy gets illegal immigration at top of EU-Africa summit agenda', *El País* (April 2014).

Kingsley, P, 'This wall, we will not accept it', *The Guardian* (22 June 2015).

'Portugal to grant citizenship to descendants of persecuted Jews' *The Guardian* (29 Jan 2015).

Queiroz, B, 'Vistos Gold: nem tudo o que reluz é ouro!', *Público* (17 Nov 2014).

'Renzi says Italy will do what EU can't' *Ansa* (16 June 2015).

OFFICIAL DOCUMENTS

Committee on the Elimination of Racial Discrimination, General Recommendation 30, Discrimination against non-citizens, 64th session, 2004.

Commission, Communication to the Council and the European Parliament on the Development of the Schengen Information System II, COM (2001) 720 final.

Commission, Communication on Improved Effectiveness, Enhanced Interoperability and Synergies among European Databases in the Area of Justice and Home Affairs, COM (2005) 597 final.

Commission, Communication from to the European Parliament, the Council, the European and Social Commitee and the Committee of the Regions preparing the next steps in border management in the European Union, COM (2008) 69 final.

Commission, Communication to the European Parliament, the Council, the Economic and Social Committee and the the Committee of the Regions examining the creation of a European Border Surveillance System (EUROSUR), COM(2008) 68 final.

Commission, Communication to the European Parliament and the Council on guidance for better transposition and application of Directive 2004/38/EC on the right of citizens of the Union and their family members to move and reside freely within the territory of the Member States, COM(2009) 313 final.

Commission, Communication on an area of freedom, security and justice serving the citizen, COM 2009 (262).

Commission, Communication to the European Parliament and the Council on Smart borders—options and the way ahead, COM (2011) 680 final.

Commission Staff Working Document Impact Assessment accompanying the document Proposal for a Regulation of the European Parliament and of the Council establishing an entry/exit system to register entry and exit data of third-country nationals crossing the external borders of the Member States of the European Union COM (2013) 95, Brussels, 28 February 2013.

Council of the European Union, 'Draft Council Conclusions on access to Eurodac by Member State police and law enforcement authorities', Brussels, 20 April 2007.

Council of the European Union, 7007/ 14, An Effective EU Return Policy, Brussels, 2014.

European Commission proposal (COM(2005) 391 final) for a Directive of the European Parliament and of the Council on common standards and procedures in Member States for returning illegally staying third-country nationals, Brussels, 2005.

European Commission proposal (COM(2011) 873 final, for a Regulation of the European Parliament and of the Council Establishing the European Border Surveillance System (EUROSUR), 2011.
European Commission amended proposal (COM(2012) 254 final), for Regulation of the European Parliament and of the Council on the establishment of 'EURODAC' for the comparison of fingerprints for the effective application of Regulation (EU) No [.../...] (establishing the criteria and mechanisms for determining the Member State responsible for examining an application for international protection lodged in one of the Member States by a third-country national or a stateless person) and to request comparisons with EURODAC data by Member States' law enforcement authorities and Europol for law enforcement purposes and amending Regulation (EU) No 1077/2011 establishing a European Agency for the operational management of large-scale IT systems in the area of freedom, security and justice, 2012.
European Commission proposal (COM(2013) 95 final) for a Regulation of the European Parliament and of the Council establishing an Entry/Exit System (EES) to register entry and exit data of third country nationals crossing the external borders of the Member States of the European Union, 2013.
European Commission proposal (COM(2013) 97 final) for a Regulation of the European Parliament and of the Council establishing a Registered Traveller Programme, 2013.
European Commission proposal (COM(2016)194 final) for a Regulation of the European Parliament ando of the Council establishing an Entry/Exit System (EES) to register entry and exit data and refusal of entry data of third country nationals crossing the external borders of the Member States of the European Union and determining the conditions for access to the EES for law enforcement purposes and amending Regulation (EC) No 767/2008 and Regulation (EU) No 1077/2011, 2016.
European Council, 13440/08, European Pact on Immigration and Asylum [2008].
European Council, Presidency Conclusions, Tampere, 15, 16 October 1999.
Extraordinary Council meeting of 20 September 2001, Doc.1219/01 (Presse 327).
European Council, Presidency Conclusions, Seville, 21-22 June 2002 (SN 200/02).
European Council, 2005/C53/01, The Hague Programme: Strengthening Freedom, Security and Justice in the European Union, [2005] OJ C53/1.
European Council, 2010/C, The Stockholm Programme—An open and secure Europe serving and protecting citizens, [2010] OJ 115/01.
European Council, Conclusions, EUCO 23/11, 23/24 June 2011 [2011].
European Council, Conclusions, EUCO 22/15, 25/26 June 2015 [2015].
European Parliament Resolution on EU citizenship for sale, 2013/29995 (RSP), 16 January 2014.
Joint Supervisory Authority Opinion on the development of the SIS II, 19.05.2004.
Opinion of the European Data Protection Supervisior on the Proposal for a Regulation of the European Parliament and of the Council concerning the Visa Information System (VIS) and exchange of data between Member States on short stay-visas (COM(2004)835 final), OJ C 81, 2005.
Opinion of the European Data Protection Supervisor on the Proposal for a Council Decision concerning access for consultation of the Visa Information System (VIS) by the authorities of Member States responsible for internal security and by Europol for the purposes of the prevention, detection and investigation of terrorist offences and of other serious criminal offences (COM (2005) 600 final), OJ C 97, 2006.

Opinion of the European Data Protection Supervisor on the draft SIS II legislation, OJ 91/38, 2006.

Opinion of the European Data Protection Supervisor on the amended proposal for a Regulation of the European Parliament and of the Council concerning the establishment of 'Eurodac' for the comparison of fingerprints for the effective application of Regulation (EC) No (…/…) (establishing the criteria and mechanisms for determining the Member State responsible for examining an application for international protection lodged in one of the Member States by a third-country national or a stateless person), and on the proposal for a Council Decision on requesting comparisons with Eurodac data by Member States' law enforcement authorities and Europol for law enforcement purposes, OJ C 92/1, 2010.

Opinion of the European Data Protection Supervisor on the amended proposal for a Regulation of the European Parliament and of the Council on the establishment of 'EURODAC' for the comparison of fingerprints for the effective application of Regulation (EU) No […/…] [….] (Recast version), 2012.

Opinion of the European Data Protection Supervisor on the proposals for a Regulation establishing an Entry/Exit System (EES) and a Regulation establishing a Registered Traveller Programme (RTP), 2013.

Opinion of the European Data Protection Supervisor on the Communication from the Commission to the European Parliament and the Council entitled 'Strengthening law enforcement cooperation in the EU: the European Information Exchange Model (EIXM), 2013.

Opinion of the European Data Protection Supervisor on the Second EU Smart Borders Package Recommendations on the revised Proposal to establish an Entry/Exit System, 2016.

UNHRC, 'General Comment 31: The Nature of the General Legal Obligation Imposed on States Parties' (29 March 2004) UN Doc CCPR/C/21/Rev.1/Add.13.

REPORTS AND OTHER SOURCES

Amnesty International, 'Italy—The regularisation should protect the rights of migrants workers' Amnesty International Publications, 2012.

EUROPA—Press Releases—Special Eurobarometer: Right to Move and Reside Freely in the EU and Right to Good Administration Are the Most Important Citizens' Rights, July 7, 2011.

European Union Agency for Fundamental Rights, Fundamental rights of migrants in an irregular situation in the European Union, Comparative Report, Draft Final.docx.

'House of Lords European Union Commitee, Schengen Information System II (SIS II), 10 of July 2006'.

Conclusions of the Fundamental Rights Conference 2014 on "Fundamental Rights and Migration to the EU", 2014.

Council of the European Union, *Doc nr 6387/03: Summary of discussions*, 25 February 2003.

Dimitris Avramapoulos, 'Fundamental Rights: the Pillar for EU Migration Policy'—European Commission Speech, 10 November 2014.

EU Parliamentary question for written answer to the Commission, 16 June 2015.

EU Parliamentary question for written question to the Commission, 15 January 2014, OJ C 288.

European Commission, Study on the situation of third-country nationals pending return/removal in the EU Member States and the Schengen Associated Countries—HOME/2010/ RFXX/PR/1001, 11/03/ 2013.

European Data Protection Supervisor Press Release, EDPS/09/11, Law enforcement access to EURODAC: EDPS expresses serious doubts about the legitimacy and necessity of proposed measures, Brussels, 8 of October 2009.

European Data Protection Supervisor Press Release, EDPS/12/12—EURODAC: erosion of fundamental rights creeps along, Brussels, 5 September 2012.

European Parliament, 'Briefing—Irregular immigration in the EU: Facts and Figures' 2015, www.europarl.europa.eu/RegData/etudes/BRIE/2015/554202/EPRS_BRI(2015) 554202_EN.pdf.

Fundamental Rights Agency (FRA) Comparative Report on Fundamental rights of migrants in an irregular situation in the European Union, 2011.

Fundamental Rights Agency (FRA), Report on the Criminalisation of migrants in an irregular situation and of persons engaging with them, 2014.

Meijers Commitee, Note on the Proposal for a Regulation establishing the European Border Surveillance (COM (2011) 0873), CM1215, 12 September 2012.

Meijers Committee Note on the Smart Borders proposals (COM (2013)) 95 final, COM (2013) 96 final and COM (2013) 97 final, CM1307, 3 of May 2013.

Meijers Committee, House of Lords European Union Commitee, Schengen Information System II (SIS II), 10 of July 2006.

Recommendation of Immigration Ministers on 30 Nov/1 December 2002 (SN 4678/92, WGI 1266, 16 Nov 1992), published in Elspeth Guild and J Niessen, 'The Developing Immigration and Asylum Policies of the European Union: Adopted Conventions, Resolutions, Recommendations, Decisions and Conclusions' (Kluwer 1996).

Report from the Commission to the European Parliament and the Council on the evaluation of the Dublin system, COM 299 final and SEC 742, [2007].

Report from the Commission to the European Parliament and the Council on the application of Directive 2004/38/EC on the right of citizens of the Union and their family members to move and reside freely within the territory of the Member States, COM(2008) 840, [2008].

Report from the Commission to the European Parliament and the Council on the development of the Visa Information System (VIS) in 2012, COM(2013) 232 final, Brussels, [2013].

Report from the Commission to the European Parliament and the Council COM(2013) 232 final on the development of the Visa Information System (VIS), [2013].

Schengen Joint Supervisory Authority Activity Report—December 2005—December [2008].

Statement by First Vice-President Frans Timmermans, High-Representative/Vice-President Federica Mogherini and Migration and Home Affairs Commissioner Dimitris Avramopoulos on the recent incident in the Mediterranean, Statement /15/5480, Brussels, 06 August 2015.

The Statement of the United Nations Commissioner for Refugees (UNHCR) (2008).

US Department of Justice, Office of the Inspector General, A Review of the FBI's Handling of the Brandon Mayfield case, March 2006.

Viviane Reding, Speech at the European Parliament Strasbourg Plenary Session of 15 January 2014—'Citizenship must not be for sale'.

Index

www.ingramcontent.com/pod-product-compliance
Ingram Content Group UK Ltd.
Pitfield, Milton Keynes, MK11 3LW, UK
UKHW020812290926
15470UKWH00003B/1118

9 781509 912872